MIRACULOUS MESSAGES

MIRACULOUS MESSAGES

From Noah's Flood to the End Times

David W. Balsiger
and
Charles E. Sellier

Bridge-Logos
Alachua, Florida 32615

Bridge-Logos

Alachua, Florida 32615 USA

Miraculous Messages:
From Noah's Flood to the End Times
by David W. Balsiger and Charles E. Sellier

Printed in the United States of America.

Library of Congress Catalog Card Number: 2007942795
ISBN: 978-0-88270-467-8

Scripture taken from the *Holy Bible, New International
Version®, NIV®* Copyright© 1973, 1978, 1984 by
International Bible Society. Used by permission of
Zondervan Publishing House. All rights reserved.

G1.316.N.m804.35230

SPECIAL DEDICATION

This book is dedicated to the brave 20th and 21st century explorers and expeditioners who have advanced the search for Noah's ark on Mount Ararat in eastern Turkey, and those who have advanced the horizon of academic research regarding Noah's Flood. Those who stand above all others for their contributions and are most deserving of this appreciative dedication include Chuck Aaron, Ray Anderson, Dr. Ahmet Ali Arslan, Dr. Carl Baugh, John Bradley, Dick Bright, Dr. Walt Brown, B.J. Corbin, Bill Crouse, Eryl and Violet Cummings, Ed Davis, Scott Van Dyke, Bob Garbo, Rex Geissler, George Hagopian, Professor Jim Hall, Col. James Irwin, Mary Irwin, Yavuz Konca, Elfred Lee, John Libi, John McIntosh, Dr. John Morris, Fernand Navarra, Don Shockey, Gunnar Smars, A. J. Smith, Bob Stuplich, and Dr. Charles Willis.

Expert Interviews

Experts who granted interviews for this book and the television special are usually not footnoted. All interviews were conducted in 1992 and 2007.

ACKNOWLEDGEMENTS

The authors wish to express their deep appreciation to Debbie Pursell for her editorial and writing assistance on this book and to the numerous experts quoted herein who granted interviews for this book and the various related television specials that we have produced over the past fifteen years. Additionally, we want to thank Judy Wood and Michelle Miller for their typing and formatting assistance on this book. We would be amiss not to mention Michael Morrell, who with Bridge-Logos did the final edit on this book. Finally, we wish to thank John McIntosh for his research and consulting on both this book and the TV/DVD documentary related to this book.

—David W. Balsiger/Charles E. Sellier

Contents

Significance of Finding Noah's ark

Archaeologists have uncovered Flood stories in cultures all over the world. As an historian I find this powerful evidence that a Flood really did take place. If we find an ark on Mt. Ararat it will be the greatest archaeological discovery of all time…it would not only have enormous impact on the academic community, but it would simply confirm what archaeologists have been doing now for about 200 years…and that is, finding that what the Bible teaches is true.

Phil Mitchell,
Center for Western Civilization, University of Colorado

Imagine having an artifact to study from before the Flood. We know very little about that period, and it might shed much new light on the interpretation of the early chapters of Genesis. These chapters are among the most attacked by liberal scholars who maintain the Flood account is largely myth.

Bill Crouse,
Publisher, *Ararat Report*

If the ark exists at about the 15,500-foot elevation, and its details match those described in Genesis, we would all be descended from Noah and his family, who lived about 5,000 years ago. This would mean that we were all cousins. What would the world be like if most people understood that?

Walter Brown, PhD,
Author/Mathematician/Physicist

The discovery of Noah's ark, in my estimation, would prove conclusively the authenticity of the Genesis account of a worldwide Flood. It constitutes the one remaining link to the pre-Flood world.

Roger Oakland,
Author/Science Educator

I think the potential discovery of Noah's ark could have great implications in this overall creation/evolution question which is raging around the world today. You see, evolution is based on the assumption of uniformity...that things have been uniform throughout the past. But, of course, the Bible tells that there have been episodes of Earth's history dramatically different from anything even possible today. Noah's Flood would be one of those episodes. If we were to find that 500-foot boat on top of a 17,000-foot mountain, catastrophism would prove to be the rule of Earth's history—not uniformity.

John D. Morris, PhD,
Author/Professor of Geology

The only common denominator of the three major Western religions that we know of is Noah's ark. Islam, Christianity, and Judaism all say that there was in fact an ark. If it were found in this time of crisis in the Middle East, would it not have a tendency to unite the people...Can it be wrong to look for it under this circumstance?

Jack Donohue,
International Government Consultant

No event in Scripture is doubted as much as Noah's ark and the accompanying global Flood. To find the ark would silence the detractors and increase the faith of many.

Carl Baugh, PhD, ThD,
Author/Museum Curator

The discovery of Noah's ark would be extremely important for our understanding of this Earth and man's life upon it. The editor of National Geographic Magazine *told us, "If the ark of Noah is ever discovered it would be the greatest archaeological find in human history, the greatest event since the resurrection of Christ, and it would alter all the currents of scientific thought." He added, "I would have to reconsider the origins of man."*

Such a discovery would help confirm many of the Scriptural accounts which many skeptics have put into the realm of myths and fables … Finding Noah's ark is far more than just identifying the past, it could well help us identify the future, and motivate us to want to live to be a part of it.

Elfred Lee,
Archaeological Illustrator/
Ararat Explorer

Many historians and scientists have virtually ignored the possibility of a universal Flood, in spite of the fact that virtually every civilization has deep Flood traditions. If the ark of Noah is found and verified, then we're going to have to reexamine almost everything we think we know.

Chuck Missler,
Biblical Expositional Commentator

ONE

ANCIENT MYSTERY IMPACTS WORLD

The process of scientific discovery is, in effect, a continual flight from wonder.
—Albert Einstein

A GREAT MYSTERY LIES HIDDEN on a permanently snow-covered mountaintop in eastern Turkey. This mystery has influenced all the civilizations of the world and is reflected in their literature throughout the ages. This mystery has perplexed and challenged explorers for nearly 5,000 years.

A man-made artifact, the object of this mystery has attracted the attention of the CIA and the Russian KGB. Both Russian and U.S. spy satellites as well as reconnaissance planes from these countries and NATO allies have secretly photographed this strange object protruding from the snow-capped summit. Many of the photographs have remained "top secret" and are stored in underground military vaults in the United States and hidden in the KGB chambers of the Kremlin.

Treasure of Aghri Dagh

For centuries hundreds have traveled to Aghri Dagh—in Turkish, Ağrı Dağı, "the Mountain of Pain"—hoping to get even a glimpse of this

1

legendary treasure. Many explorers have not survived the arduous climb up into steep, unstable slopes covered with volcanic rock, ice, glaciers, and deep, snow-covered crevasses. On this mountain, violent storms with high winds can develop, quickly dropping temperatures to more than fifty degrees below zero. The hazards to climbers from avalanches, thieves, wild animals, poisonous snakes, and even modern-day terrorists have taken the lives of many adventurers.

The very few who have been fortunate enough to avoid injury or death and have come back with eyewitness accounts of this ancient artifact—even with photographs to back up their stories—have met with calamities. All the privately held photographs of this mysterious object have disappeared. In one case, the owner was murdered for his pictures. Many of the other eyewitness photographers have long since died, taking to the grave the whereabouts of their pictures documenting this ancient mystery.

What is this mysterious artifact explorers risk their lives trying to find? Why is it so important for the superpowers to keep the photographs locked in top-secret military vaults? Why do Washington and Moscow refuse to declassify these pictures? The only specific historical document that can be used to identify this object is the Holy Bible. In the Book of Genesis, the Bible records the landing of a large, wooden boat "on the mountains of Ararat." Could it really be the biblical ark of Noah that rests on Mount Ararat? Maybe it's some other large boat or even an ancient building. And if it's not Noah's ark, how did this other artifact get buried in the ice and snow at such a high elevation? What ancient people would have put it there, and why?

A Far-Fetched Idea

The very idea of Noah's ark on Mount Ararat does seem farfetched. Just as Pompeii was buried and thought to be only a legend for 1,500 years, and the Great Sphinx of Giza was hidden in sand with its existence questioned for 2,000 years, the mysterious Noah's ark hidden for nearly 5,000 years may still be waiting to be discovered. Critics, however, scoff at the biblical account as mere legend.

The ancient city of Troy was also considered to be a legend until Heinrich Schliemann, who dreamed of finding it from the time he was a boy, hired diggers and found this notable city in Turkey. Maybe once again Turkey is about to reveal to the world the greatest archaeological find of this millennium. Mount Ararat could indeed be the resting place of the ark of Noah that the Bible claims saved mankind and the animal species from the devastating global Flood described in Genesis.

Still, this mystery raises more questions than it answers. If it's Noah's ark, why is our government being secretive about it? Does disclosing the photographs of this wooden boat endanger U.S. national security? What scientific evidence substantiates the incredible claims that Noah's ark not only exists but has been found on a mountaintop? How could a wooden ship possibly survive to the present day when many ancient cities made of stone have already crumbled into rubble?

Consider this even more provocative question: How could Noah, a citizen of an ancient civilization, build a giant vessel sturdy enough to survive a cataclysmic worldwide flood? Where did he get his engineering plans and tools to build the ark? And where is the evidence that the flood described in Genesis even occurred?

What Solving the Mystery Could Mean

Even if we can answer scientifically all the questions that surround this mysterious and controversial biblical account, does finding Noah's ark have any real relevance in our world today?

"For many of us today, religious beliefs seem old-fashioned, unscientific, and not particularly relevant in people's lives," says Dr. Tim LaHaye, best-selling author of numerous self-help books and co-author of the well-known *Left Behind* book series.

If the ark of Noah can be discovered, it will mean that the Bible cannot be written off as just a collection of legends, but must be considered more as fact ... The discovery of the ark will make us reexamine what religious teachings of all faiths have to say about very important issues such as death, immortality, and how we live our daily lives.

Another perspective on the significance of finding Noah's ark comes from Jack Donohue, who has been a U.S. presidential advisor and consultant to heads of state around the world.

The three major religions in the world, Judaism, Christianity, and Islam, all have in their sacred writings the story of Noah's ark. Suppose we can prove the ark exists. Suppose we can prove that the Genesis account is not a fairy-tale. These groups have been tearing each other apart in the Middle East for centuries. Just think what a unifying force the ark could be for the Jews, Muslims, and Christians—for all the peoples of the world!

As the late editor of *National Geographic* said several years ago regarding Noah's ark: "It will be the greatest archaeological find in human history and the greatest event since the resurrection of Christ. It will alter all the currents of scientific thought."

Finding the physical artifact of Noah's ark resting on a mountaintop in eastern Turkey is only part of an ancient mystery waiting to be solved. Equally as important is its connection to our past, present and future. It's the source for understanding all the geological anomalies on planet Earth. It's connected to our present-day concern about Global Warming. It's the background setting for all the modern day strife between Muslims, Jews, and Christians. It further reveals how the world will finally come to an end, and embedded within the Noah account is the crucial message of how people can escape the End Times catastrophe.

The Noah Flood account goes back to ancient times, but it is a living breathing story that will continue to impact our lives and unfold until the last day on planet Earth as we know it.

Today, there's a lot of talk about "codes"—the Da Vinci Code, the Healing Codes, and others. But those who gain insight into the integrated connections of Noah's ark and the Great Flood will unlock a biblical spiritual code of understanding that explains why the world is where it is today, and where humanity is heading.

This book is about more than the search for an ancient ship on a mountaintop. It is ultimately about how this one past event has impacted our lives and will determine our future. For those who come along for the investigation surrounding Noah's ark will indeed gain an understanding of the real world around us–in a perspective not seen on the evening television news.

Beginning Your Journey

Join us now for a thought-provoking journey as we turn back the hands of time and look at the world through the eyes of Noah—as we scientifically examine the entire Noah's ark and Flood accounts recorded in the Bible.

Modern technology and experts in virtually every scientific field have been utilized to objectively and thoroughly scrutinize all of the available evidence regarding this biblical ship. Reports of those who claim to have been inside of this mysterious vessel have been carefully examined, and satellite photos obtained from foreign governments have been analyzed in an effort to verify the accounts. Wood brought back from the ship by eyewitnesses has been scientifically tested and dated.

Absolutely nothing in our investigation of the mystery of Noah's ark has been intentionally eliminated or overlooked. This book is foremost a scientific and archaeological search to discover, identify, and report the truth. The quest for tangible evidence of truth will lead us to even greater discoveries within the historical ark.

The evidence alone will challenge your understanding of our past and stimulate your thinking about our future as we journey along the path to the incredible discovery of Noah's ark and the miraculous messages it reveals for our time and the distant future.

Our journey begins with a highly probable event one day long, long ago ...

Two

PREPARING FOR DOOMSDAY

It is a blessed thing that in every age someone has had the individuality enough and the courage enough to stand by his own convictions.
—Robert G. Ingersoll (1833-1899)

SALTY BEADS OF SWEAT BURNED as they fell into Noah's eyes. He stopped hammering the heavy plank above his head and wearily wiped the perspiration away with his dusty forearm. Stepping back on the platform, he surveyed the noisy activity around him—pounding hammers, the cracking of huge beams, men cursing and shouting commands.

Almost twenty men were working on the third level of the ark—and he could have used fifty more. It had been a long, difficult job to build this enormous craft; a task filled with delays, injuries, and unforeseen dangers.

Noah cupped his mouth with his callused hands. "Stop working!" he yelled. "Let's rest for a while and get a cool drink. Go tell the others." Noah waited patiently as his message was called down to those working at the other end of the massive structure—nearly 450 feet away.

The sounds of hammering and sawing quickly died down and Noah took a deep breath. The rich, warm air was filled with the smells of freshly hewn wood and boiling sap resins. Lost in his thoughts, Noah sat on a stack of planks and drew a long drink of water from his goatskin bag before splashing a little on his face.

His rough, sweat-drenched tunic clung to his body, and he seemed to ache all over. But nagging worries irritated him more than sore muscles. Finding and keeping good workers was a constant and growing problem. He also had difficulty keeping the materials and completed work safe from thieves and vandals. Noah and his sons took turns guarding the construction site at night, but even that wasn't always enough.

Silently, he cried out to God in sheer frustration. He wondered how and when they would ever be able to finish this monumental project. Nothing seemed to go smoothly anymore, and no one seemed to care that the end was so very, very near.

"Something troubling you, Father?" Japheth, the "fair one" jumped down on the platform from the scaffolding above. The youngest of Noah's sons, he was slender but strong, with a smile just like his mother's. He drank from Noah's goatskin bag.

"Oh, I am just thinking about the work that still needs to be done and the number of men we'll need when it's time to load the provisions. The grain ..." Noah paused and dropped his head, sighing deeply.

"We finished fifteen cubits of wood this morning and if we have enough men tomorrow, we can probably make fifteen more," Japheth said encouragingly. "The ark will be finished soon. You should be happy, not sad. So what's troubling you?"

Noah gave Japheth a doleful glance. "It's nothing, son. You and your brothers have done a good job and the work will be over soon. I just ..."

"You're really thinking about the workmen who will die if they still refuse to believe, aren't you, Father?" Japheth sat quietly beside Noah. "You've done your best to warn them; each man must decide for himself." Noah looked up and smiled at the son too young to be so wise. Japheth gave his father a reassuring pat on the shoulder before scrambling back up the scaffolding again.

Noah was a man of extraordinary courage and faith who found favor in the eyes of God. He lived with his wife, Naamah, and their children in the lush, green valley of Mesopotamia surrounded by gently rolling hills. The land was beautiful, but the people were violent and cruel.

Unimaginable Wickedness

In the Bible, Genesis chapter six, tells us:

The Lord saw how great man's wickedness on the earth had become, and that every inclination of the thoughts of his heart was only evil all the time. The Lord was grieved that he had made man on the earth, and his heart was filled with pain. So the Lord said, "I will wipe mankind, whom I have created, from the face of the earth—men and animals ..." (Genesis 6:5-7, NIV[1]).

So God said to Noah, "I am going to put an end to all people, for the earth is filled with violence because of them. I am surely going to destroy both them and the earth. ... I am going to bring floodwaters on the earth to destroy all life under the heavens, every creature that has the breath of life in it. Everything on earth will perish" (Genesis 6:13, 17).

9

Although the people of Noah's day were intelligent and advanced in their achievements, they sought pleasure through unimaginable wickedness. They flaunted their evil in blatant sexual abuse. They sacrificed their children to pagan gods. They practiced violence and lawlessness as a way of life. Finally, their evil became intolerable to God.

"Whatever other sins that ancient man was guilty of ... the biblical record, anthropological findings, and archaeological evidence indicate ancient civilizations were violent and in continuous conflict," according to Dr. Clyde McCone, professor emeritus of anthropology at California State University in Long Beach, California.

"Apart from the Bible, we find independent accounts telling us much the same story about the conditions in civilization at the time," says Father Michael Hanifin, an Old Testament Bible educator and parish priest in southern California. "Both ancient Greek and Hebrew writings indicate that there was a great deal of corruption and brutality among the populace. There were many murders—human life was cheap indeed."

Genesis 6:11 states: *"Now the earth was corrupt in God's sight and full of violence."* Biblical Prophecy tells us that in the End Times "it will be like in the days of Noah," which we will discuss in the concluding chapter of this book (See Matthew 24:37-39).

The world had become such an evil place in Noah's day that it had even lured away some members of Noah's own family—a fact that was a constant source of pain in his heart. Only his wife, Naamah, and their three sons, Shem, Ham, and Japheth, believed God and his instructions to Noah—and even they had moments of doubt.

His sons loyally worked on the ark in spite of the mocking, brutal people who took great delight in harassing them. The ark was a burning reminder of Noah's preaching of repentance, and it seemed to make the people angrier all the time. Although it was a dangerous time to go against the crowd, the young men and their wives believed the warnings of God's coming judgment and chose to trust Noah. His fate would be theirs, too.

Out of the corner of his eye, Noah noticed a loud group of extremely tall men talking to some of his workers and offering them wine. They were the Nephilim. Giants, these men were enormous, cunning, and evil. Their presence meant trouble. Noah scanned the platforms and dirt below for his oldest son, but the brawny Shem was nowhere in sight.

"Hey, old man," one of the giants yelled, scooping up a rock from the dark soil and hurling it in Noah's direction. "We'll turn this into a nice big brothel when you finally finish it. There'll be plenty of room for everyone—even animals!" The men howled with laughter as they passed around a jug of wine.

Some of the workers resting in the shade laughed, too, and quietly started egging the Nephilim on, hoping for a fight that would delay their return to work.

Noah faced the giants squarely, his voice firm and bold. "You will soon face God's judgment if you …" But they drowned out his words with swearing, crude gestures, and laughter as they turned to walk away, beckoning the workers to follow.

"Judgment from God? What god? And rain?" they sneered. "Who's ever heard of water falling from the sky? You're crazy, you old fool, and one of these days ..."

"Back to work men—now!" Noah shouted as he quickly descended the ladders. "There will be no pay if you do not work a full day."

On the ground, the Nephilim looked even more imposing than from above. Noah was dwarfed by the fierce-looking men with the bronzed, muscular bodies. As he marched closer to them he was almost overwhelmed with the stench from their wine and filthy clothes. Their piercing eyes were filled with a wild hatred. Noah suppressed the uncomfortable fear welling up inside and spoke in forceful tones.

"If you want to go with these men, then go, but if you are here to work, then get back to work now! I will only pay if you work a full day."

"Don't listen to him; come and have some fun," one of the drunken Nephilim demanded. Then he stepped forward and pointed at Noah. "And as for you, old man, you haven't seen the last of us."

With a silent prayer and steely determination, Noah stood his ground and repeated his command.

His second son ran up and stood by his side. Together they stared silently at the giants and their crew, wondering what would happen next ...

Supermen

Who were the Nephilim? We know very little about them apart from what is recorded in the Bible. Genesis 6:4 tells us:

> The Nephilim were on the earth in those days—and also afterward—when the sons of God went to the daughters of men and had children by them. They were the heroes of old, men of renown.

"The Nephilim were the unnatural offspring of man and fallen angels," says Bible commentator, Chuck Missler, author of thirty books, including *The Flood of Noah, The Rise of Babylon,* and *The Persian Gulf Crisis.* "This unnatural intervention in the lives of mankind was the reason for the Flood, and Noah's uncontaminated genealogy was a factor in his being selected to survive it."

The theory that the Nephilim were the offspring of demonic beings and humans is still controversial. Some scholars maintain that the term only refers to the line of Cain, the wicked son of Adam and Eve, intermarrying with righteous descendants who followed God. Many believe the Nephilim were giants, as the King James version of the Bible translates. Whether giants or normal-sized human beings, they had become very evil and violent. The results of their immoral carnage are well documented by ancient historians.

The World of Noah

The world Noah and his family lived in was quite different than you might imagine. Instead of being primitive, the ancient civilizations destroyed by the Flood were highly advanced in many fields, including astronomy, metallurgy, agriculture, weaponry, mathematics, and architecture. Their remarkable intelligence, abilities, and accomplishments have intrigued scientists for centuries.

But when did Noah live? What do we know about the pre-Flood world? How do we know that ancient men even had the tools and technology necessary to build a great ship like the ark?

Chronology is the science dealing with the division of time, enabling us to arrange events in order of their occurrence, or to assign correct dates to ancient events—such as when Noah lived! We can use one or more of four different types of chronology to determine this answer: astronomical, geological, archaeological, and political-historical.

"We can accurately calculate when Noah lived," says Gene Faulstich, founder of the Chronology History Research Institute in Ruthven, Iowa, "using astronomical data and historical data from the Bible and other ancient manuscripts. The ancients kept very accurate and detailed records of their observations of the sun, moon, and sky.

"Astronomy is an exact science, and by examining the astronomical information recorded by these ancient astronomers, it's possible for us to determine on our calendar when these events actually took place. In other words, based on Noah's records found in the Genesis account, and astronomical computer analysis, we have determined that he began building the ark in 2465 B.C., with the first rains falling in 2345 B.C.," explains Faulstich.

Ancient Man's Achievements

Let's look at some of the archaeological evidence of ancient man's abilities and achievements to get a better idea of the world in which Noah lived before the Flood and immediately thereafter. According to Roger Oakland, a respected author-lecturer and science educator:

"If we look at the evidence left to us by ancient civilizations, we find that the further back we go, the more amazing are the accomplishments.

"The ancient Minoans on the island of Crete were highly advanced. Some of the reconstruction of their temples that were destroyed catastrophically reveals that they had tremendous abilities, architectural skills, and artistic design in their buildings. They used inlaid stone, natural ventilation and air-conditioning.

"We can look at ancient Egyptian artifacts such as daggers—some of which are electroplated. Electroplated artifacts have been found literally around the ancient world.

"The ancients were also able to make batteries and generate electricity. The ancient Mayans were able to calculate the solar year to be 365.2420 days—accurate within 2/10,000th of a day.

"Even more amazing is the recent discovery of a Chinese woman buried over 2,100 years ago. Today, her body is still so perfectly preserved that X-ray technicians were able to determine the contents of her last meal. Her body was buried at the base of a mound and when it was excavated, they found a very complex system of coffins. Within the sarcophagus, they found many interesting things—a compact containing rouge, lipstick, powder, brush, silk gloves, and a silk scarf. They also found lacquerware and musical instruments—exactly what the Bible claims the people of the past were able to do!"

Other ancient achievements are just as amazing and leave researchers with numerous difficult questions. For instance, the largest stone in the Third Pyramid in Egypt weighs more than 319 tons and was cut with a precision that rivals what modern man can cut using lasers and computers today. Many of the stones in this pyramid and in ancient temples around the world fit together so perfectly that you can't even slip a piece of paper between them—astounding architectural achievements by ancient man.

In England, researchers have found that the stones composing the strange ruins of Stonehenge weigh fifty tons each and apparently had to be moved uphill at least a hundred miles to their present location. Scientists still can't be certain what Stonehenge was used for, but possibilities include an enormous lunar calendar, a pagan temple, a navigation school, and an eclipse predictor. A worship site is the most likely explanation, as pagan worshippers still periodically assemble there for rituals.

How could ancient people construct temples and pyramids so mathematically and astronomically precise? Such incredible feats can be compared with the information we are only able to obtain today through the latest satellites and computers. Were these people really that advanced?

"We tend to think of ancient man as being very uncivilized," says Dr. Donald Chittick, holder of several patents in alternate fuels, and a retired professor of earth science and chemistry, who has lectured around the world. "However, archaeological evidence shows us that the contemporaries of Noah had a very high level of scientific activity. For example, researchers have found ancient electric batteries in the Middle East. They used copper and iron instead of carbon and zinc like we do, but the batteries definitely worked and were used to electroplate daggers and other objects with gold."

Besides electroplating applications, it's believed these "Baghdad" batteries, found in 1936 in an archaeological site near Baghdad, Iraq, were used to illuminate underground crypts and tombs. Both

Babylonian and Egyptian high priests, and perhaps even common folks, may have been adept at producing electrical energy.

The world's first known working seismometer (a device that registers earthquakes) was built in A.D. 132. More than 2,000 years ago a Chinese astronomer noted the moons of Jupiter—long before Galileo "discovered" them. The first model airplane, found in 1898 in a Middle East archaeological dig and now on display in the Cairo Museum with a replica shown at the Smithsonian Aviation Museum, shows ancients understood flight. This 2,200-year-old model airplane has wings that angle slightly downward at the ends—the exact same improved wing design first used in modern times on the supersonic Concorde!

"Archaeologists have also found an analog computer on a sunken ship in the Aegean Sea," notes Dr. Chittick. "It was used to make maps that were generally more accurate than the ones we could make before the advent of satellites. In fact, until very recently, we believed that their maps were in error because they showed two bodies of land representing Antarctica. Now we've found that their maps were accurate and ours were in error.

"In California," Dr. Chittick says, "a geode was found with an ancient version of a spark plug inside ... Now, these artifacts are not unique. There is ample evidence to show that there were very advanced civilizations spanning the globe. Then they were inexplicably wiped out—presumably by the Flood."

Tubal-Cain Forged Metals

The Bible gives us another clue to the abilities of the people in Noah's day. According to the Book of

Genesis, Tubal-Cain "forged all kinds of tools out of bronze and iron." The Bereshith Rabba Jewish tradition tells us that Naamah, the sister of Tubal-Cain, was Noah's wife. If that is true, then it would be logical to assume that Noah had access to metal tools to aid him in the construction of the ark. Artifacts found in that region of the Middle East confirm that the people of Noah's day not only had metal tools but also metal household objects and metal pagan idols, some with elaborate decorations.

"There was an exciting discovery in 1934 of a wood-handled metal hammer encased in sedimentary deposited limestone (Ordovician stone)," says Dr. Carl Baugh, a museum curator and archaeological excavator. "The metal was analyzed and found to contain 96.6 percent iron, 0.74 percent sulfur and 2.6 percent chlorine. In order to compound chlorine with metallic iron it requires a process perfected only within the last ten years. Therefore, it had to be natural circumstances under which this ancient hammer was forged because of the elemental constituency requiring complete elimination of ultraviolet radiation. This artifact confirms that ancient man had extensive knowledge of metallurgy and used metal tools before the Flood."

According to Roger Oakland, ancient belt buckles have been found in China that were made from an alloy of 5 percent manganese, 10 percent copper, and 85 percent aluminum. Scientists are amazed that ancient man knew how to extract aluminum from bauxite ore because it involves using temperatures in excess of 1,000 degrees plus electrolysis!

Also in China, archaeologists have found swords dating back more than 2,200 years that were made of thirteen different metals alloyed together. In the

Mount Ararat region alone, Russian scientists have found 500 ancient furnaces presumably used for smelting bronze. The ability of ancient man to mine and use a number of different metals has been proven by artifacts found around the world.

It seems obvious, then, that the tools and technology necessary to construct an enormous ship were available to Noah. But what do we know about the ark itself? Let us again turn back the hands of time and view the ark under construction.

Built to Last

"Now compress the pieces of wood together with these rocks," Shem instructed the workman struggling under the weight of a stack of unfinished beams and planks. "Once the gopher wood is cured, it will be as strong as your ax."

The man muttered something under his breath as he stacked the planks.

Using a coarse brush, Shem spread some of the boiling sap resins on a huge strip of wood and then added another layer. The air was filled with the fragrance of freshly hewn wood and the sticky resins boiling over a fire nearby. Several men were using the same procedure on another stack of planks not far away—layering strips of wood with sap resins, then using large stones to compress the boards as they dried.

All around them were thick planks drying in the sun and stacks of hardened wood ready to be used on the ark. Workmen were swarming over the massive three-story ship now nearing completion. The man by Shem broke off a toothpick-size sliver from a plank and put it between his teeth as he stretched his arms in the bright noonday sun. "Why not just use whole beams of wood to build this crazy ship?"

he asked, helping Shem lift the heavy planks up to the workbench. "Why go through all of this extra work?"

"Because, my friend, once these strips are coated with that boiling sap, they'll be so strong nothing can break them. This great ark will last forever."

"It may last forever," the man laughed, "but it's never going to see any water this far inland ..." The historical account in Genesis 6:14-16 outlines God's instructions for building the ark:

So make yourself an ark of cypress wood; make rooms in it and coat it with pitch inside and out. This is how you are to build it: The ark is to be 450 feet long, 75 feet wide and 45 feet high. Make a roof for it and finish the ark to within 18 inches of the top. Put a door in the side of the ark and make lower, middle and upper decks.

What is "cypress wood," or "gopher wood," as it is called in some translations? The answer is still being debated, but for many years scientists believed that the gopher wood referred to in the Bible was either white oak, cypress, cedar, or larch. All of these species are strong and durable. They were used by various ancient civilizations for shipbuilding and could be found growing in the rich, pre-Flood area of the Middle East.

"Gopher Wood" Was Lamination Process

Dr. Don Shockey, a cultural anthropologist and founder of the Foundation for International Biblical Exploration and Research, has recently discovered a startling new explanation for the term "gopher wood":

The ancient term for *gopherwood* in Hebrew was not the name of a particular species of wood but rather the term for a unique lamination process using resins made from sap. It's ingenious. I met a man raised in Jerusalem and he told me that in the past, they would cut the bark of a certain tree and collect the sap. Then, if you put this protective sap on two pieces of wood, clamped them together and left them overnight, by the next day, you could not break the splice. The wood on either side would break first.

He said that they do not use this system any more because it discolors the wood. After he told me that, a light went off in my head. We obviously don't have a "ply" tree, yet we have plywood. The idea of *gopherwood* being a process rather than a species makes perfect sense to me. From an engineering point of view, a laminated beam made from several different types of wood glued together, cured and hardened, would be structurally superior, in terms of tension and resiliency, than just a single block of wood.

We've found that this process is currently being used in Canada to commercially produce a laminated wood product. In this process, they take small strips of wood with resin hydrocarbons, heat and pressurize it and then cure it with microwaves. Once it's cured, the wood becomes harder than steel. We know that in England and in Russia, they have been using this process to make weapons of war—including gun barrels—and there are indications that our own Stealth Bomber has some of this in it because it is vegetable material and cannot be detected like metal.

It is absolutely amazing, and there are endless uses for it. Insects won't bother it, and this process makes the wood water-resistant, fire-resistant—practically indestructible. I am convinced that Noah had this technology and used it building the ark.

"Scoffers who say that Noah's ark would not have been strong enough since he used wood as the building material need to consider the fact that Noah did not use regular wood—he used *gopherwood*, with its amazing strength and properties as described," comments Arnold Mendez, Noah's ark and Early Man researcher.

It is interesting to note that several of the eyewitnesses who have reported seeing the ark on Mount Ararat specifically mentioned that the mighty beams they saw looked as if they were made of laminated wood. A piece of wood brought back from Mount Ararat by a twentieth-century ark expeditioner, and believed to be from the ark, generated this unusual note from a Carbon-14 lab:

The dark bituminous-like coating turned out not to be just surface coating but distributed throughout the wood. This was very surprising as we have only encountered this before in dealing with pressure-penetrated woods. Still further of a mystery is how this material [bituminous coating] could be impregnated so deeply within the wood fibers without the use of present-day technology.

As we can see from the discussion above, "gopher wood" is most likely not a particular type of wood, but a wood process. Researcher Arnold Mendez adds some interesting observations about

the significance of God's specifics in Genesis 6:14:
Make yourself an ark of gopher wood, cover it (or pitch it) inside and outside with pitch.

"The word 'gopher,' which is the word from gopher wood, is very similar to the word 'pitch' and the word 'atonement' or 'cover' used in Leviticus 16. In other words, the words *gopher* wood, *pitch*, and *covering* or *atonement* (atonement being a type of covering) are all very similar."

Relating the connection between these words, could it be that the ark was not only a physical shelter or *covering* for Noah, his family, and the creatures aboard, but in addition, an atoning spiritual *covering* in the judgment of the Floodwaters?

Additional significant details—Noah was instructed to cover the ark with pitch *inside and out*. Webster's dictionary defines "pitch" as a thick, dark, sticky substance derived from either the sap of a conifer or made from the distillation of coal tar, asphalt, or petroleum. Pitch, a bituminous substance, is found in oil-bearing regions like the Middle East, and during Roman times, it could even be found floating in great lumps on the Dead Sea. It was usually mixed with straw or reeds to fill cracks in the hull of a ship to make it waterproof. However, it was generally used only to coat and seal the *exterior* of a ship.

Why would God tell Noah to coat the ark *inside and out*—especially if gopher wood was actually the name for laminated beams glued together and covered with resins? Wouldn't that be overkill? Or, is it possible that God wanted the ark to be waterproofed and completely sealed inside and out to ensure that it would survive all of the natural elements—to the present day?

Missler, Biblical Expositional Commentator, founder and president of Koinonia Institute, relates in his recent interview the significance of the use of *pitch*—to preserve the ark to our present day:

> Another provocative aspect of God's instructions to Noah was to pitch it "within and without." Now you don't need to pitch it on both sides for floatation, but you would for preservation. That ark sat in Noah's driveway for 120 years as a testimony to an unbelieving world of a coming judgment. There are some of us that suspect that that may be its destiny once again. Once the ark is discovered, it once again may prove to be a testimony to an unbelieving world of a forthcoming judgment.

Dr. John Morris, geologist and author of *Noah's ark and the Ararat Adventure,* refers to the pitch as a "preservative," and in a recent interview shared what this means to the continued search for the ark:

> The Bible says he was to pitch it within and without, and I think that really means... probably injecting the wood...it would be a preservative...and maybe that's why we're still looking for it. Because the evidence is that it's up there, and maybe that preservative is part of that evidence. It's kept the ark there. I think every part of this story [of Noah and the Flood] has a supernatural flavor to it. God designed the ark, God protected it and, well, we're still looking.

The Size of Noah's Ark

God told Noah to build the ark and make it 300 by 50 by 30 cubits. In ancient times, the cubit was defined as the distance between an average man's elbow and fingertips, ranging anywhere from 17 inches to 24 inches in length. Using 18 inches as the cubit measurement most frequently cited by the ancient Hebrews, this would make the ark 450 feet long, 75 feet wide, and 45 feet high. An enormous craft by any definition.

Presumably constructed out of laminated wood, stained dark with resins, and covered with a shellac-like pitch, the ark would have resembled a dark brown, rectangular barge or a shoe box. "The Book of Genesis says that the ark was an 'ark.' And, an ark did not have to have a prow; it did not have to have a bow, because it wasn't being propelled. It didn't have to have sails, it wasn't sailing. The word 'ark' means 'box' or 'chest.' So, when we think of the ark we should think more along the lines of a large barge, a box-like configuration and not necessarily the shape of a boat," Mendez comments.

So it's not sophisticated looking, but very functional. Once again, that's essentially the same description as that given by many of the eye-witnesses, including those who have never read or heard the biblical account.

Consider the spiritual implications for such a box-like "lifeboat"—without any type of sail or steering mechanism—Noah had to have tremendous faith, for he was completely dependent on God, not himself, for the direction and safety of the ark when he entered inside and the door was sealed closed.

Let's use some comparisons to visualize the size of the completed ark. Experts tell us that the ark was the length of one and one-half football fields, or approximately the size of a four-story apartment building a block long.

"Noah's ark is one-half the size of the great ocean liner, the *Queen Mary*," says George Williamson, an avid ark researcher and hobbyist from the Chicago area. "The roof of the ark could have easily held twenty volleyball/basketball courts and the interior of the ark contained 1.5 million cubic feet—enough room for 170 railroad boxcars!"

Imagine! It would have taken 280,000 cubic feet of timber—between 9,000 and 13,000 planks—to construct the ship, which has been estimated at a little more than 4,100 tons deadweight.[2]

With ocean water figured at 35 cubic feet per ton, the ark, completely empty, would float with its bottom about 4.3 feet below water. Loading the ark to where it would sink to a depth of 15 feet would require 10,000 tons of cargo, and to 20 feet, 15,000 tons. Assuming the weight of the animals as 100 tons, and allowing each animal twenty times its own weight in food plus twenty times its weight in water for a year, the cargo would weigh about 4,000 tons. We don't know, of course, how many tons of animals were aboard, but these calculations are within reason and extremely conservative. It is calculated that the fully loaded ark probably weighed about 24,300 tons.

The ark was undoubtedly a great ship, very different from the Sunday school drawings and cartoons so many people are familiar with. A massive vessel, it was built to withstand the violent forces of the greatest catastrophe the earth has experienced to date.

Windows in the ark

"You shall make a window for the ark, and finish it to a cubit (18 inches) from the top ..." (Genesis 6:16, NASB).

"The design is absolutely ingenious," claims Dr. Elfred Lee, an internationally acclaimed archaeological illustrator and college professor. He has worked with several of the ark eyewitnesses to re-create what they've seen on Mount Ararat. "The only window on the ark was about eighteen inches high and spanned the center of the ship for 450 feet. A small overhang covered this window to keep the rain out. It would have appeared kind of like a catwalk down the center of the rooftop. This unique design provided light and ventilation to all three levels and, because of its position, probably kept out the water from even the most violent waves. It was a simple, yet marvelous design."

Stable and Seaworthy

Shipbuilders have discovered that the ark's length to breadth equals a ratio of six to one, meaning it would be a slow-moving vessel. In 1604, Pieter Jansen, a Dutch merchant, commissioned a shipyard to build a scale model of the ark according to the measurements given in the Book of Genesis. This craft proved to be not only more seaworthy than contemporary vessels, but its gross tonnage was one third larger than ships built to more modern designs.[3]

Rev. Eddie Atkinson, a pastor and model ark builder who has studied the design of the ark for many years, explains:

> The ark was exactly six times longer than it was wide, and it set the standard for all other oceangoing vessels. Had the ark been square,

for instance, it would have just spun around in circles. The dimensions of the ark made it so stable in rough seas that the same length-to-width ratio is still being used by modern shipbuilders today. In fact, during World War II, the USS *Oregon* and the USS *New Mexico* were built specifically on this model, using the same length-to-width ratio as the ark.

"The ark was very seaworthy," as Mendez demonstrates in his recent interview:

There have been many computer models that have been done on its stability. These models that have been built have actually been floated in some of the tanks in which they look at various designs of ships. The 1:6 ratio of the ark's dimensions made it extremely stable. Marine architects say that this is the most stable ratio there is when you want to increase carrying capacity. It is estimated that we would be able to have a 200-foot wave and if the ark met it head-on, there would not be any problems.

Scoffers of the Genesis story ran computer models several years ago to see how large a boat could be built out of wood. They say that about 300 to 340 feet is the longest that one can be built to operate and remain stable in water. Other than that it would probably be tossed to and fro in the sea and would break up. What the skeptics did not consider is that the Chinese, 600 years ago, were actually building wooden ships more than 600 feet long. In the harbor at Nanjing, they have discovered an old rudder. And, the proportion of the rudder and the size of the rudder indicates that it was used to turn a ship about 600 feet long. Some of these ships that the Chinese built had nine masts, were 600 feet long, and some of them were 171 or 180 feet across. So, it's already been done. Noah's ark being at about 450 feet would have been just a bit smaller than the Chinese treasure ships that have already been built.

Marine engineering experts agree that with its low center of gravity, the ark was exceptionally stable and could have remained seaworthy indefinitely—even through the most violent waves and storms.

Geologist John Morris claims that at the time of the Flood, some of the waves were probably as high as 1,000 feet, yet the ark was designed to be able to survive the turmoil of the Flood. The important design factor that he cites from the experts in a recent interview, is the cross section of the ark:

Experts have noted that the cross section of the ark, 450 feet long or so by 75 feet wide and 45 feet high, that cross section would keep the ark stable. There's a "riding couple" that it's called there—the weight of the ark pulling down, but the buoyancy force of the water pushing up—the ark then could tilt. Any degree of tilt up to 90 degrees or so and a riding couple of the two forces would tend to bring it back to right side up. It would be almost impossible to capsize. The length of the ark would keep the ark facing into the waves so that it would not be hit broadside by some of these super waves. So, the ark had to be marvelously well designed.

"In terms of the hydrodynamic forces," the late Dr. Henry Morris, professor emeritus of hydraulics engineering, claimed, "this ark would have been very stable. In fact, the balance between the buoyant force, the gravitational force, and the wave force would be such that the ark would right itself if it were tilted anywhere from zero to 90 degrees. It would be practically impossible to capsize."

We wanted to test the various stability theories put forth by Dr. Morris. So we had a model ark built to the same proportions as the biblical ark. We had our tests conducted in San Diego, California, by an internationally known hydraulics laboratory that asked us not to disclose its name. The following interview was conducted with the hydraulics lab project director after the testing:

Q. *How high a wave could the ark have survived?*

A. The tests showed that the ark could survive waves higher than you would ever encounter in the ocean.

Q. *What is the maximum height of a wave the ark could have survived based on your test results?*

A. More than a 200-foot wave without capsizing. But there are no waves that large in the ocean.

Q. *What about tidal waves—would they ever be high enough to capsize the ark?*

A. A peaked up tidal wave could maybe reach 100 feet or more, but this would happen only close to shore in shallow water, not in the ocean.

Q. *Then because of the ark's unique design ratio, it could have survived any type of wave produced by the ocean?*

A. If it were hit broadside by a gigantic wave, it's conceivable that it could have been capsized. However, the surprising thing revealed by the tests was that the ark naturally propelled its bow into the waves. It's a remarkably stable vessel.[4]

Like the giant ships of today, the ark's low center of gravity gave it remarkable stability. The deeper it sank in the water because of its heavy cargo, the more stable it became. The results of these tests proved conclusively that the ark was not only seaworthy and remarkably stable, but that it had a natural tendency to propel its bow into the waves—making it almost impossible to capsize.

Ark Inspired Later Shipbuilders

The ark was a masterpiece of engineering that has inspired shipbuilders and mariners throughout history. Our investigation of other aspects of this mysterious vessel will continue in later chapters, but let's examine what we know to be true about the ark so far.

We know that Noah had access to the metal tools and technology necessary to build this great ship and that it was begun in 2465 B.C.. The ark was constructed with a variety of indigenous woods laminated together with resins, then coated inside and out with pitch. It had three levels, with a window down the length of the roof, and it didn't have sails or a rudder.

This incredible design, as given to Noah by God, kept a very precious cargo—the only remnants of selected human and animal life on earth—safe and dry for a year while floating on the dark, cold turbulent seas that covered the entire planet.

"We'll go with them to have some fun," one of the builders of the ark scoffed with wine dripping from his chin, "but we'll be back after we've used up our money. And when this ship is finished, we'll put it to good use—long after you're gone."

Five of the workers left with the Nephilim, and Noah turned back toward the ark without a word.

"Father, aren't you going to try to stop them?" Ham demanded angrily. "We need their help."

"No, son, it would be useless. Besides, what good will they be to us full of wine? We can finish with the men we have left. Come now, the time is short and we have much to do to get ready ..."

Endnotes

1 Note : All scripture quotations, unless otherwise indicated, are taken from the *Holy Bible, New International Version*®. NIV® Copyright© 1973, 1978, 1984 by International Bible Society. Used by permission of Zondervan Publishing House, All rights reserved.
2 Frederick A. Filby, *The Flood Reconsidered* (Grand Rapids: Zondervan Corporation, 1971), p. 88.
3 Ibid., p. 100.
4 David W. Balsiger and Charles E. Sellier, *In Search of Noah's Ark* (Los Angeles: Sun Classic Books, 1976), pp. 117–118.

THREE

CREATURES ON THE ARK

By perseverance the snail reached the ark.
—Charles Haddon Spurgeon

HEAVY CRATES, BAGS OF GRAIN, and enormous water jugs were stacked all over the compacted dirt near the massive wooden loading ramp of the ark. The air was heavy and still cool in the early morning light.

Japheth yawned and stretched his back and was bending down to pick up another crate when he spotted them.

"Father, look!"

"It's unbelievable!"

"Shem, Naamah, everyone come quickly!" Noah cried out. "Hurry, we must help them."

"Quick. Open the cages," Naamah called to her daughters-in-law. "Put the birds inside. Gently ..."

From every direction—walking, crawling, or drifting down from the sky—animals and birds of every kind were making their way to the ark. All were moving quickly as if they were being driven by an unseen force.

Noah and his family had been loading provisions on the ark when Japheth first spotted the deer tentatively coming close to the ramp—the only door to the ark.

33

"Look, they're coming to us on their own! They're walking into their cages. It's amazing!"

"Here, drop some grain and see if they'll follow you inside."

"Look, Father, they want to come inside," Japheth laughed. One deer was eating grain out of his hand and the other was nuzzling his leg as he backed up the ramp. "All right, all right, come with me."

"Look at all the birds. Here. Scatter grains near the cages. See if they'll go inside."

"They trust us."

"I can't believe it. They want to come inside!"
"It's wonderful."

"This is just as the Lord said it would be," Noah laughed. Suddenly his voice turned somber. "We need to get them all safely into their stalls and cages because the time is short." He surveyed the darkening sky. "Very short. The animals can sense it."

In chapters six and seven, the writer of Genesis records this spectacular event. God told Noah:

I am going to bring floodwaters on the earth to destroy all life under the heavens, every creature that has the breath of life in it. Everything on earth will perish. But, I will establish my covenant with you, and you will enter the ark—you and your sons and your wife and your sons' wives with you. You are to bring into the ark two of all living creatures, male and female, to keep them alive with you. Two of every kind of bird, of every kind of animal and of every kind of creature that moves along the ground will come to you to be kept alive. You are to take every kind of food that is to be eaten and store it away as food for you and for them. Noah did everything just as God commanded him.

The Lord then said to Noah, "Take with you seven of every kind of clean animal, a male and its mate, and two of every kind of unclean animal, a male and its mate, and also seven of every kind of bird, male and female, to keep their various kinds alive throughout the earth. Seven days from now I will send *rain on the earth for forty days and forty nights....* "

On that very day Noah and his sons, Shem, Ham and Japheth, together with his wife and the wives of his three sons, entered the ark. They had with them every wild animal according to its kind, all livestock according to their kinds, every creature that moves along the ground according to its kind and every bird according to its kind, everything with wings. Pairs of all creatures that have the breath of life in them came to Noah and entered the ark. The animals going in were male and female of every living thing, as God had commanded Noah. Then the Lord shut him in (Genesis 6:17-22; 7:1-4, 13-16).

Probably nothing in the biblical account of Noah's ark and the Flood creates more controversy than the animals themselves. Critics pose a number of tough questions that need scientific answers: How did Noah capture the animals? How many different kinds of animals were aboard? How could eight people care for the animals? With the help of scientists and Bible scholars, these questions can possibly be answered.

How Noah Captured the Animals

First, how could Noah possibly gather or "trap" representatives of every kind of animal on earth?

The late Dr. Arthur J. Jones was a scientist at Bournville College in Birmingham, England, who did years of research on the questions raised by the Genesis account of Noah's ark, and carefully studied the original Hebrew terminology in his search for answers. In an article in the *Ararat Report*, the world's only regularly published newsletter on Noah's ark research activities, Dr. Jones wrote:

> The Lord commanded Noah to "cause [the animals] to come into the ark" [Genesis 6:19] and to "take to you [into the ark—Genesis 7:1] all the behemah and birds [Genesis 7:2-3]." He was told that they would come to him for this purpose.[1]

The Bible says in several other places that the animals came to Noah. There wasn't any need to trap them. Genesis 6:20 says "pairs of all shall come unto you." Genesis 7:9 says "two by two they came unto Noah." Genesis 7:15 says "they came unto Noah unto the ark two by two." Genesis 7:16 says "the coming ones came male and female of all flesh."[2]

But, why would the animals go to the ark on their own? It doesn't seem to make sense; we do not see wild animals walking up to people in today's world.

"Animals are directed by instinct to respond naturally to numerous stimuli," says Dr. Ken Cumming, a retired Harvard-trained professor of biology at the San Diego–based Institute for Creation Research, who still acts as a consultant.

> Scientifically, we've learned that animal response to potential disaster seems linked to magnetic field fluctuations in the brain—and it's also connected to how they respond to polarized light.

> You can actually see many animals react to imminent danger right before natural disasters such as hurricanes or earthquakes

and before magnetic disturbances such as thunderstorms.

The earth-shattering tectonic events that released the waters from under the surface of the earth would have affected the earth's magnetic fields and could have produced the stimuli that warned the animals of pending danger. Their natural instinct to seek safety and shelter may well have been what drew them to the ark.

Interestingly, even today predators and prey will run together or stay in close proximity for long periods without incident while fleeing forest fires and other natural disasters.[3]

In addition, we know from the fossil record that the climate of the pre-Flood earth was very different from that of the post-Flood earth—something we will discuss in a later chapter. Tropical plants have been found frozen in Arctic regions, and fossil evidence has shown that desert regions were once covered with lush vegetation. If the entire pre-Flood earth had a similar temperate climate, it's possible that representative animals of all kinds on the earth at that time could have been found in the general area where Noah built the ark. They wouldn't have had far to travel after they sensed the coming disaster.

How Many Animals Came Aboard?

Another frequently asked question involves the number of animals on the ark. According to taxonomists, there are more than 1,072,000 known species of animals in the world today.

Dr. Richard N. Vineyard, a biology professor in Utah and a critic of the biblical account of Noah, says, "The question I would ask is quite simple: How could two of every living animal be brought aboard any vessel? The sheer numbers and weight would overwhelm a fleet of arks. I don't believe we can take the story of the ark literally."

But Dr. John Whitcomb, a retired professor of Old Testament Studies at Grace Theological Seminary who co-authored the book *The Genesis Flood,* explains:

It doesn't say in the biblical account that "two of every single animal on earth was taken aboard the ark." There were certain animals that didn't have to go on board, such as fish, water snakes, whales, insects, and other marine life that could survive in the water.

Also, it says that only two or seven of each "kind" were taken. The extra animals taken aboard the ark fell into the clean-animal categories and were to be used for sacrifices to God following the Flood. Some may have also been used for food and clothing in the post-Flood world.

"Each family of creatures on the earth today has a single pair of ancestors," says Dr. Kenneth Ebel, professor of biology at Christ College in Irvine, California. "Even though there are over 300 varieties of dogs in the world today due to selective breeding ... they all have a single common ancestor.

Arnold Mendez, a chemistry instructor at Texas A&M who holds a Masters in biology and thirty years of experience as a researcher of Noah's ark, explains the concept of "biblical kinds":

The ark did not carry animals based on species, but on what we call the "biblical kind." And, if you read the first chapter of Genesis the "biblical kind" referred to are animals that reproduce other animals like themselves. So, generally speaking, a "kind" contains a lot of species.

Consider the canine species. The canine species include the wolves; they include the jackals, the foxes, and coyotes, all of these dog-like animals. In reality, all of these species could be contained in probably one or two biblical kinds. Because the biblical kinds were all interrelated to each other, Noah did not have to load the ark with a wolf, a jackal, and a dog, and a coyote. He could have loaded one biblical kind, which would give rise to all of these modern day species.

Well, just how many common-ancestor kinds went aboard the ark? According to Dr. Whitcomb, "We can deduce that only the following numbers of animal groups would have possibly been on the ark—3,700 known kinds of mammals; 8,600 kinds of birds; 6,300 kinds of reptiles; and 2,500 kinds of amphibians."

This would leave hundreds of thousands of different kinds of fish, tunicates (marine chordates like sea squirts), echinoderms (marine creatures like starfishes and sea urchins), mollusks (mussels, clams, and oysters), coelenterates (corals, sea anemones, and jellyfish), sponges and protozoan (microscopic single-cell creatures) to survive in the water.

In addition, aquatic mammals (whales, seals, porpoises), certain amphibians, a large number of the arthropods (lobsters, shrimps, crabs, water fleas, barnacles), as well as many species of worms and some insects could have survived outside the ark.

"According to my calculations," says Dr. Whitcomb, "there could have been as few as 2,400 animals on the ark or up to as many as 50,000 animals on the ark. While that seems like a huge discrepancy, it can be explained by the different estimates and definitions of the kinds of animals on the earth before the Flood.

"These 'kinds' never evolved or merged into each other by crossing over the divinely established lines of demarcation, but they have been diversified into so many varieties and sub-varieties (like the races and families of humanity) that even the greatest taxonomists have been staggered at the task of enumerating and classifying them.[4]

"Noah did not have a hopelessly impossible task," concludes Dr. Whitcomb. "The biblical record is totally credible."

Dr. Ebel agrees, saying there would have been "room left over for Noah's family and supplies. Considering the number of kinds of animals required to be put aboard the ark, there would have been ample room to load the ancestors of all the species we know today."

John Woodmorappe, author of *Noah's Ark: A Feasibility Study,* explains:

If people think there should be millions and millions of species of animals on the ark, well that is absolutely false. To begin with, the Genesis account in the Bible clearly talks about land animals and air-breathing animals, which rules out fish ... obviously it's talking about land vertebrates—not insects, not microscopic organisms—it's talking about land and air-breathing mammals, birds and reptiles and their counterparts ... animals that can interbreed according to the original creative kind mentioned in the Bible. So, when we take both of these things into account—it comes out to about 16,000 animals, a male and female of each kind and then seven of each so-called "clean" animal.

When you do a size distribution of the animals, you find that the vast majority of them are small. So, if you were to line up all 16,000 animals from the biggest to the smallest, have a parade of 16,000, you find that the 8,000[th] animal—that's the middle one, right in the middle, would be about the size of a large rat, 200 grams. The vast majority of the mammals are small, even more the vast majority of birds are small, and a majority of reptiles are small. Only 15 percent of the animals were sheep-sized or larger.

Now for the larger ones, there at the end of the parade line, there are several hundred large ones … but these could have been taken as young animals onto the ark, which would greatly have reduced the spacing problem even for the large animals, and the younger would have needed less food and water.

In my book, I did account for all the sizes of animals on the ark and I only used this value of the median, the 8,000th animal being the size of a large rodent, or rat, simply for purposes of reference. I actually have weight categories for each category of animal beginning in the ten to one hundred ton size range which would be the adult version of the sauropod; then the one to ten ton size, when an adult would have been the size of elephants and hippos; then the one hundred kilogram to one ton size as an adult size for horses, cows and pigs; and ten to one hundred kilogram size that would be about the weight and size of a human; one to ten kilogram that would be the size range of cats and rabbits; one hundred grams to one kilogram that would be the sizes of squirrels and large rodents that I mentioned; ten to one hundred grams that would be the size of mice and a large fraction of all birds; and the smallest would be one to ten grams, the smallest the size of shrews and some of the smaller lizards. So you have many orders of magnitude of sizes and the largest ones, I have represented as juvenile animals on the ark and all of the calculations are done as entirely workable for housing them and feeding them and providing them water.

Pairs of Clean and Unclean

Genesis classifies some animals as "clean" and some as "unclean."

Pairs of clean and unclean animals, of birds and of all creatures that move along the ground, male and female, came to Noah and entered the ark, as God had commanded Noah (Genesis 7:8-9).

What do "clean" and "unclean" mean? Clean animals are generally described as non-flesh-eating, chewing a cud, and having a divided hoof. Many non-predatory birds are considered clean, while camels (which chew the cud but do not have a divided hoof) and pigs (which have a divided hoof but do not chew the cud) are considered unclean. Unclean animals, in contrast, are ones that do not have a divided hoof or chew the cud, and eat flesh.

It is difficult to determine exactly which animals in the "clean" and "unclean" categories were on the ark. However, after studying numerous other biblical references, Dr. Jones came up with the following list of "clean" animals: deer, giraffes, pronghorns, cattle, antelopes, sheep and goats, pigeons, dodos, sand grouse, megapodes, curassows, grouse, pheasants, guinea fowl, turkeys, sparrows, finches, ducks, geese, and swans.

The "unclean" animals would include predatory and scavenging land birds, most water birds, bats, small rodents, lizards, and predatory mammals.

God's first instruction to Noah was that he bring the animals into the ark in pairs. Later, Noah was told the number of pairs. There would be one pair—male and female—of the unclean animals, but seven pairs of the clean animals—male and female—or fourteen animals in each clean group.

Bible students disagree on this point. Some contend there were only seven of each clean group, or three pairs plus one, which Noah would sacrifice after the Flood.[5]

Dr. Jones, however, argues the seven-pair theory:

Four times (Genesis 6:19-20; 7:2-3, 8-9, 15) the account emphasizes that all the animals were taken into the ark in pairs. The account also makes it clear that the purpose was propagation: "to keep seed alive upon the face of all the earth" (Genesis 7:3).

The reason for taking seven times more clean animals than unclean seems straightforward: first, clean animals were required for sacrifice; second, they would be required to provide clothing and food (Genesis 9:3) after the Flood (the environment being radically changed);

third, as these were becoming vulnerable prey animals they required a head start for survival (Genesis 7:3).[6]

Carrying Capacity of the Ark

Assuming the average size of all the animals on the ark was the size of a small dog (since there are relatively few large animals, and even those could have been represented by young of their kind), how many animals would the ark hold?

Arnold Mendez, researcher and presenter of Noah's Ark/Early Man seminars, has constructed various sized scale models of the ark in order to demonstrate the size and carrying capacity of the ark. In a 2007 interview, using various scale models he illustrated the ark's size and capacity:

The Bible indicates that Noah's ark was 300 cubits long, fifty cubits wide, and thirty cubits tall and we consider that the cubit was approximately eighteen inches. This would mean that Noah's ark was about 450 feet long, at fifty cubits wide it would be seventy-five feet wide, and at thirty cubits tall it would be forty-five feet tall. Now this means that the ark would have a carrying capacity of 1.5 million cubic feet. I have a 6-foot ark model based on the cubit being eighteen inches and that gives us a scale of 1/75th, so approximately 1/75th scale model of Noah's ark. Now, for comparison purposes, consider a 44-foot railroad stock car. This 44-foot railroad stock car is able to carry approximately 250 sheep-sized animals. Now the ark would be able to carry approximately 570 railroad stock car capacities inside of it … if we put these railroad cars together in a long train, that would be a train 5 $\frac{1}{2}$ miles long. To give you an idea, if you've ever come up to a stop sign when the railroad boom lowers, if we had that 5 $\frac{1}{2}$ mile long train going by you at thirty m.p.h., it would take approximately eleven minutes for that train to pass by you. Therefore, we can see that the ark was very, very large and it had a very, very large capacity.

Now here we have a Ferrari scale model about 1/75th, a Ferrari car, and this is also at a 1/75th scale model, approximately fourteen feet long. The ark could carry inside of it, stacked on top of each other, about 5,000 full-sized family cars–which means, if we put four people in each car you would have 5,000 Ferraris with 20,000 people packed into the ark. So, once again, I just want to give you an idea, or dispel the notion that the ark was a very small bathtub sized boat, when in actuality it was a very, very large immense ship.

Many scoffers of the Scriptures say that the ark could not possibly have carried all the animals. They say that the ark was not large enough. Now if we assign each animal to about the size of a small dog (even though, in reality most mammals are about the size of a small rat or rodent), then the ark-load at about 35,000 animals would have taken up about 22 percent of the ark's capacity. If we look at about 16,000 animals, it would have taken up about 12 percent of the ark's capacity. If we look at 2,000 animals, it would have taken up a little bit less than 2 percent. So in reality, when we're looking at the biblical kinds, not species, the ark very easily could have carried all of the animals with room left over.

It has commonly been estimated that only 36 percent of the ark would have been filled with animals. However, since the ark was designed for long-term living rather than short-term transport, extra room would have been needed. Some of this space would have been taken up by the subdividing created for stalls, cages, and ramps and by all of the food required for man and animals for one full year. There also had to be enough internal free space for ventilation and water storage, and plenty of room for waste disposal, which most experts believe filled the bottom deck.

Mendez has also built a 1/32nd scale model based on the biblical 18-inch cubit for his Noah's ark demonstrations in which a 6-foot tall man is represented by a 2 1/4 inch tall figure. When Mendez exhibits the ark model with proportional-sized scale models of numerous pairs of animals including giraffes, elephants, and other large animals arranged on the three decks, it gives an idea to his audience of how large the ark actually was. He concludes, "When we look at the ark and we look at the statistics behind it and its carrying capacity, we can see that it would very easily have carried all of the animals."

How could eight people possibly care for that many animals? Wouldn't it have been impossible? Let us imagine what it was like for Noah and his family after all the animals were on board.

How Noah Cared For the Animals

"Father, all of the animals are locked in their cages," Shem said, chewing on a piece of straw.

"Yes, we checked on all of them," Ham interjected wearily as he slumped down on a pile of rugs stacked against the dark brown wall.

"All of them?" Noah asked, surprised.

"Yes, all of them." Japheth nodded with his arm wrapped around his new bride. He squeezed her gently and she giggled.

"Good. Now we must divide up the responsibilities."

Noah looked around the large room at his tired family. This room on the first floor of the ark would be their communal kitchen and main living area for more than a year, so they had worked together to make it as comfortable as possible. It had a large, low table surrounded by cushions and blankets. Covered storage boxes that could be used for sitting or sleeping lined the walls.

Sunlight streamed through their only window, which ran the length of the ship high above them. They had oil lamps to use when it became dark, but for now, the sun cast streaks of light across the dark wood of their living area.

This was the first time they had stopped moving and come together since the door of the ark had been sealed shut. Looking at his beloved family, Noah felt a tightening in his throat as his eyes filled with tears.

"First, we must thank the Lord for bringing us safely …" Noah paused, listening to the muffled voices of people laughing and yelling outside.

"Hey, Noah, what are you doing in there? We don't see any water yet."

"Yea, what are you doing in there? Trying to make water yourself?"

"You'll have to come out and face us sometime."

Noah shook his head and spoke softly to his family, his voice cracking. "They will not be laughing soon." Clasping his rough, callused hands together, he bowed his head and led his family in a prayer.

The voices outside caused Noah pain—but not because the people were mocking him. Even though the end was just a few days away, the people still did not believe; there would be no other chance to escape the coming judgment. The door was sealed.

"Oh, my loved ones," Noah said, turning to look at each of them before glancing sadly toward the voices outside, "this has been a difficult journey already—just building the ark and getting the animals safely inside. It's impossible to imagine what it will be like when the waters come and all life outside ..."

"We'll take care of preparing the food," Naamah interrupted, nodding her head toward her daughters-in-law. "And we will help to feed the birds and the other small animals on this level, dear." She looked down at her lap and smoothed out the folds in her skirt, unable to look at her husband's distraught face any longer.

"Yes," Japheth's beautiful young wife encouraged, "and we'll help with the larger animals too. It'll all work out."

"Good. Thank you. Your youth will serve you well." Noah smiled faintly. "This voyage to our new life will not be easy, but God will be with us and see us safely through this terrible time. It is good to know that the Lord is merciful to those who seek his mercy." Noah bent down and kissed Naamah on the top of her head, then straightened up and smiled.

"Now, with all of the larger animals on the second level ..."

"Father, I'll take the cats," Ham offered.

"I'll be happy to feed the elephants and the other large animals in the middle cages," Shem chimed in.

"I don't mind taking care of the livestock, Father," Japheth pronounced.

"Good. Thank you, my sons. Well, then, let's rest for a short time. The judgment of the Lord on the earth will begin soon."

Skeptics discard the possibility that eight people could have fed the thousands of animals on board the ark. To support their argument, some have pointed out that during a twelve-hour day, each member of Noah's family would have had to feed one animal every three minutes.

Scientists tell us, however, that the living conditions on the ark, including the falling temperature, the reduced light, the restriction of movement, and the rocking of the ship would have caused most of the animals to go into a state of inactivity—like cows locked in their barn stalls during Midwestern winters. Motion and semidarkness are both known to have a calming effect on animals. These circumstances would have also caused most of the animals to eat less and sleep more than normal, and many animals would have gone into some form of hibernation.

Hibernation is only a small part of a wide spectrum of animal behavior. In the tropics, for example, many small animals go to sleep to avoid the peak of the dry season, a phenomenon called *aestivation*, which is very similar to hibernation. Even an occasional short period of unfavorable conditions is slept through by many animals. As for larger animals, such as bears, they will remain in a semi-dormant state in their dens for months at a time during the winter.

"Practically all reptiles and amphibians have the capacity of hibernation," says Dr. Henry Morris, coauthor of *The Genesis Flood.* "Mammals, being warm-blooded, do not have as great a need for it, and so at present, relatively few practice it. Nevertheless, it is probable that the latent ability to do so is present in practically all mammals."[7]

When animals are hibernating, they do not remain in that condition indefinitely, but arouse periodically in a rhythmic manner every few days or weeks. As soon as conditions on the ark improved, the animals probably awoke and ate. The ability to enter a prolonged sleeping period, however, is a fairly common property among animals.

"In the ark, we would expect that there would be a lot of darkness, mainly due to the storm above," says Dr. Cumming. "Under these quieting conditions, with lack of food and sleep in semidarkness— all of this added together would make the family of Noah more than adequate to care for the animals for even up to a year."

So the experts tell us that it would not have been difficult for eight people to look after their animal cargo. "The ratio of human caretakers to animals on the ark is similar to that in many modern zoos around the world," according to Dr. Whitcomb.

In addition, all animals before the time of the Flood ate only vegetation and did not fear man, (Genesis 1:30). This changed after the Flood.

Critics of the ark point out the huge amount of space that zoo animals need and the numbers of specialists that are needed in zoos as proof that it would be totally impossible for eight people to take care of thousands of animals for a year. According to John Woodmorappe, the author of *Noah's Ark, A Feasibility Study*:

Comparing the ark to a zoo is nonsensical since a zoo is primarily for long-term display of animals in lifetime captivity, whereas the ark was just for temporary housing for a year. A zoo is designed with humanitarian considerations, and the comfort of the animals. In the ark we're concerned about survival, saving their lives and their seed and their descendants for all time, which was a totally different purpose. Most importantly, these attentions that are needed for animals in the zoo, a lot of them are based on comfort and are not required for the animal to live... whereas in the ark you are primarily interested in letting the animals live even if its in difficult and stressful conditions.

Another argument of critics that Woodmorappe addresses in a 2007 interview is that of animals requiring very specialized diets, like koalas needing fresh eucalyptus leaves (which zoos do provide.) It turns out that when the first koalas were taken by ship from Australia to England, (in 1880, before airplanes were invented), they discovered a group of koalas that could survive on dry eucalyptus leaves because there were no fresh eucalyptus leaves aboard the ship during the long journey. Yet they lived, and they made it to the London zoo surviving on dried leaves. So even though koalas are extremely exclusive in their diet, it is possible to find some individual koalas that will live on dried eucalyptus leaves or even common foods on which eucalyptus oil has been sprayed.

The panda is another example, in their need for bamboo. It turns out that they will eat dried bamboo and they will even eat thick, large grasses. (Bamboos are members of the grass family.) So, it is possible to get pandas to subsist on other foods. And the same thing can be said about various other animals with exclusive dietary habits. Of course, this assumes that animals have not changed since the Flood, which if they have become more specialized; they may have been less specialized before the Flood than they are now. But even without that assumption, it can be concluded that even the most difficult animals could have been cared for on the ark.

From what the Genesis account tells us, it appears then, that Noah would not have had an impossible task collecting or caring for the animals put into his care on the ark.

Rev. Eddie Atkinson, a pastor and ark-model builder, has studied the account of Noah's ark in the Bible as well as numerous other ancient Flood traditions. He also has built several scale models of the ark. The most elaborate one contains more than 1,100 hand-carved animals and includes minute detail of what the ark's interior was like fully loaded with animals and supplies. Based upon his research, he believes that animals were placed only on the top two levels of the ark.

The top floor held all of the birds from one end to the center of the ark. Then, there was probably a catwalk over the cages of the elephants and giraffes on the second floor. The other half of the top floor held the rodent cages, storage, the kitchen and living quarters for the eight members of Noah's family.

Then, on the second floor, there would be all the different kinds of cats including lions and tigers in cages at one end, then the cages for hippos and rhinos, with the cages for the elephants and giraffes in the middle, open from above. Next, on the second level, would be the horses, zebras, sheep, livestock, and storage areas of food for the animals. The bottom level was undoubtedly used for garbage and waste.

Animal care involved more than feeding, of course. Stalls and cages would have had to be cleaned daily—at least when the animals were not hibernating. Manure would most likely have been stored on the lower deck. Computations by some San Diego zoologists indicate that up to 800 tons of manure accumulated in the lower deck during the year aboard the ark.[8]

How Noah and Family Lived in the Ark

How Noah and his family lived in the ark is also intriguing. Room would have been ample for food, water, and sanitation storage, and for exercising of the animals, with sufficient internal free space to prevent unbearable fouling or heating of the air. So the ark was built to maintain the best possible conditions for life.

With such provision for the animals, it is logical to assume the eight persons aboard also were comfortable. We must not ignore, either, the woman's touch to the living quarters. We can surmise Noah's wife and daughters-in-law made their cabins as pleasant as possible under the circumstances.

What kind of beds did they sleep in?

A bed in Bible days was simply a mat or blanket that could be carried in the hands. The poor often had no bed, except their outer garment. We can hardly consider Noah poor; he would have had to have wealth to hire work crews for the ark. Wealthy people had quilts or mattresses filled with cotton, which they spread on the floor or on a divan.

Divans were platforms about three to four feet wide. Sometimes they extended across one end of the room or around three sides and were elevated from six inches to a foot above the floor. By day, they were used as a sofa, by night for sleeping.[9] It is possible that there were built-in divans in the family's living quarters.

Noah's family probably had other furniture, maybe even crude wooden tables for eating. Modern Arabs usually have nothing but a piece of skin or leather, a mat, or a linen cloth spread upon the ground for a table. Ancient Hebrews are supposed to have used a similar "table."

We don't know, of course, what the living customs were during pre-Flood times, but can assume that furnishings after the Flood evolved from the craftsmanship, designs, and traditions of Flood survivors.

What did the people on the ark eat?

Noah was commanded to bring food aboard the ark for both the animals and his family.

Genesis 9:2-3 implies that before the Flood, people were vegetarians. After the Flood, God put the fear of man in the animal kingdom and told Noah, "Every moving thing that liveth shall be meat for you; even as the green herb have I given you all things." Meat became part of the post-Flood diet. The phrase, "even as the green herb," strengthens the evidence that Noah and his family were vegetarians before and during the Flood.

We can assume their diet included milk, eggs, bread, nuts, fig cakes, raisins, cheese, grains, grapes, herbs, olives, wheat, and other similar foods, since all these existed in ancient biblical times.

To make bread, Noah's family would have needed some means for baking. One type of oven still used in the Middle East is a great stone pitcher. A fire is made in the bottom among small flints and the dough is soon baked. Sometimes the dough is rolled out very thin and stuck on the outside surface of the heated pitcher. When it's baked, it falls off. Perhaps such an oven existed in Noah's day.

Frying pans existed in Old Testament times (Leviticus 7:9). There were deep vessels of iron used for boiling meat or baking bread. Also in existence were thin, flat iron plates on which bread could be quickly baked as on the griddles we have today. Conceivably, such baked foods were part of Noah's diet.[10]

Other cooking and eating utensils could have included earthenware pots and bottles, and skins. These were common in Bible days. We also know from the Bible that pre-Flood craftsmen were skilled in metal-works. It is conceivable that some of Noah's utensils were made of copper, gold, or silver. They could have been quite fancy.

Noah and his cargo were aboard the ark for about one year and ten days. They undoubtedly had their hands full feeding and caring for the animals and looking after their own needs, but it's obvious that their task was not impossible. Their ingeniously designed craft was well suited for the needs of both people and animals on a long voyage into a new world.

Woodmorappe's Feasibility Study, motivated by the many objections against the possibility of the ark account, is founded on seven years of work and 1,200 references based on animal care. He concludes:

Most arguments of its impossibility are based on ignorance. On the other hand, what I have is actual research in practical, simple animal-care methods. How long does it take to care for animals if you have the proper layout? How long would it take eight people to take care of 16,000 animals? How much food and water would you actually need? How much space do animals actually need in an emergency survival situation for one year?

When you actually do a study and see how much floor space you need for animals compared with laboratory animal housing, you'll see there easily is space on the ark for 16,000 animals ... same with the feeding and the care of the animals—if you actually study how long it takes to feed and provide water for animals based on actual studies, time travel studies of confined animals, how long it takes people to do it under such circumstances, without any modern technology, you find that it is workable.

The account of Noah's ark raises other questions that critics are quick to point out in discrediting the story. If a flood were going to destroy the earth, where would all the water come from? And where would it all go afterwards? Even the people of Noah's day scoffed at the sight of the enormous barge resting on a dry plain near Shuruppak in Mesopotamia—now modern Iraq.

Endnotes

1 Bill Crouse, *Ararat Report* 19 (Nov—Dec 1988), pp. 1-5. Published by Christian Information Ministries International, Richardson, TX.

2 Ibid., pp. 1-5.

3 Tim LaHaye and John Morris, *The Ark on Ararat* (Nashville: Thomas Nelson, Inc., 1976), p. 251.

4 John C. Whitcomb and Henry M. Morris, *The Genesis Flood* (Phillipsburg, NJ: Presbyterian and Reformed Publishing, 1961), p. 66.

5 Dave Balsiger and Charles E. Sellier, *In Search of Noah's Ark* (Los Angeles: Sun Classic Books, 1976), pp. 129-130.

6 Ibid., p. 130.

7 Ibid., p. 71.

8 Balsiger, *In Search of Noah's Ark*, p. 134.

9 Ibid., p. 135.

10 Ibid., p. 136.

FOUR

A WATERY GRAVE

The elements that unite to make the Grand Canyon the most sublime spectacle in nature are multifarious and exceedingly diverse.
—John Wesley Powell

SEVEN DAYS HAD PASSED since the dark, monolithic ark had been sealed shut. On the first day, many of Noah's neighbors had come to jeer and watch the last of the provisions and animals being taken aboard. But the number of people had dwindled as the days went by and nothing happened.

It was a hilarious sight to the people, and travelers went out of their way to see the huge ark. Strangers couldn't believe the gossip that there were actually thousands of animals inside, so big discussions would ensue with the local experts. Men would stroke their beards and sometimes share a jug of wine as they pontificated on why a wealthy man would lose his mind and build a great ship so far inland—and then fill it with animals!

Everyone wanted to know what was going on in there, and many hurled more than just insults at the ark.

"Noah, when's your water falling from the sky?"

"Hey, did your gods forget?"

"Maybe you just heard them wrong."

"You'll have to come out and face us some-time."

But mocking and laughing at Noah's folly could only consume so much of one's time. Only a passion-ate few spent their days and nights outside of the ark —mostly watching to make sure that Noah and his family didn't try to sneak out and slip away unnoticed.

"Noah, we're still waiting."

"Hey," a man yelled, laughing, between bites of fruit, "it doesn't look like your boat has gone very far yet."

Preaching judgment to the people and calling for their repentance over the years, Noah had made many bitter enemies—enemies who wanted to hu-miliate him and settle the score.

"He's not going to tell us how to live our lives," a large woman with only a few teeth was telling a stranger. "We made sure of that. And when he comes out, I want to be here. Some of the men have plans for that Noah."

"Yes, that will be a celebration day," a young Nephilim sneered. "They have to come out eventu-ally, and we'll be ready for them when they do."

The soft magenta sky was unusually dark this seventh morning, but no one was alarmed at first. Even when the first drops of rain fell, everyone had an explanation for them—birds, most likely.

But the sky, brewing ominously, grew very dark.

Even the "ark-watchers" dismissed the idea that Noah was right until the sky became like a dam bursting in the heavens.

Great sheets of rain pelted the earth and quickly turned the dust into puddles of mud.

The earth groaned like a woman about to give birth, and people became terrified as wrenching earthquakes below and thunderous explosions above signaled the violent pangs of judgment.

The shrill whistling sound of objects falling through the sky was carried in every direction by the wind. In a panic, the people who had been laughing and cursing Noah for years raced to the ark, covering their ears, screaming.

"The sky is falling!"

"Help us! The sky is falling!"

"Get out of my way," a man yelled, viciously knocking an old woman out of his way.

"We're going to die!"

They pounded on the solid, high walls and clawed at the only entrance, begging Noah to open the ramp. In desperation, people climbed on top of others in an effort to reach the roof of the ark.

"Please, Noah. Save our children."

"Open the door—now!"

"Let us in there you …"

Their unanswered pleas quickly turned into vile cursing as they kept pounding on the walls and screaming in vain. The wind lashed the rain like a whip, stinging their unprotected faces.

More and more people came running to the ark, shrieking at Noah and his family to let them in as the muddy fields turned into deepening lakes and the rumbling in the earth turned into a roar.

Their muffled pleas could be heard by everyone inside, who stood in stunned silence, eyes wide with horror. There was nothing they could do. The door had been sealed shut. No one could come in.

Noah shook his head sadly and gazed at Naamah. "It's started. The judgment has begun."

Genesis, chapter seven, gives us only a brief account of this event:

Noah was six hundred years old when the floodwaters came on the earth. And Noah and his sons and his wife and his sons' wives entered the ark to escape the waters of the Flood ... And after seven days the floodwaters came on the earth.

The animals going in were male and female of every living thing, as God had commanded Noah. Then the Lord shut him in.

For forty days the Flood kept coming on the earth, and as the waters increased they lifted the ark high above the earth. The waters rose and increased greatly on the earth, and the ark floated on the surface of the water. They rose greatly on the earth, and all the high mountains under the entire heavens were covered.

The waters rose and covered the mountains to a depth of more than twenty feet. Every living thing that moved on the earth perished—birds, livestock, wild animals, all the creatures that swarm over the earth, and all mankind. Everything on dry land that had the breath of life in its nostrils died. ... Only Noah was left and those with him in the ark.

The waters flooded the earth for a hundred and fifty days (Genesis 7:6-7, 10, 16, 17-23).

Flood Story Raises Questions

This passage sparks many questions. Where did all of the water come from, and where did it all go after the Flood? How could forty days and nights of rain alone provide enough water for a worldwide Flood? How could floodwaters possibly cover all the highest mountains? And what would have initiated such a massive deluge?

Modern-day meteorologists tell us that even if all of the water in our atmosphere were to precipitate at the same time, it wouldn't produce more than two inches of water across the globe—hardly enough to float the ark, much less destroy all life on earth. We asked a number of scientists as well as Bible scholars to help us answer these difficult questions and explain some of the prevalent theories regarding our ancient earth.

Where Did the Water Come From?

"The Bible says that water both from above and below flooded the earth," says California Bible educator and parish priest Father Michael Hanifin. "Rain from the heavens fell and the oceans flowed up over the land. There are different theories to explain where the water came from and why, but the Bible is clear, this Flood covered the entire earth."

"Most people don't realize how much water is on the earth," says Dr. Walter Brown, the former chief of science and technology at the Air War College and author, *In the Beginning: Evidence for Creation and the Flood.* "There's actually ten times more water in our oceans than land above sea level. In fact, if we could flatten out our earth and make it as smooth as a billiard ball, the water would cover the earth to a depth of nearly 9,000 feet."

While there is a great deal of water on and in our planet, very little moisture exists in the atmosphere above. However, the fossil record and other evidences show that the earth and its atmosphere experienced a radical change during the Noachian Flood. According to the late Donald W. Patten, a Seattle, Washington based geographer and planetary catastrophist, the earth's pre-Flood atmosphere was comprised of approximately three to five times as much water vapor as is in today's atmosphere. And, like today, this water vapor was concentrated in the lower troposphere.

A Pre-Flood Water Canopy

The climate of the pre-Flood earth was moderate around the globe. Many scientists attribute this to a so-called "greenhouse effect" on ancient earth. This enormous global canopy of water existed as vapor, or in a frozen, crystallized form at the upper levels of our atmosphere.

"The first chapter of Genesis describes a firmament or atmosphere above the earth," says Dr. David Clark, a professor of New Testament Studies and chairman of the Division of Religion at Vanguard University. "God created this to separate the waters above the firmament from the waters below the firmament. In describing the waters above the earth, the Bible suggests that in the time before the Flood, there was a water vapor or canopy surrounding the earth. This rich, dense cloud cover protected the earth, moderated the climate, and provided dew instead of rain prior to the Flood, as we see from Genesis 2:5-6."

"The idea of a water vapor or canopy surrounding the earth sounds somewhat bizarre," says Dr. Larry Vardiman, Chair of the astro-geophysics department, on staff with the Institute for Creation Research, who has spent years researching the concept. "But actually, canopies are quite common among the planets of our solar system. Venus, Jupiter, and Saturn all have cloud canopies and thick gaseous envelopes surrounding them."

Dr. Vardiman further explains:

Under a water-vapor canopy, earth would have had a relatively warm, uniform temperature, high humidity, and increased atmospheric pressure. The climate may have been tropical from pole to pole and may have contributed to giantism in plants and animals and much longer life spans.

The vapor canopy would have precipitated at most 40 feet of water directly. In addition, water released by volcanic eruptions during the Flood would have kept heavy rain falling for forty days and nights becoming lighter as our present-day weather regime came into existence. Soon after the Flood, precipitation would have turned to snow on high mountains and in the polar regions causing the "Ice Age."

Pre-Flood Canopy Allows Dinosaurs to Thrive

Explains Dr. Carl Baugh, archaeological excavator and author, *Panorama of Creation*:

We've been doing extensive research into the context that produced the enormous sizes of plants and animals that can be found in the fossil record, and this equates with a pre-Flood model mandating that there had to be a pre-Flood canopy of some sort compressing the atmosphere.

We know that the great dinosaurs such as Tyrannosaurus Rex had a relatively small lung capacity, and yet tests indicate paleontologically, from the fossil record that is, that some of the dinosaurs reached tremendous heights. Seismosaurus, for example, could raise his head almost 70 feet in the air. Now something has to explain this anomaly compared to today's atmosphere. How could the largest dinosaurs oxygenate their deep cell tissues with such a small lung capacity?

At sea level today we have 14.7 pounds per square inch of atmospheric pressure. The largest dinosaurs needed more atmospheric pressure than that to oxygenate their deep cell tissues. Tests have determined that at two atmospheres of pressure, the entire blood plasma becomes saturated with oxygen. Therefore, a canopy, a firmament above the earth, compressing the atmosphere, would explain how the dinosaurs were able to survive and why plants were able to grow so much larger than they are today.

Also, from analyzing air bubbles trapped in fossilized tree resin, we have found that the pre-Flood atmosphere contained 30 percent oxygen as compared to our 21 percent oxygen today. With the ancient canopy over the earth creating approximately 27 pounds per square inch of atmospheric pressure and the air containing 30 percent oxygen as compared to our present 14.7 pounds per square inch of atmospheric pressure and 21 percent oxygen today, tests have determined that a man would have been able to run approximately 200 miles without getting winded.

We know that this canopy surrounding the entire earth performed several different functions. Water by its very nature filters out the ultraviolet rays that are harmful to man. In addition, the charged hydrogen in this water vapor or canopy of crystalline content would glow a magenta—that we would call pink. This perfect wavelength would have created a gentle pink glow in the sky.

Researchers have found that this is the exact wavelength that encourages the large growth and reproductive cells of plants. That means that this canopy would have increased the life span of man and the longevity of all biota.

Biosphere Experiments

Dr. Baugh, in a 2007 interview, shares some of the amazing results from modern experimentation in a man-made Hyperbaric Biosphere, which simulates the hypothesized pre-Flood atmosphere:

After approximately forty years of research on the parameters of the pre-Flood world, we have designed and built a hyperbaric biosphere simulating those conditions. We've been able to essentially double the atmospheric pressure, increase the electromagnetic energy, elevate the oxygen and carbon dioxide levels, filter the sunlight specifically and, as a result, we've been able to produce phenomenal results.

We know that the diameter of the Earth was slightly smaller—10 to 12 percent—that gives us an indicator as to what kind of gravitational attraction and atmospheric pressure would be involved. So, we have almost doubled the atmospheric pressure. In addition to that, we have increased the electromagnetic field because we do have tests indicating that the Earth's electromagnetic field was about ten times its current moment or energy level. In addition, we have filtered the light in the appropriate spectrum, we've elevated the carbon dioxide, we elevated the oxygen at specific levels and, as a result, we have more than a hyperbaric chamber, we actually have a Hyperbaric Biosphere—a living, ecological context.

In this [living, ecological] context, we have placed *Drosophila melanogaster* (fruit flies), we've placed *Crotalus* and *Agkistrodon contortrix* (those are rattlesnakes and copperheads). In the second generation, we tripled the adult lifespan of the fruit flies. That's the equivalent of you as a human living to be 200 years of age even with your damaged DNA.

Now with the snakes, we were interested in their venom. After 4 weeks in the biosphere we took the snakes out, we milked them with a professional herpetologist, we took the venom to a professional independent laboratory and, to their amazement, they found that we had actually strengthened and orchestrated the venom. If you've ever seen snake venom under scanning electron microscopic analysis, it looks like gnarled spaghetti, but at the laboratory they found that just by having the snakes in the Biosphere, it had completely changed and orchestrated [strengthened at the microscopic level] their venom.

In addition to that, we have eliminated certain protein expressions, we have strengthened some, we've diminished some, and we've expressed protein that is not expressed in the ambient context. In other words, in this scientific laboratory experiment, where we have simulated the conditions before the worldwide Flood—we have been able to produce an explanation for the large, gargantuan sizes we find in the fossil record, such as the dinosaur, and the long-lived specimens.

We are in the process of building a much larger full-scale laboratory hyperbaric biosphere that is sixty-two feet long, weighing

92,000 pounds, with an airlock and an internal 48-foot chamber. In the larger Biosphere, we will be able to run multiple experiments simultaneously. I will be able, along with my colleagues and scientific participants, to go in and out of the Biosphere on a regular basis and the results should be astounding.

In that chamber, we're going to essentially double the atmospheric pressure, introduce stronger electromagnetic energy in pulse form consistent with Earth's magnetic field. In addition to that, we're going to elevate the oxygen and carbon dioxide, and filter most of the ultraviolet from the light spectrum. In this Biosphere, we plan to run various exotic experiments. For instance, we're going to place flying squirrels in this chamber. Flying squirrels have bug-eyes, which indicate that they can see in many directions simultaneously. In today's conditions, in order to fly they have to glide from limb to limb at a lower profile. However, in two atmospheres of pressure they should have no difficulty flying from one end to the other.

We're also going to place dragonflies in the chamber. The largest dragonflies found today have a 4- to 5-inch wingspan. But, in the fossil record there were dragonflies, known as Meganeuropsis, that had up to a 36-inch wingspan. So, if we can produce a dragonfly with a 10-inch wingspan, we have demonstrated scientifically that under these conditions, in spite of damaged DNA, living systems would be much larger like we find them in the fossil record. This is another demonstration of the fact that the pre-Flood world of Noah's day explains far better the biota, the living systems we find introduced in the fossil record, than does evolutionary development. We believe the scientific data confirm that there was a worldwide Flood, that living systems were caught in that Flood and, hence, fossilized.

We're very excited about getting the experiments run in many, many dimensions, and perhaps this will benefit medical science, perhaps it will explain the biota for biologists and for geologists, and it can go a long way toward explaining that there was a worldwide Flood.

Other tests with controlled environmental conditions have also produced surprising results. In the mid-1980s, Dr. Kei Mori, professor of science and technology at Keio University in Tokyo, Japan, while testing light energy transmission systems for future consumer applications, unknowingly applied some pre-Flood atmospheric conditions to a tomato-plant test. To a cherry tomato plant he added increased atmospheric pressure around the stalk and filtered out the ultraviolet radiation. After two years his cherry tomato plant had not only thrived, but was a tree—sixteen feet tall—and had produced 903 tomatoes. Eight years later his plant was thirty feet tall and had produced more than 8,000 tomatoes. His test was an excellent scientific verification that the pre-Flood context would produce very large sizes such as we find in the fossil record.

Pre-Flood Scenario

What do we know about the floodwaters that came according to the biblical account? Genesis 7:11-12 says:

In the six hundredth year of Noah's life, on the seventeenth day of the second month—on that day all the springs of the great deep burst forth, and the floodgates of the heavens were opened. And rain fell on the earth forty days and forty nights.

From this account we can surmise that there were three sources that produced enough water for a global Flood: the water vapor canopy, subterranean pressurized reservoirs, and the sinking of landmasses or the rising of the ancient ocean seabeds.

Is there any significance in the fact that Genesis 7:11 says the subterranean waters "burst forth" before the "floodgates of heaven were opened?"

On the pre-Flood earth, a secondary source of water existed in vast subterranean heated and pressurized reservoirs either in the primeval crust or in the earth's mantle. Such a situation still exists today, although in lesser quantity.

A number of things could have triggered the eruption of the underground waters and caused the cataclysm. Dr. Henry Morris suggests a simple explanation:

"The pressurized waters below the crust suddenly erupted at a point of weakness. Collapse at one point would cause a chain reaction leading to similar eruptions at many other points around the world."[1]

The resulting atmospheric turbulence, combined with immense amounts of dust blown skyward from erupting volcanoes, would begin condensation and precipitation of the canopy, he says. The process would be similar to modern-day cloud seeding to cause rain.[2]

Thus we see the possible significance of the order of destruction mentioned in Genesis 7:11. Subterranean upheavals within the oceans, volcanic eruptions and earthquakes, and the gushing forth of those waters triggered the canopy waters to pour upon the earth as torrential rains for forty days and forty nights before slacking off to light rain for the next 110 days.[3]

Dr. Frederick A. Filby, in his book *The Flood Reconsidered,* says:

> Using the metaphors of ancient languages, the Bible records that the *windows* of Heaven were opened and the *fountains* of the Great Deep (abyss) were broken up. In other words, Noah was conscious of torrential rain and the oncoming of a huge tide, not from swollen rivers, but from the Great Deep—the ocean.

> That the latter (ocean and subterranean water) was much greater than the former is clearly shown by the fact that the ark (both in the biblical and the Babylonian accounts) was carried northwards towards Armenia, whereas a river flood resulting from rain and geyser-type eruptions would have carried it out to the Persian Gulf.[4]

The Hydroplate Theory

Picking up on Dr. Filby's contention that great earth movements occurred during the yearlong Flood, we again turn to Dr. Brown. This former professor of mathematics at Massachusetts Institute of Technology (MIT) and author, *In the Beginning: Evidence for Creation and the Flood,* has advanced the scientific Hydroplate Theory to explain the geological and other events that took place during the Flood. "Hydroplates" are approximately 10-

mile-thick, continental-size plates, which, before the Flood, had considerable water under them.

In a 2007 interview, Dr. Brown expounds his theory:

We can see on our planet twenty-five major features that can now be systematically explained as a consequence of a global Flood that erupted from subterranean chambers with an energy release exceeding the explosion of 30 trillion hydrogen bombs.

This hydroplate explanation solves the origin of the Mid-Oceanic Ridge, salt domes, metamorphic rock, volcanoes, and magnetic patterns on the ocean floor and shows us just how rapidly our major mountain ranges formed.

It explains the coal, oil and methane deposits, the rapid Continental Drift, and why on the ocean floor there are huge trenches, hundreds of canyons and tens of thousands of volcanoes. This theory also explains the Ice Ages and it gives the primary reason for Global Warming. It explains the formation of the layered strata and almost all fossils, the frozen mammoths, and major land canyons, especially the Grand Canyon. Surprisingly, it explains the origin of comets, asteroids and of meteorites.

Noah and all other pre-Flood people probably lived on one very large super-continent with lush vegetation, inland seas and major rivers. The mountains were smaller than today's, but perhaps six thousand feet high. Before the Flood, about half the Earth's water was in interconnected chambers about ten miles below the Earth's surface. This formed a thin, spherical shell almost a mile thick.

Crack in Earth's Crust

What caused these chambers to erupt and flood the entire earth? Dr. Brown explains:

Pressure in the subterranean chamber had been increasing for centuries because the gravity of the sun and moon produced tides in the subterranean water that lifted and lowered the Earth's massive crust twice a day. This tidal pumping added gigantic amounts of energy to the subterranean water. It became what is called "super-critical water," a very high-energy explosive form of water. This increasing pressure in the subterranean water steadily stretched the crust as a balloon stretches when the pressure inside increases.

Failure in the crust began as a microscopic crack that grew in both directions at almost three miles per second. The crack, following the path of least resistance, encircled the globe in about two hours. As the crack raced around the Earth, the overlying rock crust opened up like a rip in a tightly stretched cloth.

The subterranean water was under extreme pressure because of the weight of the ten miles of rock pressing down on it. So, the water exploded violently out of the rupture, fountains of water jetted supersonically almost twenty miles into the atmosphere. As the Bible states (Genesis 7:11), "On the same day all the fountains of the great deep burst open." Then it says, "And the rain fell." The fountains of water jetted supersonically into and above the atmosphere. The spray from these enormous fountains produced torrential rain such as the Earth has never experienced, before or after.

The Bible even gives us a precise date for that day: "… the six hundredth year of Noah's life, on the seventeenth day of the second month." All of these events, which happened about five thousand years ago, can now be tied together scientifically.

Dr. Brown continues the vivid description of the course of events that followed:

The "fountains of the great deep" and the expanding steam produced violent winds. Some of the waters jetting high above the cold stratosphere froze into super-cooled ice crystals and produced some massive ice dumps—burying, suffocating, and instantly freezing many animals—including the frozen mammoths of Siberia and Alaska.

The high-pressure supersonic fountains eroded the crumbling rock on both sides of the widening crack. This produced huge volumes of sediments that settled through the floodwaters, trapping and burying plants and animals forming the fossil record. Vegetation uprooted by the floodwaters accumulated in various regions where it was buried and compressed, quickly becoming coal and oil by processes we can duplicate in the laboratory today.

Eventually the crack became so wide that the compressed rock beneath the subterranean chamber sprung upward, giving birth to the Mid-Oceanic Ridge that wraps around the Earth like the seam of a baseball. The continental plates (the hydroplates), with lubricating water still beneath them, slid downhill away from the rising Mid-Atlantic Ridge.

After the massive, slowly accelerating continental plates reached speeds of approximately forty to fifty miles per hour, they ran into resistances, and like a runaway crashing train, they compressed, crushed, buckled and thickened, rising out of the floodwaters. Today's major mountains were all pushed up in hours. The portions of the hydroplate that buckled downward formed ocean trenches. Those that buckled upward formed our mountain ranges. This is why the major mountains are generally parallel to the oceanic ridges from which they slid.

This also explains why today's continents do not have a jigsaw fit against each other that so many textbooks mistakenly claim. For example, one of the deliberate distortions in these textbook pictures is the shrinking of Africa in area by 35 percent. However, the continents do fit snugly against the base of the Mid-Atlantic Ridge where the rapid Continental Drift began.

Dr. Brown's theory not only describes where all of the water of the Flood came from, but also gives an answer for where all the water went when the Flood receded:

The continental plates (the hydroplates), in sliding away from the Oceanic Ridges opened up very deep ocean basins into which the floodwaters retreated.

As the hydroplates crashed, they thickened and rose out of the water, forcing the floodwaters over the continents to recede. Simultaneously, upward-surging subterranean water was choked off. As the floodwater drained off the continents, every continental basin was left brimful of water, producing many post-Flood lakes.

The Grand Canyon is Formed

During the following centuries, some lakes breached their boundaries by either spilling over their rims or undercutting their banks. The rapid catastrophic discharge of these lakes, much like the collapse of a large dam, carved canyons.

Several centuries after the Flood, two very large ancient lakes, Grand Lake and Hopi Lake, sitting on top of the high rising Colorado Plateau, breached their boundaries and carved the Grand Canyon in just a few weeks. The massive canyon was not carved by the relatively small Colorado River over millions of years. According to Dr. Brown, that river is a consequence of the carving of the Grand Canyon.

Dr. Steven A. Austin, professor of geology at the ICR Graduate School in San Diego, California, has been studying the Mount St. Helens eruption and comparing what is observable there to the possible formation of the Grand Canyon. He claims this eruption is the most significant geological event of the twentieth century because it tells us much about strata, coal, and canyon formations.

The eruption of Mount St. Helens in Washington State on May 18, 1980 was initiated by an earthquake and rockslide. Pressure was released inside the volcano where super-hot water turned to steam. The northward-directed steam explosion released energy equivalent to twenty million tons of TNT, which toppled 150 square miles of forest in six minutes. An enormous water-wave in Spirit Lake, north of the volcano, stripped trees from slopes as high as 850 feet above the lake. The total energy output, on May 18, was equivalent to 400 million tons of TNT—20,000 Hiroshima-size atomic bombs. Dr. Austin explains what happened during the eruption:

> Deposits of strata up to 600 feet in thickness have formed at Mount St. Helens since 1980. What is unique is that these strata accumulated in short periods of time—in some cases in less than a day. In the past, it was thought that these strata layers were formed slowly over hundreds or thousands of years.
>
> Rapid erosion occurred during the volcanic eruptions of Mount St. Helens. Mudflows were responsible for the most significant erosion. A mudflow on March 19, 1982, eroded a canyon system in the headwaters of the North Fork of the Toutle River Valley. This canyon, known as the "Grand Canyon of the Toutle River," is a one-fortieth scale model of the real Grand Canyon—and, it was formed in less than a week.

So, modern eyewitness scientific evidence does exist confirming that not only can layered strata be laid down rapidly, but hills and gullies—or even the Grand Canyon—could have formed in very short periods of time instead of during the course of thousands or millions of years.

Dr. Walt Brown's theory of a massive, worldwide catastrophe in antiquity supports the biblical story of the deluge in every detail. However, what other evidence exists to support his amazing theory?

Dr. Brown interprets some of the ongoing scientific findings:

"In 1970, I predicted that large pools of salt water would be found beneath major mountains. That prediction has been confirmed in several ways: by gravity studies, by seismic studies, and by electromagnetic studies."

A paper published in the April 2001 issue of *Science Magazine* announced the discovery of an electrically conductive layer under the Tibetan Plateau. The article suggested that such high conductivity at depths of approximately 10 miles could be achieved by a layer of "aqueous fluids," some 1.6 kilometers thick and containing 10 percent brine—in other words, salt water.

"This is only the first of a series of discoveries and other predictions that are being confirmed. Just how big these subterranean layers of water will turn out to be no one really knows. However, the article points out that the high electrical conductivity is evident across the entire Tibetan Plateau, a distance of hundreds of miles," says Brown.

Other evidence came in the late 1990's when a three-pound meteorite that had crashed to the ground near a playground was later cracked open by NASA scientists. They discovered that the meteorite contained salt crystals and liquid water.

Dr. Brown explains:

The NASA scientists who investigated this meteorite believe it came from an asteroid, but that is highly unlikely because asteroids in the vacuum of space cannot sustain liquid water, which is required to form salt crystals. It is also too cold and there is too little gravity.

Earth is the only body in the solar system that can sustain liquid water on its surface.

I believe this demonstrates the enormous power of the subterranean super-critical water, the fountains of the great deep, that launched water and rock fragments into orbit around the sun.

These rock fragments are still returning to the Earth as meteorites. Scientifically examined meteorites have been found to contain Earth-like material, including many types of living, but dormant, bacteria. This means that meteorites and their bacteria did not originate in the vacuum of space. Meteorites are literally tiny chunks of the Earth itself returning home.

Scientists are also puzzled over another recent discovery. On the Kola Peninsula in Northern Russia, they have created the world's deepest hole, extending to a depth of 7.5 miles. At this depth, what they expected to find was a layer of basalt—earth's most common type of volcanic rock. What they actually discovered was something entirely different. The hole did not reach the basalt underlying the granite continents, but to everyone's surprise, they did reach hot salty water flowing through crushed granite. Geologists are mystified, but according to Walt Brown the Hydroplate Theory provides a simple explanation.

The Cataclysmic Trigger

Getting back to the onset of the global Flood, we must ask the question, what was the trigger that set the events of the Flood in motion?

Some scientists theorize that the gravitational pull from a close planetary flyby caused the waters to "burst from the deep," and they cite numerous evidences to support this theory.

"We have records from ancient civilizations around the world," claims Donald Patten, a geographer and planetary catastrophist, "that say the Flood was caused by a close planetary flyby and the ancient astronomers all state in their accounts that it was caused by Mars. In the Sumerian account it was Mars, in the Assyrian account it was Mars, and in the Chaldean account it was Mars. In India, it was Mars and in the Egyptian Book of the Dead, it was Mars. Almost all of the ancient civilizations left records of catastrophic flybys attributed to Mars.

"The Flood then," Patten continues, "was caused by the gravitational conflict created when Mars flew perilously close to the earth. The tides arose in the Indian Ocean to 5,000 or 6,000 feet high because the gravitational pull on the water was such that which way was up and which way was down became totally confused."

In his book *Worlds in Collision*, Immanuel Velikovsky also examines the records of ancient civilizations and concludes that they were almost universally afraid of Mars and, in some instances, Venus and tried to appease those planets—sometimes with human sacrifices. In addition to the civilizations cited by Mr. Patten, Dr. Velikovsky also lists the Romans, Greeks, Aztecs and Voltecs, Mayans, Chinese, Indo-Iranians, Pawnee Indians, and Israelites as recording catastrophic events on earth caused by close flybys of either Venus or Mars.

Still, many scientists are not convinced that a close planetary flyby caused the worldwide

Noachian Flood, because only legends and traditions exist supporting that idea.

California astronomer David F. Coppedge says, for example:

It's clear from observation of the moons and planets of the solar system that many of them have undergone periods of heavy meteorite bombardment. Even on the earth, with its higher erosion rates, over a hundred such ancient impact sites have been discovered. It is certainly plausible that one of these triggered several cataclysmic events that resulted in the Great Deluge.

According to Jeremy Auldaney, a science researcher and meteoricist:

The most likely cause of the Flood was the close approach of an astronomical meteoroid or the impact of one or more asteroids. An asteroid is actually a very large meteorite or group of meteorites, which contain iron, carbonaceous chondrites or other elements. It is very common for small meteorites to hit the earth. An iron meteorite, for example, is very rare in space, but very common on the earth.

We have found elements of carbonaceous chondrite meteorites in the iridium layer found in the last strata left by the Flood, leading us to believe that a carbonaceous chondrite meteorite exploded coming through the upper atmosphere, destroying the canopy, and that an iron meteorite possibly penetrated the earth, releasing the water inside.

While doing research for a previous book, *In Search of Noah's Ark*, the authors of the present text found sufficient evidence to suggest that a gigantic meteorite colliding with Earth could have jarred the Earth's crust so tremendously that it set off the universal cataclysmic conditions necessary to have caused the rising of sea-beds, earthquakes, volcanoes, and the collapse of the water canopy.[5]

The *Encyclopedia Britannica* states that the number of meteorites falling in the centuries before Christ was higher than today. Indeed, in early times, men regarded iron as the metal that fell from the sky.[6]

The meteorite that fell in prehistoric times near Winslow, Arizona, made a hole 4,500 feet across and 600 feet deep. It flung out masses of rock weighing up to 7,000 tons and is estimated to have hurled out altogether 400 million tons of rock. The pressure of the impact exceeded 1,000,000 pounds per square inch, turning silica into new forms known as coesite and stishovite.

How big would a meteorite have had to be to cause the Flood? And, how would it have sparked the Flood?

When a huge meteorite, say up to 500 miles in diameter, hits a planet, fast-moving compressive waves move through the globe, followed by slower surface waves. They converge at a point opposite the meteorite impact, shattering land forms and leaving the area in shambles.[7]

Scientists are quite sure this happened when a huge meteorite collided with Mercury and created the 800-mile wide Caloris basin. The fast-moving compressive waves followed by surface waves moved through the planet, shattering the landforms opposite Caloris and creating what scientists call the "weird terrain." Similar shattered landforms exist on the Earth's Moon opposite great crater basins.[8]

Off Its Axis

The earth's axis was also changed dramatically during the Flood. This change gives us some fascinating clues as to what took place during that horrific time of multiple cataclysmic events. While researchers cannot say definitively what caused the earth's axis to change, the data show conclusively that it was changed around the time of the Flood.

"The tilt of the earth's axis today," says Dr. Bill Overn, retired visiting professor of physics at Concordia College and aerospace computer engineer, "is about 23 1/2 degrees. In the past, it was changed quite radically, and we know this from reliable ancient records as well other data."

According to Dr. Overn, there is a grave misconception among many scientists today that the ancients did not know the earth was round. The Babylonians and Assyrians measured the tilt of the earth's axis, and in 250 B.C. the Greeks measured the circumference of the earth to within less than 25 miles of its present value. Dr. Overn asserts:

Using ancient records and artifacts along with other data, we can see there has been a change in the earth's axis and we know that that change occurred during the Flood. Right after the Flood, the tilt of the earth's axis was about 27 degrees and it has since changed to its present 23 1/2 degrees.

It is normally accepted that the less the tilt of the earth, the less severe the winters are. Under the old, higher tilt caused somehow during the Flood, the earth would have experienced an Ice Age for 300 to 400 years, becoming less severe as the value or degree of the tilt decreased.

Scientists writing in the May 15, 1970 edition of *Science* magazine were able to determine the date that the axis shifted by studying data on the position of the sun and the solstices (positions of the sun creating the longest and shortest days of the year). Their conclusion—2345 B.C.—is the same date that, according to its astronomical analysis, the Chronology History Research Institute says Noah's Flood started.

Viewing the Evidence

There is sufficient evidence to suggest that a canopy of water vapor or ice covered the planet before the Flood. This canopy compressed the earth's atmosphere and helped to moderate the temperature and climate. In addition to the atmosphere, the earth's axis and geology were also vastly different than they are today.

In or around 2345 B.C., the earth's surface was drastically affected; and geological evidence supports that a Flood covered the entire earth for a year, created by water from underground reservoirs combined with surface water and the water from a collapsing canopy. Solid evidence supports its occurrence and that the Flood changed our planet forever.

As we shall see in a later chapter, this Flood is the only event in human history that can be found in some oral or written form in practically every culture and civilization subsequent to Noah's. No other single event in human history carries this distinction. Now let us return to our passengers aboard the ark.

Weathering the Storm

The violent waves rocked the great ship and the darkness made the wind cold. The animals settled down and made little noise. Most huddled together for protection from the rocking and the unknown sounds carried by the wind.

Noah's family eventually got their "sea legs," too, and were able to walk down the hallways to check on the cages without falling over.

Naamah took an oil lamp and followed her worried daughter-in-law down a dark hallway to the room she shared with Japheth. He had been very sick and looked pale by the light of the lamp. Naamah gently brushed his hair off his forehead, and he opened his eyes halfway.

"How are you feeling, son?" Naamah asked Japheth as she felt his forehead and cheeks.

"Oh, better. I just need to ..."

"It's okay. You rest for now. Your father and brothers have all of the animals under control, so you just lie here until you feel better." Naamah adjusted the wet cloth on his forehead and smiled at Japheth's young wife.

"He'll be fine. It's just the rocking of the waves that has made him sick."

Naamah walked unsteadily back down the hall to the small private room she shared with Noah. She lay down on the blankets next to him in the semidarkness and stared up at the ceiling, unable to go back to sleep. Even though she trusted God, she could not help wondering how they would all survive this terrible ordeal.

Endnotes

1 Henry M. Morris, *Scientific Creationism* (San Diego: Creation-Life Publishers, 1974), pp. 124–125.
2 Dave Balsiger and Charles E. Sellier, *In Search of Noah's Ark,* (Los Angeles: Sun Classic Books, 1984), p. 58.
3 Ibid., p. 59.
4 Frederick A. Filby, *The Flood Reconsidered* (Grand Rapids: Zondervan Publishing Corp., 1970), pp. 7–8.
5 Balsiger and Sellier, *In Search of Noah's Ark,* p. 62.
6 *Encyclopedia Britannica,* Vol. 15, pp. 275–276 (1966).
7 Balsiger and Sellier, *In Search of Noah's Ark,* p. 62.
8 Kenneth F. Weaver, "Mariner Unveils Venus and Mercury," *National Geographic,* June 1975, p. 861.

FIVE

EVIDENCE FOR A WORLDWIDE FLOOD

*Facts do not cease to exist because
they are ignored.*
—Aldous Huxley

NOAH REACHED INTO A CAGE and gently grabbed one of the gray doves with one hand while stroking its head tenderly with the other. Birds of all types and colors in the other cages were making a variety of sounds—cooing, clucking, chirping, and squawking at him in the semidarkness. Noah spoke to them softly, reassuringly, with a chuckle as he latched the cage and then, holding the dove, walked back down the dark hallway to the main living area.

Noah took the dove and climbed up a ladder to the window he had made and set it free.

"Go, little dove, and find us dry land."

It spread its wings and was lifted high by the gentle breeze. He watched it soaring in the pale blue sky until it flew out of view. The breeze was still such a new sensation; he stuck his hand out of the window to feel it on his skin.

Noah turned away from the window and looked at his son Shem. "If this dove doesn't return, it'll be a sign that enough dry land is above water for the dove to live outside the ark."

Noah and his family had already been in the ark several months. Tired of being locked up in it, they all wanted to look at the sky and walk on dry land again. They had many questions on their minds, and the waiting for the waters to subside was getting frustrating for everyone.

"God will let us know when it is safe to leave the ark," Noah reassured them. "He will tell us through the birds when it's safe to leave. Until then we must wait."

Waiting had been the hardest part all along. They had huddled in fear during the rumbling explosions that started the Flood and thankfully waited as the storms slowly subsided and the mighty ark drifted endlessly day after day after day. Finally, seven months after the Flood began, the ark came to rest on the mountains of Ararat.

During the many long months, they had finally grown used to the gentle rocking of the boat, the sound of the water lapping against the hull and the creaking of the great timbers inside. They had settled into the routine of caring for the animals and now had plenty of time on their hands to think. Too much time.

They couldn't see anything outside—which added to their frustration. The warm sunlight came in from above, but there was nothing they could see in any direction except water and the pale blue sky. Even though the ark had already run aground on Mount Ararat, other mountain peaks were not yet visible. It was difficult and frustrating not being able to see other land and never really knowing what would happen next. Every day required blind faith and trust in God. Everything about their lives had been changed forever, and it scared them.

The water all around them carried an eerie silence and they believed that no one outside their immediate family had survived. No one. They were all alone in the world; the thought was frightening.

Viewing the Biblical Record

According to Genesis, chapters seven and eight:

Every living thing on the face of the earth was wiped out; men, animals, and the creatures that move along the ground and the birds of the air were wiped from the earth. Only Noah was left, and those with him in the ark. The waters flooded the earth for a hundred and fifty days.

But God remembered Noah and all the wild animals and the livestock that were with him in the ark, and he sent a wind over the earth and the waters receded. Now the springs of the deep and the floodgates of the heavens had been closed, and the rain had stopped falling from the sky. The water receded steadily from the earth. At the end of the hundred and fifty days, the water had gone down, and on the seventeenth day of the seventh month the ark came to rest on the mountains of Ararat. The waters continued to recede until the tenth month, and on the first day of the tenth month the tops of the mountains became visible.

After forty days Noah opened the window he had made in the ark and sent out a raven, and it kept flying back and forth until the water had dried up from the earth. Then he sent out a dove to see if the water had receded from the surface of the ground. But the dove could find no place to set its feet because there was water over all the surface of the earth; so it returned to Noah in the ark. He reached out his hand, took the dove, and brought it back to himself in the ark. He waited seven more days and again sent out the dove from the ark. When the dove returned to him in the evening, there in its beak was a freshly plucked olive leaf! Then Noah knew that the water had receded from the earth. He waited seven more days and sent the dove out again, but this time it did not return to him (Genesis 7:23-24; 8:1-12).

Although this part of the story raises many key questions, it also tells us much about the developing post-Flood. The account indicates that a new weather regime had started with the blowing of wind. It reveals how ancients kept their calendar, where the ark landed, and how the post-Flood culture used birds for gathering important information.

A Universal Story

The Noachian Flood is the only event that appears in the oral history or written records of almost every society on earth. It was the last event shared by all of mankind. Critics who claim that this is a result of teaching by Christian missionaries can't explain why no other event or story in the Bible is so universally known.

If Flood traditions around the world stemmed from missionaries teaching Bible stories, then one could conceivably find widespread variations of the story of Jonah and the whale, Sodom and Gomorrah, the feeding of the 5,000 by Jesus, or many of the other miracles found in the Old and New Testaments. Noah's Flood stands alone because the eight members of Noah's family were the only human survivors of this unique worldwide catastrophe, and these eight survivors passed the story on to their descendants, and it has continued to be passed on.

Phil Mitchell, Assistant Director of the Center for Western Civilization and History Professor at the University of Colorado, comments:

Geographers and archaeologists have discovered Flood stories among many, many cultures around the world—separated by thousands of miles and never having had contact with each other over thousands of years—yet in every case the story is the same: Some great Flood or a catastrophic deluge destroyed every plant and animal on the Earth, but one man and family were preserved along with animals and birds from this great catastrophe in some type of large boat.

According to historians and cultural anthropologists, "there does seem to be historical evidence of Noah and the Flood, 272 historical mentions to be exact," says Mitchell, and stories of the Flood can be found in more than 217 different cultures around the world. In the Middle Eastern and African cultures, for example, there are 17 Flood traditions; in the Pacific Islands, 38; in the Far East, 21; in Europe and Asia, 34; and, among North American Indians, 58 Flood accounts. Additional accounts exist in Central and South America, including the Aztec and Inca cultures.

"As an historian, the evidence is overwhelming," Mitchell emphasizes in his 2007 interview for this book and the Noah television documentary. "I find that the most powerful piece of evidence for the historicity of Noah's ark is the fact that in virtually every civilization and culture around the world there are Flood stories that report that a Flood did, indeed, take place. There is lots of historical evidence as well."

Three different ancient Babylonian Flood stories remain on cuneiform tablets—all are intimately related to the biblical Flood story. Some of these tablets were found in the ancient library of King Ashurbanipal in Ninevah.

George Faber, in his book *Origin of Pagan Idolatry*, published in London in 1816, says:

A very large part of heathen mythology originates from the history of the deluge, and many of the more ancient nations have preserved almost literal accounts of an universal deluge, which corresponds in a very wonderful manner with the history of it as detailed by Moses.[1]

"I have researched the story of the great Flood in languages and cultures throughout the world," says Dr. Charles Berlitz, author of more than 200 books and one of the fifteen most eminent linguists in the world. "Not only does it appear in the Christian Bible, but also in the *Koran*, the bible of Islam. There it tells the story of Noah—'Nuh' in Arabic—who escapes the Flood and survives with his family.

"In all the stories of the Flood I've studied, the stories are practically identical in all different sorts of languages, whether Persian, Babylonian, Assyrian, Egyptian, Chinese, or Sanskrit. The only thing that changes is the name of Noah but the story is essentially the same. This is a worldwide phenomenon."

In his book *The Lost Ship of Noah*, Dr. Berlitz says, "There are over 600 variations of this legend among the ancient nations and tribes, and the story has been told through the millennia in all quarters of the globe. The variations in accounts of the catastrophe, as could be expected, occur principally in regional modifications of the same story, such as the description of the ark, the reasons for heavenly displeasure, the way chosen individuals were saved, and even the possibility of the doom happening again."[2]

Dr. Steve Deckard, a professor of science education at a California graduate school, gives us an interesting comparison of the Flood legends from around the world. "Similar Flood legend accounts in various cultures imply a common source for the cultures or a common event, or both."

According to Dr. Deckard, "The eleventh tablet of one of the Babylonian Flood stories known as the *Gilgamesh Epic* is considered to be a remarkable confirmation of the Genesis account. This cuneiform fragment was found near the Israelite city of Megiddo. The date of this cuneiform account is unknown but it most likely dates back to the time of Moses—about 1400 B.C.. Comparison of the Genesis Flood account with the *Gilgamesh Epic* and more than 200 other Flood legends show a remarkable similarity in a number of respects." Dr. Deckard's similarities include:

- 95% talk about a global Flood.
- 95% state the catastrophe was a Flood alone.
- 88% report there was a favored family.
- 73% say animals played a part.
- 70% claim the people survived due to a boat.
- 67% say the animals were saved.
- 66% say man's wickedness was the Flood's cause.
- 57% report survivors ended up on a mountain.

- 35% claim birds were sent out.
- 13% state survivors performed a sacrifice afterward.

However, critics of the Noah account point out that Flood traditions name more than fifty different mountains as the landing site of the boat. What sets apart the biblical Flood story from all the others?

"This is one area where the Hebrew account in the Bible is unique from the other Flood accounts," says cuneiform expert, Dr. Arthur Custance, a fellow of the Canadian Royal Anthropological Institute. He has authored fifty-two treatises relating to ancient history, anthropology, archaeology, biblical history, and philosophy. Dr. Custance explains:

In extra-biblical accounts, the survivors always land on a local mountain. In the Hebrew account, the ark lands far from Palestine in a distant country "on the mountains of Ararat"— a place of which most Hebrew people had no firsthand knowledge.

This circumstance surely suggests that here in the Bible we have the genuine account. And it also underscores the great respect that the Hebrew people had for the Word of God and the requirement that they never tamper with it. It would surely, otherwise, have been most natural for them to land the ark on their most famous mountain, Mount Zion.[3]

Dr. Ethel Nelson, a Chinese pictograph linguist who has authored two books on ancient Chinese pictography, has made some startling discoveries about some of the oldest Chinese pictograph characters found written on the inside of Chinese bronzeware and on ancient oracle bone.

The Flood record has been found on such artifacts as the Akkadian, Sumerian, and Babylonian cuneiform tablets now on display at the British Museum. These tablets date back to about 700 B.C.. But there is a more ancient pictograph record found in ancient Chinese bronzeware and oracle bone pictograph writing. This pictograph writing dates back to about 1700 B.C.—within 600 years after the Flood!

Dr. Nelson, writing in her book, *The Discovery of Genesis*, with coauthor C. H. Kang, states that by dissecting ancient Chinese characters, they found that many of the characters ideographically explain the story of Noah and the Flood, and other parts of the book of Genesis.

"The Chinese claim to be the descendents of a man called "Nua" who overcame a great Flood. Also, the Chinese character for ship has within it the character for *eight* and *persons*. The first ship (the ark) had eight people on it. According to their tradition, these are the Chinese," adds Archaeological Illustrator, Elfred Lee, who has spent much of his life researching Noah's ark and searching for it on Mt. Ararat.

In addition to ancient Flood traditions providing evidence for Noah's Flood, a large bronze coin struck 1,700 years ago at Apameia Kibotos in Asia Minor (modern Turkey), near the mountains of Ararat, depicts the story of Noah's ark. The coin, now on display at the Israel Museum, is believed to be the only coin type known to bear a biblical scene. Containing Greek inscriptions, the coin pictures three portions of the Flood story on one side. Noah and his wife protrude from the ark, the dove with an olive branch rests on the ark's roof, and then Noah and his wife are shown standing to the right of the ark with arms upraised in prayer. The side of the ark is inscribed with the Greek letters for *Noah*.

Geological Evidences

According to Roger Oakland, science author and former biology professor at a Canadian college:

There's an extensive amount of evidence for a global Flood. And I see most of that evidence in the fossil record. Worldwide fossils of animals and fish have been found buried in swimming positions, suddenly and catastrophically preserved in a moment in time.

One of the most fascinating fossil finds, which show animals in swimming positions including rhinos, hippos, and zebras, is found in Nebraska. Hundreds of dinosaurs in Alberta, Canada, drowned in flood-deposited volcanic ash. In Scotland, tons of fish have been found in positions of terror, fins extended and eyes bulging. Another fossil graveyard in Geiseltal, Germany, shows a mixture of plants and insects from all climatic zones.

When these kinds of fossils are found together at such a great distance from their apparent place of origin, this is usually indicative of widespread global flooding and rapid burial. The only conclusion anyone can make is that it was caused by a flood of a universal nature.

The late Harry S. Ladd of the United States Geological Survey told of a petrified "fish bed" in Santa Barbara, California, where "more than a billion fish, averaging 6 to 8 inches in length, died on four square miles of bay bottom."[4] The question is, how did they get trapped there, if not by a flood?

Another graveyard believed to be related to flood action is found near Diamondville, Wyoming. This deposit, now a tourist attraction, is furnishing some of the most perfect specimens of fossil fish and plants in the world. Fish from 6 to 8 feet in length and palm leaves from 3 to 4 feet wide have been uncovered.

This confirms the geological theory that the climate was tropical, unlike the blizzard-ridden, rugged terrain of Wyoming today. The deposit contained an assortment of other odd remains—alligators, garpike, deep-sea bass, sunfish, chubs, herring, pickerel, crustaceans, birds, turtles, mollusca, mammals, and varieties of insects.[5]

Such a mixture of organisms from different habitats and climatic regions of the world is characteristic of the most important fossil deposits. Many scientists believe this happened by the *allochthonous process* in which materials are rapidly transported to their final locality and deposited under flood conditions.[6]

This is illustrated by the famous Baltic amber deposits in Eastern Europe, extensively investigated by Dr. N. Heribert-Nilsson, late director of the Swedish Botanical Institute. He says, "The insects discovered there are of fairly modern types (not prehistoric) and their geographical distribution can be ascertained. It is then quite astounding to find that they belong to all regions of the Earth."[7]

"The Morrison Formation," says Dr. Ariel Roth, retired director of the Geoscience Research Institute at Loma Linda University in California, "is spread over 400,000 square miles in the western United States. It runs from Texas to Canada and is well known because it contains lots of dinosaur fossils. This formation is indicative of what you'd expect to be laid down during a global Flood because of its uniformity in strata layers and its widespread coverage. This is what you would expect from a worldwide catastrophe such as described in the Bible."

Rapid Deposit of Earth's Layers

"An obvious indicator that there was a global Flood is the fact that we have sedimentary layers of rock and coal deposition around the world," stated museum curator and scientific researcher Dr. Carl Baugh in a 2007 interview.

Now in order to get these sedimentary layers, material has to be ripped apart, transported, has to be water-laid, and the only mechanism to explain this is the global Flood. Inside these sedimentary deposits, we have fossils. Now fossils do not form under general atmospheric conditions. They require a very rapid immediate burial in the deposition—free of aerobic and anaerobic microbes, free of free-oxygen. Otherwise, they would biodegrade very rapidly. When they are recovered, then very slowly osmosis occurs, where each cell is replaced. This requires a very rapid sedimentation and we have this expressed over the entire globe.

Fossils are unique in that they represent living forms of the past that have been covered very quickly and preserved until this very day because of their hard parts. And quite often, in addition to the bone, the wood fiber, or the shells, we have soft parts preserved, meaning, in each case they had to be covered in sedimentary deposit away from free-oxygen very rapidly. The only mechanism to account for this is a global Flood like that of Noah's day.

Further confirmation for rapid deposit of the sedimentary layers comes from Dr. M.E. Clark, who has studied flood sedimentation deposits worldwide. "My view," says Dr. Clark, a professor of hydraulics as well as theoretical and applied mechanics at the University of Illinois, "is that the whole geologic column is composed of conformal layers laid one on top of the other with usually a fine line of demarcation between them. This necessitates a very rapid deposition of these individual layers."

Dr. Clark, and his colleagues, Andrew Rodenbeck and Ian Jube, have conducted sediment studies to scientifically demonstrate the evidence for rapid layering. "We're trying to relate the sedimentary column to the Bible, and in the Bible they have a great hydraulic event called the Flood of Noah. According to the evolutionary scenario, the sedimentary layering that we see worldwide in the road cuts and the canyons took tens, sometimes hundreds of millions of years, to form. However, is that really accurate? The scientific sedimentation experiments, explained below, provide an alternative explanation."

Dr. M.E. Clark and Dr. Henry Voss, a fellow faculty member at the University of Illinois, have designed an experiment apparatus with a circular flume that can simulate the mechanisms that would produce the sedimentary layering that can be seen worldwide in canyons and road cuts along roads and highways. Dr. Clark clarifies that water was the cause of these patterns of layers: "In the road cuts we have conformal layering all starting out in a horizontal direction and possibly being moved around by tectonic activity to tangled layers, but essentially the water mechanism was horizontal, and so the layers come out that way. As you're driving along, you see the predominance of a horizontal mechanism, which had to be a water-created layer of sediment."

Dr. Clark demonstrated the scientific sedimentation experiment for us in a 2007 interview. The experiment involves a flume that accommodates a surface like that of the globe, completely saturated and covered with water. The flume also accommodates the effect of the moon gravitationally on this open body of water. The premise of the experiment is that if you have emulsified materials, such as the expulsion of the fountains of the great deep, in a global body of water effected by the moon bringing those waters into resonance and wave-like action—then we should be able to produce from those emulsified materials the stratographic layering that we see on earth, as well as the fossils in those layers.

This simulation process is done experimentally and scientifically. The flume channel is half filled with water, then the water is filled with sand and dirt material, and then stirred into action much as the moon would do, bringing the waters into resonance.

"The experiment is designed to see if this simulated process can actually produce the sedimentary deposits that we find on planet Earth worldwide. If so, this will confirm that it did not take, and does not require, tens of millions or hundreds of millions of years to produce the sedimentary layers, but instead it can be done overnight in a globe of deposited water," says Clark.

After the flume channel is half filled with water, then a paddle is pumped down to agitate the water and the sediments that have been added to the chamber. The mix is completely homogenized, and then the paddle is pulled up to let the water come to rest by itself, so that the sediments that are in it will become stationary in their position. At the conclusion of the experiment, the researchers make radial and circumferential cuts in the sediment, as well as cross-sections of the sediment, in order to clearly display the layering within it.

"The layers that have been produced in the experimental chamber are just as they are observed in the geologic record, or as seen in road cuts along highways—some are very fine layers, some thicker layers, and some layers of great purity, almost white, whereas some layers are more mixed," explains Clark.

Andrew Rodenbeck, who has experience in fluid dynamics, comments about the results from the experimental chamber:

The significance of these results is that here we have an experimental laboratory demonstration of exactly how sedimentary layers in the fossil record are actually produced. This is exactly what we see in actual sedimentary rocks. This is not an irrefragable projection of how they might have formed, but rather this an experimental demonstration of how these rocks really formed, how these layers are really laid down. It doesn't take very long at all—these [layers] fall out in fifteen to twenty minutes, and they fall out simultaneously. One layer does not grow as a given time period and then another as a given time period, but rather they all advance together simultaneously, and so you cannot use the principle of superposition to indicate that a given layer is a given time period. That's just not how it really works.

"Cross bedding" is another important evidence for the rapid sedimentation theory.

Ian Jube, one of the scientific experimenters, explains:

Cross bedding is a rather unusual formation that we see fairly common in the sedimentary record. Sedimentary layers are stacked on top of each other, and then within those layers are very unusual curves downward with a slope, and then a curve leveling off again.

Conventional interpretation, which automatically rejects the idea of a global Flood, interprets these as fossilized sand dunes. There are many problems with that interpretation. First, how can a sand dune be fossilized without a whole pile of water? It just doesn't happen. Secondly, you can see the curves in one layer, but where's the other side of the sand dune? It's gone. You won't find it. If you do find it, it's hundreds of miles away. The layers extend for hundreds of miles without a break, literally over the distance of [several U.S.] States; and they can be fifteen, twenty, twenty-five feet thick. To produce thicker layers in our experiments, all that is required is to upscale the speed and volume of the water, although all that it takes is the increase in water volume, not the speed, to produce thicker layers.

Now, within the cross beds, you will find very unusual fossil track waves. The interesting thing about these track waves is —they always go uphill. Some of the track waves, although they're sideways, they're walking sideways uphill with the toes pointing up. Now if these tracks had been made in a sand dune, why would they only be going uphill?

Some have suggested that only the tracks on the leeside of the sand dune were preserved, but that doesn't make sense. That means all the animals were going one direction in the desert at all times. It's completely illogical. Some have suggested the tracks are preserved going downhill. At the sand dunes in White Sands National Monument, you can see tracks are preserved both ways. The tracks go in all directions—uphill, downhill, across, on an angle.

Now let's relate all of this to the Flood. We can observe that in the sand dune tracks that only go uphill, within a span of feet the tracks will go from deep to shallower to only claw-prints, and then completely vanish. How can that be explained? Did the animal walk to a tiptoe across the desert floor and then just fly away? It makes no sense unless explained within the context of a global Flood, that these layers were laid down by water.

The linear flume that we built demonstrates that water can produce cross beds. Now some of the skeptics have suggested that the angle is indicative, that the cross bedding could only be formed in a dry desert environment. The first question that arises is, which one makes deeper slopes—dry sands, or wet sticky sand? The wet sticky sand of course, so it makes more sense that the steeper slopes would be made by water.

Some have refuted that the slopes can only be made up to about 25 to 30 degrees in water, yet in our experiment in the flume chamber, a 37-degree cross-bed was made. All it took was fast moving water traveling in one direction and running into standing water. And there's a number of ways you can get standing water with the encroaching floodwaters coming on, carrying sediments, and dropping them rapidly, producing these cross beds. Unquestionably, they were formed under water, the most logical explanation.

Even more compelling evidence for rapid sedimentation and fossilization, as opposed to the evolutionary millions of years, is that of polystrate fossils—a fossil tree or animal that is evidenced in the rock layers of having been covered up by ten or twenty layers. Dr. Clark explains: "The tree could not have stood for thousands of years while that many layers were being laid down gradually. This is very compelling evidence for very rapid deposition of the sedimentary layers that we see throughout the geologic column."

According to Mace Baker, a paleontological researcher and author:

The dinosaur fossils point to a worldwide Flood. Dinosaurs are often found in mass burials with up to a hundred dinosaurs in one location such as the ones that have been found in New Mexico and Germany. These mass burials are encased in enormous quantities of rapidly formed sedimentary rock layers, which are deposited by water. These mass quantities of dinosaur fossils indicate that they were buried catastrophically and very rapidly.

Ordinarily, when animals die their flesh is soon consumed by scavengers and their bones are left to decay and return to the soil. During the time in which the bones are decaying they most generally may be found in one of two positions: (1) they may be found on their side with their legs outstretched, or (2) the bones are sometimes found in a disarticulated condition. The latter condition is due to the work of scavengers.

In the case of armored dinosaurs, we find that a large number of them have been overturned and then fossilized in an upside-down position. To find one dinosaur fossil in this position would not be significant. To find so many in the upside-down position, however, speaks very clearly of a great catastrophe involving the force of raging waters.

Another example of rapid burial is a fossil of a *Compsognathus*, a small bipedal dinosaur that was found in Germany with the fossil remains of a lizard in its stomach and a *Pterosaur*, a type of flying reptile, [that] was found with food in its stomach and in its beak. So these, among many other evidences, clearly indicate that the dinosaurs did not perish over a long period of time, as most scientists believe, but were wiped out and covered very rapidly by a catastrophic flood.[8]

Seashells and fossils of fish and marine mammals have been found on the highest mountain ranges on earth—further evidence of a universal deluge. Skeletons of whales have been found in the Himalayas, the world's highest mountain range. The bones of crocodiles have been found in the Swiss Alps.[9] Fossils of fish, sea snails, and clams have been found atop Mount Everest.

Geologists who have climbed Mount Ararat—the landing site of Noah's ark—have discovered a variety of seashells and other evidence that this mountain was once underwater.

"I've noticed two things in particular on Mount Ararat from a geological point of view that indicates this 17,000-foot volcanic mountain was once underwater," says Grant Richards, a former geologist-geophysicist and field associate with the San Bernardino County Museum in California. "First is the occurrence high on Mount Ararat of what is called pillow-lava. This alone indicates that the mountain was at one time underwater. Secondly, we have found salt crystals on Mount Ararat which could only have been formed under water."

Dr. Clifford Burdick, a geologist commissioned by the Turkish government many years ago to study Mount Ararat, discovered more impressive evidence of a Flood. He found cube-shaped salt clusters as large as grapefruit near the 7,000-foot elevation of Mount Ararat.[10]

Pillow lava has been found as high as the 14,000-foot level of Ararat, implying that lava issued from inside the earth while Ararat was underwater. The water rapidly chilled the lava, creating circular formations resembling pillows. This would support Genesis 7:20, which says the Flood covered the highest mountains to a depth of 22 1/2 feet.

Dr. Burdick says most of Ararat was formed by volcanic action, and if the glacial ice cap on Ararat did not exist, one would probably find pillow lava all the way to the summit.[11]

Could this pillow lava have been formed during the time of the Flood or because of it?

"Presumably so," Dr. Burdick says. "We don't know of any other time that a mountain that high—17,000 feet—would have been underwater. You just have to connect the two. There's no other historical or geological record of the ocean being that high except at that time."[12]

Conglomerate cones found on Ararat, Dr. Burdick says, are further evidence of a universal Flood. The conglomerates are various sizes of rocks fused together. They are a mixture of rounded stones, solidified by a cementing medium like calcium carbonate. Lava flow and violent water action are needed to produce them. Finding a conglomerate cone at the 12,000- or 13,000-foot level of Ararat indicates that at one time the area was underwater.[13]

Exciting evidence of a global Flood can also be found in the study of coal deposits. Coal is formed by compacted, decayed vegetation, and scientists estimate that it takes anywhere from 5 to 10 feet of compacted plant material to form 1 foot of coal. At a ratio of seven to one, then, a 10-foot seam of coal represents 70 feet of compacted plant material.

When we realize that coal seams can be up to 400 feet thick, we begin to understand how much more vegetation flourished in the pre-Flood world than exists on earth today.

Dr. Harold Coffin, a retired scientist at the Geoscience Research Institute, has done extensive research into the formation of coal beds and has concluded that a 400-foot seam of coal would represent a fantastic 4,000 feet of peat at an average of 10 feet of peat or vegetable matter for 1 foot of coal. Few peat bogs, marshes, or swamps anywhere in the world today reach even 100 feet, and most are less than 50 feet. The only logical conclusion to explain the creation of a 400-foot seam of coal, then, is a tremendous force collecting and compressing all of this vegetable matter.[14]

"The concept of a global deluge," Dr. Coffin says, "that eroded out the forests and plant cover of the pre-Flood world, collected it in great mats of drifting debris, and eventually dropped it on the emerging land or on the sea bottom is the most reasonable answer to this problem of the great extent and uniform thickness of coal beds."[15]

The fossil record, then, clearly indicates that the fish and animals found perfectly preserved in sedimentary layers worldwide were not a result of these animals dying naturally and then being slowly covered with sedimentary layers over a long period of time. They had to have been caught suddenly in a tremendous deluge that compressed them quickly between various sedimentary layers before they could decompose. There is absolutely no other logical explanation for the fossils and enormous coal deposits other than a worldwide Flood.

Pre-Flood Artifacts

"I would seriously doubt and question that any so-called man-made objects would be found in ancient coal beds," says field geologist Tom Hill of Irvine, California.

If manmade artifacts can be found in either sedimentary rock layers or in coal deposits, only one of two alternative conclusions can be made: "Either man has been on the earth for millions and millions of years, or the entire sedimentary deposits of the Geologic Column are in error, and all of that [the sedimentary columns] is flood deposit ... In addition, it indicates recency in the creation of planet Earth, and also means that the widely accepted 'geologic column' taught in schools is in error," comments Dr. Carl Baugh, author of *Panoroma of Creation.*

Bible scholars in the past had estimated that the pre-Flood population numbered in the millions. And more recent estimates calculate that the population was one billion. These large populations could not have disappeared without a trace—and they didn't!

Manmade artifacts actually have been found in the sedimentary deposits of the geologic column. Many such human artifacts have been found encased in either coal or sedimentary rock layers. Examples of such finds include an eight-carat gold chain, a clay figurine, a spoon, a thimble, an iron pot, nails, and other items.

Among the list is a cup that was discovered early in the last century by Frank Kanard. While working in a power plant in Oklahoma, he took a huge chunk of coal to throw into the furnace of the power plant. He could not get it in, so he took a sledgehammer nearby and broke the chunk of coal. It fell in two pieces. One side exposed this manmade cup as it fell out with the crevice still in place. In a 2007 interview, Archaeological excavator Dr. Carl Baugh explains the cup's significance:

> The cup has been analyzed. The cup or pot itself is not exotic in nature, but it is iron and it is very specific, very symmetrical, and very beautiful. Frank Kanard took it home, and then unfortunately threw the rest of the coal into the furnace. He discovered, however, that the coal that he was shoveling came from the Wilburton Coal Mines near Wilburton,

Oklahoma, and that all of the coal of those coal mines is assigned Mid-Pennsylvanian. That means that according to standard evolutionary assignment that coal is 295 million years old. That is a major problem for evolutionary dogma. Either man's been around much longer than expected, man was sophisticated from the beginning, or the entire geologic column of sedimentary deposits, including the coal, were laid down rapidly and recently.

An engraved metal bowl was found in conglomerate rock near Dorchester, Massachusetts, in 1851. An article in *Scientific American* indicates that a powerful blast made in rock near Dorchester threw out an immense mass. Some of the pieces weighed several tons. The blast scattered small fragments in all directions. Among the fragments was a bell-shaped metal pot, 4 1/2 inches high, 6 1/2 inches at the base, 2 1/2 inches at the top, and about 1/8-inch thick. It had a zinc color.

On the sides were engraved bouquets of flowers beautifully inlaid with silver. The carving and inlaying were done exquisitely by a cunning workman.[16]

Still another mystery is the discovery in England of a gold thread embedded in stone quarried from a depth of eight feet. No one knows how long this remnant of a former age had been embedded.

The late M. A. Kurtz, of Nampa, Idaho, in 1889 discovered a clay female doll at a depth of about 300 feet in a layer of coarse sand, as he was boring for an artesian well.

His discovery, called the "Nampa Image," gained the attention of the scientific world.[17] The 1 1/2-inch doll figurine was found after Kurtz had drilled through about fifteen feet of lava rock, one hundred feet of quicksand, then six inches of clay, forty more feet of quicksand, more clay, more quicksand, more clay, then clay balls mixed with sand, then coarse sand.

It has since been called one of the most curious archaeological discoveries of the nineteenth century and is currently on display at the Idaho Historical Society Museum in Boise.[18]

The significance of the image is this: It is a man-made object discovered at a depth of about 300 feet, meaning that whoever shaped it lived on that land 300 feet below the present surface, or it was washed there by the Flood. In either case, it was buried by flood action, based on what scientists know of the way sedimentary deposits are laid down.

In 1822 British surgeon Gideon Mantell chronicled that in 1791 M. Leisky of Hamburg, Germany, discovered an "ancient iron pin" in a piece of fractured flint.

The *London Times*, in 1851, reported that a miner returning from the California goldfields found an iron nail embedded near the center of a gold-bearing quartz rock.

The *Zanesville Courier*, in 1853, reported the Cusick's Mill quarry near Zanesville, Ohio, yielded the bones of a woman completely entombed in sandstone that also retained the full impression of her once fleshly form.

J. Q. Adams, writing in an 1883 issue of *American Antiquarian*, reported the discovery of a thimble trapped in a lump of lignite coal mined from the Marshall Coal Bed in Colorado.

In June 1891 Mrs. S. W. Culp of Morrisonville, Illinois, found a 10-inch gold chain embedded in a lump of coal she was breaking apart for her stove.

More recent finds include a small iron pot found in 1912 encased in a block of coal at the Municipal Electric Plant in Thomas, Oklahoma. The coal was traced to the Wilburton Oklahoma Mines. The pot, with an affidavit from the pot finder, is now on display at the Miles Municipal Museum in Eureka Springs, Arkansas.

Newton Anderson, a chemist and retired science educator living in Florida, recounts how he found a bell in coal while living in West Virginia:

> I found the bell in a lump of coal when I was ten years old. I was asked to fire the furnace. I got a large lump of coal, and when I got it to the furnace I dropped it. The coal broke and the top of the bell—the stem—was sticking out of the coal. Later, I carefully rendered the coal from the bell base.
>
> The bell has an unusual pagan god on top of the stem with both arms and wings raised upward. The god is in a kneeling position and the rest of the top is an ornate stem. This brass bell has an iron clapper inside.
>
> For a long time we've tried to learn about the bell. Historically, this pagan ceremonial bell is described very well by an account in Genesis 4:22 that say Tubal-Cain was an artificer of brass and iron. This quite likely is a pre-Flood civilization object, and it could have been carried over by Noah's Flood into the coal.

Interestingly, Anderson had a special scanning electron elemental analysis test performed on the bell and determined the elemental composition of the bell couldn't be reproduced by today's metallurgy technology. Was the pre-Flood civilization more advanced in metallurgy, or did the pre-Flood atmosphere somehow impact the elemental composition?

Pre-Flood Hammer Tested

Another equally interesting find of a human artifact containing unusual elemental properties occurred in 1934, when Emma Hahn of London, Texas, discovered a rock with a fragment of wood protruding from its surface. After breaking open the rock, she was surprised to find that the wood was in fact the splintered handle of a hammer whose iron head remained intact.

Rock formations in the immediate area and in the rock where the hammer was found have been identified as early Cretaceous, dating it by evolutionary assignment at about 140 million years. According to Archaeological Excavator, Dr. Carl Baugh, who has examined the hammer, "Either the evolutionary geological dating column is wrong, or an intelligent ancient man lived a half-billion years ago—499 million years earlier than scientists say man lived on earth!"

Critics of these conclusions regarding the hammer say that the artifact is a result of a natural process of accretion. This occurs when mineral-rich water evaporates, leaving behind deposits that build up until an object becomes completely encased.

Scientific tests, however, have revealed some intriguing properties.

"The wood in the interior of the handle is partially turned to coal," Baugh says. "The structure of the hammer has been compared to known historical hand tools recorded in the United States, and no historical equivalent could be found after an exhaustive search."

He adds, "What has intrigued scientists is that when they seared through the charred material encasing the hammer, it was shiny bright. That was in 1934, and to this date, decades since, it is still shiny bright—the hammer does not rust."

The hammer was taken to Batelle Laboratories— the labs that analyzed the Moon Stones—to determine the composition of the hammer head through a scanning electron elemental analysis. The analysis by weight shows that the hammerhead is made of 96.6 percent iron, 2.6 percent chlorine and 0.74 percent sulfur, with no silicon or nickel—a highly unusual combination. The absence of silicon and the high amount of chlorine would indicate, according to Baugh, that the hammer was not formed by any known modern means.

"It's our belief that the hammer has been formed by a totally unknown manufacturing process and that it had been formed a long time before modern manufacturing processes were developed," Baugh says. "The strength of the hammer appears to come from the strange concentration of chlorine in the iron. If the chlorine is throughout the hammer, it would account for the fact that the hammer head does not appear to corrode very easily."

Dr. Ian Taylor, a professional metallurgist in Canada, after a review of a documentary on the hammer, reported to Dr. Baugh. "In our opinion, it is a genuine pre-Flood artifact." When questioned, he answered, "Because if an area of it did not rust, that would mean there was straight FeO on the surface of the metal. Rust is Fe_2O_3 or Fe_3O_4. In a context where we add atmospheric pressure and slight humidity we can generate straight FeO, but it is not found in nature."

A tomography analysis was done on the hammer at the largest tomography lab in the world, located in Texas. Tomography is a technique using X-rays for examining the internal structure of solid objects. Dr. Baugh reports the results:

The tests revealed it was the most homogenous implement ever seen by the lab technicians. Nothing in modern technology or in ancient metallurgy can compare to the uniformity of the hammer's interior. It's impossible to produce this hammer today. We cannot compound chlorine with metallic iron. We can compound chlorine with iron dust, but not metallic iron. Physicists say the only way this hammer could be produced would be under a different type of atmospheric pressure. Here we have an enigma for the scientific community if evolution is true. On the other hand, if there was a more dense, specified pre-Flood atmosphere with greater atmospheric pressure, then this makes sense. This wrecks evolutionary hypothesis.

"A portion of the interior of the handle is *coalified*, indicating there was tremendous pressure. That is very significant," says Dr. Baugh in the 2007 interview. "Physicists have examined this, and again, a number have indicated that the only conditions under which this sophisticated metal hammerhead could be produced would be under greater atmospheric pressure—and we only find that in the pre-Flood world of Noah's day."

The Meister Print

According to Dr. Baugh, "Probably the most significant single artifact that has been found to date that is devastating against evolutionary dogma is the Meister Print."

The Meister Print was discovered by William Meister and his wife in June1968, while looking for trilobites. Dr. Baugh, of the Creation Evidence Museum, recounts in our 2007 interview the details of this significant discovery:

They found trilobites in Cambrian shale, which has been assigned by evolutionary dogma at 530 million years in age. In their search for trilobites, they took the geology pick and broke open a layer of the shale, and to their absolute amazement, they found a sandal print, manmade sandal print, with a wear on the heel and the curvature at the front of the toe, just as a sandal would be made. Stitching can be seen in the sandal print and, in addition to that, Elrathia kingi trilobites and smaller trilobites. One of our forensics experts looked at this, and he said, "This is amazing. That trilobite was crushed while he was still alive." That means that this individual stepped on the trilobite and made the depression and the print that can be seen in the shale.

If this print is 530 million years in age, that means that man has been around since the beginning of the geologic column and has not progressed in evolutionary change. But there is a far better explanation because of poly-straight interlacing fossils, and because scholars such as Professor Emmy Clark have demonstrated that you can get all of the sedimentary layering in an impact that's incredibly recent. And that explanation is that the entire geologic column has been rapidly laid down. That is, within a few weeks or months the entire geologic column could be formed, if you have a global Flood such as we had in Noah's day. Our geologists have demonstrated that there is a worldwide layer of cretaceous limestone.

"This worldwide sedimentary layer," Dr. Baugh concludes, "could only have been laid down by a global Flood."

A Shift in Geology

"The geology of the Earth has been studied with an assumption, namely, that the Earth is billions of years old," says Dr. Walt Brown. "If the ark of Noah is ever discovered, and I think it's probably there, it will change in a very drastic way people's view of a billion-year-old Earth."

According to Geologist John Morris, the scientific views of Earth's history are already changing:

Mainstream geology does seem to disallow the possibility of a global Flood. But, you know, this is an exciting time in geology. Here at the Institute for Creation Research, we do a lot of research on this, and as a geologist, I can testify that all of geology is shifting. It used to be that geology was locked into this idea called *uniformity*—that there'd never been anything that happened on planet Earth that was different from the kinds of things that are happening today. But more and more geologists are talking about big things, global things. They're talking about continents moving around, they're talking about meteorites blasting and killing off all the dinosaurs—big things, global things. Well, the Bible has been talking about this all along.

Relating this to the future implications for evolutionary theory, Morris adds:

I think the potential discovery of Noah's ark could have great implications in this overall Creation/Evolution question that is raging around the world today. You see, Evolution is based on the assumption of *uniformity*—that things have been uniform throughout the past. But, of course, the Bible states that there have been episodes of Earth's history dramatically different from anything even possible today. Noah's Flood would be one of those episodes. If we were to find that 500-foot boat on top of a 17,000-foot mountain, well obviously, it would prove that catastrophism has been the rule of Earth history, not uniformity. I think discovering the ark would be so incompatible with evolution thinking that it would just yank the rug out from under what I believe is an unscientific idea anyway, and Evolution as a way of thinking would come crumbling down.

On the Wings of a Dove

As we rejoin our passengers aboard the ark, it has seemed a long time since Noah released the dove to search for dry land. Having finished their chores for the day, the family sits quietly eating meager portions of their evening meal. Suddenly, Noah spots the dove outside of the window. Excited, he goes to the window and reaches out his hand. The dove alights on it. Under the watchful eyes of his family, he carefully draws the little bird back inside the ark and gently strokes its head.

"Well, family, it looks as if we will still be on the ark for a while. This little dove wasn't able to find dry land or else she wouldn't have come back to us."

"How long do you think we'll have to stay on the ark?" Shem asks.

"I don't know. We'll send her back out in a few days and see what happens then. I know waiting is difficult," Noah says, looking around sympathetically at his loved ones. "We have no other choice than to trust God. He knows how we are getting low on food and water. He will make a way for us."

It was natural for Noah to send out a raven and a dove to determine if the flood waters had subsided. In ancient times, animals often were used for communication and navigational purposes. Doves or pigeons, with their powerful homing instincts, have always been famous for their ability to undertake long, swift flights. To assume that Noah knew this is more than reasonable.[19]

Pigeons were used as messengers in the days of Solomon.[20] The Romans used them during battles, and the Greeks used them to carry the results of the Olympic Games. Many amazing flights were made by these birds in World Wars I and II. Through mist and storm and shrapnel, literally hundreds of pigeons carried their messages that saved the lives of thousands of wrecked airmen and troops cut off by enemy forces.[21]

Noah waited a week and again took the little dove to the window and released her into the strong wind that was blowing outside the ark. He watched her for as long as he could, then turned away from the window and silently prayed.

"Father, come quick!" Japheth was out of breath as he ran into the room. "The dove has returned with a freshly plucked olive leaf."

"Are you sure?" Noah felt a rush of excitement. "An olive leaf?"

What the Olive Leaf Proved

Olive groves are favorite places for doves to build their nests. No wonder Noah's dove returned to the ark with "a freshly plucked olive leaf."[22]

Noah apparently knew the habits of animals, and he knew that the raven—a scavenger bird—would not return to the ark if the water had subsided enough for it to perch on some slimy surface or carcass. And this is exactly what happened.

The dove is a clean bird; it would not perch on such a surface. Noah sent it out three times. The second time, the dove returned with an olive leaf in its mouth. This told Noah that the earth was returning to its fruitfulness.

While an olive tree may grow in water, it doesn't thrive at mountaintop heights and as a rule prefers slopes below 3,000 feet. Thus, Noah knew that the lower elevations were beginning to produce vegetation.[23]

In their book *The Genesis Flood*, John Whitcomb and Henry Morris say that before it was discovered by the dove, the olive leaf would have had as much as four months' exposure to sunshine in order to sprout from an asexually propagated olive branch buried near the surface of the soil.[24]

And the olive, one of the hardiest of all plants, would be one of the first to sprout after the Flood. Full-grown olive trees can survive extremely harsh treatment. Only a few months are needed from the time of implantation of olive cuttings until the leaves sprout. Branches of olive trees apparently were buried near enough to the surface of the soil to sprout shoots, thus producing a new generation of trees from asexually propagated plants, says Dr. Walter Lammerts, a California horticulturist.[25]

About a month later, Noah removed part of the ark's roof (Genesis 8:13), and saw the ground was dry. Noah waited another fifty-six days before disembarking.

Endnotes

1   Violet Cummings, *Noah's Ark: Fact or Fable?* (San Diego: Creation-Science Research Center, 1972), p. 132.

2   Charles Berlitz, *The Lost Ship of Noah* (New York: G. P. Putnam's Sons, 1987), p. 110.

3   Donald W. Patten, *A Symposium on Creation* (Grand Rapids: Baker Book House, 1972), pp. 9-10, 17.

4   Harry S. Ladd, "Ecology, Paleontology and Stratigraphy," *Science* 129 (January 9, 1959), p. 72.

5   "Fishing for Fossils," *Compressed Air Magazine* 63 (March 1958), P. 24.

6   John C. Whitcomb and Henry M. Morris, *The Genesis Flood* (Phillipsburg, NJ: Presbyterian and Reformed Publishing Co., 1961), pp. 158-159.

7   N. Heribert-Nilsson, *Synthetische Artbildung* (Stockholm, Sweden), pp. 1195-1196.

8   Mace Baker, *Evidences of a Worldwide Flood from a Study of the Dinosaurs* (Roseville, MN: Twin-Cities Creation Conference, 1992), p. 147.

9 Berlitz, *The Lost Ship of Noah,* pp. 141-142.

10 Dave Balsiger and Charles E. Sellier, *In Search of Noah's Ark* (Los Angeles: Sun Classic Books, 1976), p. 48.

11 Ibid.

12 Ibid.

13 Ibid., pp. 48-49.

14 Rene Noorbergen, *The Ark File* (Mountain View, CA: Pacific Press Publishing Association, 1974), p. 64.

15 Ibid., pp. 64-65.

16 *Scientific American* 7 (June 5, 1952), p. 298.

17 Balsiger and Sellier, *In Search of Noah's Ark,* p. 44.

18 Ibid., p. 45.

19 Ibid., p. 138.

20 *Chambers Encyclopedia,* Article "Dove."

21 Balsiger and Sellier, *In Search of Noah's Ark,* p. 139.

22 Ibid.

23 Ibid.

24 Whitcomb and Morris, *The Genesis Flood,* p. 8.

25 Balsiger and Sellier, *In Search of Noah's Ark,* pp. 139-140.

Six

REPLENISHING THE EARTH

What is a scientist after all? It is a curious man looking through a keyhole, the keyhole of nature, trying to know what's going on.
—Jacques Yves Cousteau

IN THE TENTH MONTH of their journey aboard the ark, Noah climbed up a ladder to the roof and made a hole large enough to crawl through. He then climbed out onto the roof of the massive wooden barge to look around. The ship was perched on the upper slope of a mountain that one day would be known as Mount Ararat, among the mountains of Ararat in eastern Turkey. Noah found it difficult to keep his balance in the brisk wind, but the view was spectacular.

Scattered huge clouds billowed into the pale blue sky, and the bright sunlight made him squint at first. He could see in every direction—valleys, hills, and mountain lakes brimming with water. Land! Just seeing the hills springing forth with new plant life filled him with tremendous comfort and joy.

"Oh, God, thank You for preserving us and bringing us safely through the rebirth of Your earth," he cried with outstretched arms. "How magnificent are Your works!"

125

Noah laughed and spun around, giddy with sheer exuberance over finally being out of the confines of the ark. Pacing from side to side and from one end of the roof to the other, he relished the nearly forgotten feelings of freedom and openness. His senses were bombarded with the smell of the fresh air, the sight of new colors everywhere, and the breathtaking view in every direction. This was his first, unobstructed glimpse of the landscape around him, and he felt mesmerized. Out of a tragic death was emerging glorious new life, and he knew that at that moment, he alone was privileged to witness it.

The harsh, blowing wind was cold, however; and even though he kept moving, he was shivering. Regretfully, he crawled back down into the warmth, the earthy smells, and the semidark confines of the ark.

The family chatted excitedly for hours about the new world awaiting them and even forgot about their boredom.

Noah and Naamah lay down that night with hearts full of joy, thanksgiving, and praise. Their trust in God's promises had been rewarded in the most remarkable ways, and they knew that in spite of the hardships, the best was yet to come.

As the days passed, everyone except Naamah went on the roof daily to view the landscape as it grew more lush and green. Finally, some 375 days after they boarded the ark, Noah announced that God had told him it was time to break open the seals on the ramp and lower it.

As the first one down the ramp, Noah stepped onto the dry earth and dropped to his knees. His family joined him on the rocky soil, and they offered a prayer of thanksgiving to God. Then they hugged and danced around in joy—not minding the cold wind that blew in the crisp, early morning air.

They were finally on land again. They had survived and they were finally free.

Searching for Credible Answers

The biblical account picks up the story of Noah disembarking from the ark:

By the first day of the first month of Noah's six hundred and first year, the water had dried up from the earth. Noah then removed the covering from the ark and saw that the surface of the ground was dry. By the twenty-seventh day of the second month the earth was completely dry.

Then God said to Noah, "Come out of the ark, you and your wife and your sons and their wives. Bring out every kind of living creature that is with you—the birds, the animals, and all the creatures that move along the ground—so they can multiply on the earth and be fruitful and increase in number upon it."

So Noah came out, together with his sons and his wife and his sons' wives. All the animals and all the creatures that move along the ground and all the birds—everything that moves on the earth—came out of the ark, one kind after another.

Then Noah built an altar to the Lord and, taking some of all the clean animals and clean birds, he sacrificed burnt offerings on it. The Lord smelled the pleasing aroma and said in his heart: "Never again will I curse the ground because of man, even though every inclination of his heart is evil from childhood. And never again will I destroy all living creatures, as I have done.

"As long as the earth endures, seedtime and harvest, cold and heat, summer and winter, day and night will never cease."

Then God blessed Noah and his sons, saying to them, *"Be fruitful and increase in number and fill the earth. The fear and dread of you will fall upon all the beasts of the earth and all of the birds of the air, upon every creature that moves along the ground, and upon all the fish of the sea; they are given into your hands. Everything that lives and moves will be food for you. Just as I gave you the green plants, I now give you everything.*

And God said, *"This is the sign of the covenant I am making between me and you and every living creature with you, a covenant for all generations to come: I have set my rainbow in the clouds, and it will be the sign of the covenant between me and the earth. Whenever I bring clouds over the earth and the rainbow appears in the clouds, I will remember my covenant between me and you and all living creatures of every kind. Never again will the waters become a Flood to destroy all life. Whenever the rainbow appears in the clouds, I will see it and remember the everlasting covenant between God and all living creatures of every kind on the earth."*

The sons of Noah who came out of the ark were Shem, Ham and Japheth. (Ham was the father of Canaan.) These were the three sons of Noah, and from them came the people who were scattered over the earth.

Noah, a man of the soil, proceeded to plant a vineyard.

After the Flood, Noah lived 350 years. Altogether, Noah lived 950 years and then he died (Genesis 8:13; 9:3, 12-16, 18-20, 28-29).

Critics are quick to call this part of the Noah account unbelievable: Noah was 601 years old when the ark came to rest on Ararat, and he died at 950 years of age. How could he have lived so long? How could all the races have come from Noah and his family? Furthermore, how could all the languages of the world result from a family that spoke only one? Finally, how did the animals and birds spread all over the world? Critics also dispute the belief that the Ice Age and today's weather regime came into existence as a result of the year-long Flood. Good questions from the critics—and they all need good answers from the scientific community.

The Day of Deluge

Before we deal with these difficult questions, let's set the stage by clarifying some items regarding the Flood. First, when did the Flood occur?

Dr. Gerald E. Aardsma, a nuclear physicist from Canada, believes the Flood may have occurred as far back as 12,000 B.C.. However, most biblical scholars and chronologies suggest the Flood occurred about 5,000 years ago—somewhere between 2390 B.C. and 2103 B.C.. Rabbi Jose, writing in A.D. 150, set the Flood in the year 2103 B.C., while chronologist Philip Mauro placed the date at 2390 B.C..

Chronologist Gene Faulstich, founder of the Chronology History Research Institute in Iowa, uses astronomical dating to confirm biblical events. He says:

> Ancient people did not have clocks and calendars as we do today. They dated events from the position of the sun and moon. For example, the rains began, according to Noah in the second month, on the seventeenth day. We understand that to be one lunar month

after the first day of spring—two days after the full moon.

Astronomical dating is an exact science in which we can, with the aid of computers, examine biblical events in light of astronomical occurrences. We can take the chronology data given by Noah in Genesis during the Flood and with computers, convert this data into a meaningful calendar. We also note that Noah was on the ark for one solar year of 365 days, observed the Sabbath day, and even more important, the Noah Flood events synchronize perfectly with the solstices and equinoxes, as well as with the days of the week.

In 1650, Irish chronologist James Ussher, without the aid of computers, placed the Flood in 2348 B.C.. However, with today's astronomical computer technology, we're able to accurately determine that the Flood occurred in 2345 B.C., and that the first Flood rains started to fall on May 14, 2345 B.C.. We're able to confirm all the events surrounding the Flood due to a solar eclipse which occurred at sunrise on May 16, 2344 B.C.—when he observed a bow in the sky after they left the ark three days earlier.

Once Noah's Flood chronology data is matched with astronomical-dating information on computer, Faulstich says the following scenario emerges (assume Noah is speaking):

We had the ark loaded on May 12, 2345 B.C., and we rested on Saturday, May 13. The rain broke loose on May 14, and the rains continued until the first day of summer. I could not see any land for six months, but on the first day of winter, I saw a mountain peak. The water continued to subside, and on the first day of spring, I looked out to see dry land. This was also New Year's Day in 2344 B.C.. After sending birds away from the ship, I decided to leave the ark on the anniversary of my entrance into the ark.

On Sunday, May 13, I left the ark. I built an altar for God, and on the morning of May 16th, I made the first offerings. As the sun rose, the moon came up below it and eclipsed it. This caused an awesome sight in the eastern sky, but an equally beautiful rainbow in the western sky.

Some scholars believe the Flood began and ended in our present day month of November. Many cultures around the world recognize a "Day of the Dead" that apparently was originally a commemoration of the destruction of all life on earth due to the Flood.

Dr. Filby, in his book *The Flood Reconsidered,* explains:

November 2 is All Souls' Day—the Day of the Dead. In France it is *Le Jour des Morts*—Christianized now for centuries but still at heart the old Day of the Dead when flowers are taken to the tombs. From South America to Northern Europe, from Mexico to Polynesia, gifts and flowers are placed on tombs on this anniversary of the Day of the Dead.

The Persians commenced their New Year in November in a month which was named Mordad—meaning month of the angel of death. In Peru the New Year commenced in

November. Mexicans, too, kept the Day of the Dead at the same time of the year.

Natives in parts of Australia at this time of the year paint white stripes on their legs and arms and ribs to resemble skeletons. Our Anglo-Saxon ancestors called November Blood-month! The Celtic inhabitants of England—whose traditions incidentally are among the most ancient in the world—kept their New Year in November.

The ritual has in some cases been absorbed into, or modified by, later religions, but the recollection of that Day of Judgment and death has never ceased.[1]

How Far Did the Ark Float?

Another unanswered question is—if Noah's ark landed on Mount Ararat, where was it built, and how far did it float?

According to the late Donald W. Patten, a geographer and author of *The Flood of Noah,* "The ark was built near a pre-Flood city named Shuruppak—it is so identified in the *Gilgamesh Epic,* which is a cuneiform story of the Flood found in Assyria. Shuruppak also became a post-Flood city and is located in southern Iraq.

"We know where the ark landed. It was in eastern Turkey. We know it moved 520 miles or more. It was swept north by slightly northwest high into the mountain basin of eastern Turkey."

How the Animals Migrated

The animals were led from the ark in such a way as to give the "prey" plenty of time to disperse before the "predators" were released.

"After the birds are all out, let's release the rodents," Naamah suggested. "Then we'll ask the men to release the reptiles, okay?"

Her daughters-in-law laughed. Naamah could not bring herself to even go near the snakes in the ark for more than a year and she certainly wasn't going to start now.

Just how did all the animals, reptiles, birds, and insects repopulate the new world?

Although billions of insects and fish perished during the Flood, many species survived. Fish that did not get trapped in the sedimentary deposits laid down by receding floodwaters were able to weather the Flood. Most insects reproduce by eggs and therefore many were easily capable of surviving the Flood. Furthermore, the strong evidence suggests that many insects rode out the deluge aboard floating debris atop the floodwaters. Finally, it would not be difficult to believe that some varieties of insects made it aboard the ark as stowaways or as planned passengers even though Noah was not required to include them on his embarkation list. Thus, the repopulation of insects and fish throughout the world was no doubt easily accomplished.[2]

Present-day animal distributions can be explained on the basis of waves of migrations from the mountains of Ararat after the Flood.[3]

Dr. Frank Lewis Marsh in his book *Evolution, Creation and Science,* makes these points as to how the migrations went:

The journeys from the mountains of Ararat to their present habitats were made in an intermittent fashion, each generation sending representatives a little farther from the original home. The presence of tapirs today only in

South America and the Malayan Islands, opposite sides of the Earth, is indicative of the fact that animals migrated in more than one direction.... There is no reason for believing that this distribution of animals was accomplished by any other processes than those employed in distribution today.... Increase in number of individuals of any kind causes a necessity for spreading outward toward the horizon in search of food and homes ...[4]

There is some evidence that animals could have reached their present habitats with amazing speed, crossing continents and even large stretches of open sea on their way.[5]

In 1883, the island of Krakatoa was left destroyed by a volcanic eruption. For nearly twenty-five years, practically nothing lived on the remnant of that volcanic island.

"But then, the colonists began to arrive—a few mammals in 1908; a number of birds, lizards, and snakes; various mollusks, insects, and earthworms," says Rachel L. Carson, in her famous book, *The Sea Around Us.* "Ninety percent of Krakatoa's new inhabitants, Dutch scientists found, were forms that could have arrived by air."[6]

Professor Paul A. Moody of the University of Vermont explains how large land animals have been able to cross oceans on natural "floating islands":

In times of flood, large masses of earth and entwining vegetation, including trees, may be torn loose from the banks of rivers and swept out to sea. Sometimes such masses are encountered floating in the ocean out of sight of land, still lush and green, with palms twenty to thirty feet tall. It is entirely probable that land animals may be transported long distances in this manner.[7]

We know little of the migrations of animals in the past. But what we do know shows clearly the possibility of rapid colonization of distant areas, even though oceans had to be crossed in the process.

"It would not have required many centuries to migrate from Asia to South America over the Bering land bridge," Whitcomb and Morris say. "Population pressures, search for new homes, and especially the impelling force of God's command to the animal kingdom (Genesis 8:17) soon filled every part of the habitable Earth with birds, beasts, and creeping things."[8]

The Post-Flood Earth

In addition to all of the other changes in the post-Flood earth, it is apparent from the Bible text that Noah and his family entered the ark as vegetarians but were allowed to eat meat when they disembarked.

They may not have had any choice but to eat meat when they left the ark. The new earth probably would not have produced any fruits, grains or vegetables by the time Noah's family disembarked, and they may have prudently chosen to save or ration what food they had left—especially in light of the fact that they may have been entering an "ice age" or "winter season" where nothing could grow. They may also have needed to use the skins and fur of some animals for protective clothing, leading them naturally to make use of the meat.

The world following the Flood was not as stable as the pre-Flood earth. For at least 700 years, volcanic eruptions and earthquakes were common, and weather patterns were severe and erratic. This worldwide instability resulted in the Ice Age.

Three conditions resulting from Noah's Flood would have caused the snow and ice of the Ice Age to accumulate: extensive evaporation from oceans, extensive snowfall, and reduced snowmelt.

The glacial sheets did not cover Bible lands, but they no doubt affected its climate, producing more rain, snow, and ice than occurs there today.

The patriarch Job lived in Arabia during this time. There are more references to cold, snow, ice, and frost in his book than in any other book of the Bible. For example:

• *Thawing ice and swollen with melting snow* (Job 6:16).

• *If I washed myself with snow* (Job 9:30).

• *They have nothing to cover themselves in the cold* (Job 24:7).

• *Heat and drought snatch away the melted snow* (Job 24:19).

• *He says to the snow, "Fall on the earth"* (Job 37:6).

• *The tempest comes out from its chamber, the cold from the driving winds. The breath of God produces ice, and the broad waters become frozen* (Job 37:9-10).

• *Have you entered the storehouses of the snow, or seen the treasures of the hail, which I reserve for times of trouble, for days of war and battle?* (Job 38:22-23).

• *From whose womb comes the ice? Who gives birth to the frost from the heavens? When the waters become hard as stone, when the surface of the deep is frozen?* (Job 38:29-30).

During the Ice Age, so much water was frozen that the sea level was lowered several hundred feet. Ice shelves covered parts of the oceans. This made all the continents accessible, thus allowing migration to occur. Furthermore, no competition for the uninhabited land was necessary, and since food was scarce, migration was encouraged.

Volcanic eruptions, glaciation, an unpredictable environment, a varying food supply, and intermittent warmth from the sun would present unique challenges to the animal population.

Animals inhabiting areas affected by these conditions tended to exhibit longer hair, more massive bones, and heavier teeth. Typical Ice Age mammals included the giant ground sloth, giant beaver, mammoth, saber-toothed tiger, and giant kangaroo. Most of these mammals have smaller, modern-day counterparts.

Episodes of melting snow, catastrophically ruptured glacial lakes, and sudden storms produced many fossils of land animals. Many animal types became extinct at this time. The vast numbers of mammoth fossils in Alaska and Siberia are preserved in frozen soil, not in the rocks. Only a few specimens, usually incomplete, retain frozen flesh.

Global Warming Predictions

It seems like when we hear the news, nearly every day there is talk of global warming and the catastrophic consequences that may be looming just around the corner. Is that really a threat? Is global warming really a threat? Is it something we need to be concerned about? How does the Ice Age and Noah's Flood relate to the causes of global warming that we're experiencing today? And what is the projection for the future?

Walt Brown and other scientists who support his theory believe that one has only to look at the Earth's anomalies to see that the Hydroplate Theory provides a far better explanation of the Earth's present condition than the other more prevalent, well propagated, but highly implausible theories. The current debate over global warming is a good example. In a recent interview, Dr. Brown explains this viewpoint:

> Of course, man is contributing to some global warming, but the amount is probably not large and no one really knows the extent. Those who argue that man is the sole cause of global warming have overlooked a key question: "Why does the Earth have so much ice in the first place?" In fact, worldwide there is 8-million cubic miles of ice—most of it in Antarctica and Greenland. This relates back to post-Flood conditions that led to the Ice Age.
>
> Apart from the global Flood, scientists cannot explain the Ice Age without running into major scientific problems, and they are aware of this. For a few centuries after the Flood, much of the moisture that evaporated from these warm oceans fell as snow and accumulated as glaciers on the high cold continents. But these driving forces for the Ice Age diminished over time so that ice accumulation eventually peaked; and as the amount of ice decreased on the Earth, less of the Sun's radiation was reflected off the ice sheets back into outer space, so then more of the Sun's radiation warmed up the Earth which caused more of the ice to melt, which then caused even less of the Sun's energy to go

out into outer space so that even more of the ice melted–and this cycle has been continuing, and it will continue, and it will accelerate.

The result, if all these 8-million cubic miles of ice are melted, as it appears to already have begun doing—it is just a matter of how fast it is going to happen—is that it will raise sea level 225 feet. Islands in the Pacific are diminishing right at this very moment. It's a bad outlook for locations within 225 feet of sea level. It means that a lot of Florida is going under water; New York is going under water, as well as major world cities such as London, Venice, and many others.

Since the end of the Ice Age, the sea level has already risen more than 300 feet, and that figure is undisputed. And man was not involved in that. All that took place before the Industrial Revolution. So there has been a lot of global warming since the peak of the Ice Age, and there's projected to be a lot more. Continued global warming is inevitable. To blame man for what we're seeing today, and to ignore the global warming that raised the sea level 300 feet, is simply giving man the bum rap, even though man is now contributing to some slight extent.

Dr. John Baumgardner, a retired staff scientist at Los Alamos National Laboratory, is currently working on the development of a global ocean model for investigating climate change. Dr. Baumgardner, in a 2007 interview, offers his response to the many claims being proposed, both in the scientific and political arenas, in relation to global warming:

The issue is whether or not global warming is a serious problem....And my opinion is that we are in a period of warming that began about 1800, accelerated during the Twentieth Century, and that we're about a degree warmer than we were about 100 years ago. However, this amount of warming is within the range of the warming that has occurred several times in Earth's history of warming and cooling since the Flood. We have good documentation for it in the record.

One example of another warm period was the period from about A.D. 900 to A.D. 1300, generally referred to as the Medieval Warm Period. During that time the Vikings colonized Greenland, there was abundant farming there, grasslands, and herds. Most of Europe was much warmer. There were vineyards in the northern part of England and farming was very productive. It appears to have been a prosperous time, and it was very prosperous in China during that period, which doubled its population. So, this is an example that there have been times of warmth in the past. This period in Europe was followed by what is called the *Little Ice Age*. It got so cold around the year 1600, that the Thames River in London froze over in the wintertime, and there are paintings and etchings showing that. We have clear evidence of significant variations in global temperature from man's documentation over the last 2,000 years. Therefore, this current warming is not out of that range but within the range that has been experienced by humans over the last few millennia.

One issue is, what is the cause of this warming? Is it a result of burning fossil fuel as a result of the industrial revolution? In my opinion, the case is not strong that burning fossil fuel is the main cause of the present warming. Recent research has discovered a strong connection with solar activity, magnetic activity on the sun. When this magnetic activity is strong, sunspots are strong and numerous. There is a tendency for this "solar wind" to prevent the incoming cosmic rays from reaching the Earth's surface. Cosmic rays increase cloudiness, and the clouds reflect solar radiation and cool the Earth. When cosmic rays are high, things are cloudy and the earth is cooled, but when cosmic rays are low, it is not so cloudy and the sun radiation comes in, hits the Earth and warms it. So there seems to be a connection with the amount of solar activity on the sun and the average temperature of the Earth's surface. At present, solar activity is high, there are fewer cosmic rays reaching into the atmosphere and, as a result, less clouds and higher temperatures. Many researchers are concluding that this is a much stronger driving force mechanism for global warming than the burning of fossil fuel, and I tend to agree with that. Therefore, many of the alarmists' claims, I believe, are unfounded.

As far as climate scientists, people trained in atmospheric science and ocean science, I would say the majority of them believe that the burning of fossil fuel is increasing and is responsible for the rising level of CO_2 in the atmosphere and likely will result in some warming. However, as far as having a major impact or a major catastrophic effect, very few of them believe that will happen. The main concern is that there might be some shift in rainfall patterns in various countries throughout the world that could result in political problems.

Predictive climate models are not yet capable of giving regional estimates of what the changes might be. The models, in general, show that the biggest changes are near the north and south poles. So, as far as warming is concerned, the most warming will take place in places like Canada and Siberia. Some Russian scientists think that it would be very good to have an increase of 5 degrees in the average temperature in Siberia—it would open up a lot of new agricultural land. So the idea that global warming is bad is not always true, for there are a few scientists that think that the net result will be good in that much of the Earth will be warmer, much of the Earth will get more rainfall than it gets presently, and it could result in more agricultural production. This occurred during the medieval warm period when agricultural production was higher in many places of the world. And so a little bit of warming might be a good thing and have an overall positive effect.

Greenhouse warming not only raises the temperature, but causes Spring to happen a few days earlier and the last frost in the Fall to come a little later, and it also affects rainfall patterns. In general, there will be more evaporation from the world's oceans and that water has to come down somewhere, which implies more rainfall. But just how the rainfall patterns might change is not so clear. In addition, the weather system is so complex that we do not yet have the models that can adequately predict where there might be more rain and where it might be less. Generally, the higher latitudes and locations in the northern and southern latitudes where it is warmer will get more rain and more snow. And it could be that, rather than there being sea level rise, there could even be some sea level reduction by more ice forming in places like Greenland and Antarctica as a result of more moisture falling there and turning into ice. So, those types of things are difficult to model at this point. But my point is that global warming might not be all that bad. There are going to be parts of the world that benefit from global warming.

In general, I would say there is no cause for major alarm as far as the burning of fossil fuel affecting the climate, leading to some catastrophic destruction of most of the world's cities. There is no scientific basis for that. And I personally believe that the current warming is primarily a result of activity on the sun, not the burning of fossil fuel by humans.

Overall, since the time of the Flood, the Earth has experienced a great amount of climate variation, and the Earth's climate system is designed by God to be stable. For example, when the temperature starts to rise there are mechanisms to bring the temperature down and vice versa. And so I believe there is no need for alarm for the very small changes in temperature that we have seen over the last twenty years.

Claims being made that global warming is going to melt the icecaps (the Greenland Icecap, the Antarctic Icecap), and that the sea level is going to rise—perhaps twenty feet in the next fifty or one hundred years—and flood most of the major coastal cities of the world is putting a lot of people into a panic about this. So the issue is raised, is there going to be another global Flood?

First, even if that were to take place it would be nowhere near what occurred in the Flood of Noah where the whole Earth was destroyed, where all the high mountains everywhere were covered. That represented a tectonic catastrophe where all the pre-Flood ocean flow was recycled into the interior of the planet, and there were violent currents flowing all over the continents, eroding the continents and depositing thousands of feet of sediment over much of the present continents. That type of catastrophe is not even in view here.

The estimate for global climate change potential is called an IPCC, Intergovernmental Panel on Climate Change, (a U.N. body). In the preliminary version of the report, which just came out, the IPCC revised downward their estimate of the sea level rise, so that in the current report it predicts between seven and twenty-three inches, just a few inches of sea level rise over the next century. That report, which basically attributes the warming to human fossil fuel burning, predicts that the amount of sea level rise is small and will not flood any major city.

So, it is important for people to understand that many of these claims are not based in science. In my opinion, much of it is primarily hype to push a political agenda. Bible prophecy indicates there are other things that are going to happen that are going to be much more dramatic.

In a later chapter, we will turn to the topic of what the Bible prophesies for Earth's future, and what we might expect and prepare for in terms of an impending global disaster, just as Noah was forewarned and built the ark.

Meanwhile, Global Warming may lead to the greater likelihood that the ark may be partially or fully exposed in the near future. The year 2007 has been the greatest melt-back on Mt. Ararat in several decades, and if Global Warming continues to accelerate the melting of the icecaps, the entire ark may be exposed within the next two to five years, leading to its certain discovery.

Long Live Man

One of the truly monumental questions of this biblical account is how Noah could have lived for almost a thousand years?

"A lot of people question the Bible," says Dr. Jonathon Henry, former chairman of the Department of Natural Sciences at Tennessee Temple University, "when they read of pre-Flood life spans that averaged 872 years as compared to 72 years today. There are, however, other, nonbiblical documents such as cuneiform tablets with the Sumerian King's List and the Akkadian King's List telling of kings who lived similarly long life spans.

"The famous Sumerian King's List (circa 2,000 B.C.), which makes a passing reference to the Flood, lists eight kings, each of whom is said to have ruled for an average of 30,000 years before the Flood. '[Then] the Flood swept over [the earth].' After the Flood, the reigns of kings are listed as being much lower."[9]

The idea that Noah lived 950 years is incredible enough, but for kings to live 30,000 years is totally unbelievable! But there is an explanation. "According to the ancient Sumerian King's List, preserved on the Weld-Blundell prism, eight pre-Flood rulers reigned over the lower Mesopotamian cities of Eridu, Badtibira, Larak, Sippar, and Shuruppak for phenomenally long time periods. The shortest reign is 18,600 years and the longest is 43,200 years," writes Merrill F. Unger in his famous book, *Archaeology and the Old Testament.*

The *Pictorial Biblical Encyclopedia,* written by Israeli author Gaalyahu Cornfeld, points out how the duration of these reigns are incorrectly stated because the numbering system used by the Sumerians is misinterpreted. For instance, Cornfeld points out that "King Ziusudra reigned 36,000 years" is "equivalent to 600 *ner* in the Mesopotamian numerical pattern." Therefore, the age ranges are similar to the biblical pre-Flood ages of the ten patriarchs from Adam to Noah.

Why did the people in the pre-Flood world live so much longer than we do today?

As we have shown, the earth before the Flood was encircled by a water-vapor canopy that created a greenhouse effect on the planet. Temperatures were tropical and mild from pole to pole, preventing air-mass circulations and resultant rainfall. The canopy also filtered out harmful radiation from space, reducing the rate of somatic mutations in living cells, which drastically decreased the rate of aging and death.[10]

The Flood, which marks the great division between the original and present worlds, altered the structure of the earth's atmosphere, hydrosphere, lithosphere, and biosphere by a cataclysmic change in the external behavior of the processes of nature.[11]

With earth's protective canopy gone, destructive forces were loosed. For the first time, man, animals, and plant life felt the sting of cold, the ravages of winds and storms, and the blistering temperatures of desert and tropical heat. The ravaging Flood and resultant climatic changes left planet Earth virtually ruined, its vast, once fertile land areas submerged in great oceans or under barren sands driven by hot winds.[12]

Before the Flood, man lived more than 900 years. Adam, for example, lived for 930 years (Genesis 5:5); Enos lived to be 905, Cain lived to be 910; Jared, the father of Enoch, died at age 962. Methuselah lived the longest of all at 969 years. Noah's father, Lamech, died at age 777 (Genesis 5:31). Noah lived to be 950 years, 350 of which were after the Flood (Genesis 9:28-29).[13]

After the Flood, man's life span eventually decreased to only "threescore and ten" (on the average). Shem, Noah's first son, lived to be 600. He was about 97 when the Flood began. Shem's son, Arphaxad, lived only 438 years. By the first generation after the Flood, the life span had decreased nearly 500 years.[14]

By Abraham's time, life was considerably shorter. Abraham is described as an "old man, full of years" who died "in a good old age" at 175 years

(Genesis 25:8). His wife, Sarah, was 127 years old when she died. Isaac lived 180 years, Jacob 147, and Joseph 110. A few hundred years later, King David lived to be only seventy, which is the present average life span promised by God ("threescore and ten," or occasionally "fourscore"—Psalm 90:10). Even with modern science's war against major diseases and with far better nutrition, we haven't been able to advance the average life span much beyond God's 70- to 80-year average.[15]

The declining life span seems to be linked to the dissipation of the earth's vapor canopy, say Whitcomb and Morris.[16] The most important effect of the canopy was its shielding action against the intense solar radiation bombarding the earth from space.

The canopy protected life against lethal longwave radiation. Today, ozone is concentrated in the ionosphere and fluxes down because of the global wind systems. Ozone is a highly toxic gas that reacts with the hemoglobin and lipids to create a domino chain reaction among the molecules in the human system.

Experiments have shown that not only do white blood cells rush to the lungs when ozone enters the system of an organism, but all the vital processes react. And one of the effects of ozone poisoning is aging. Ozone did not filter down before the Flood. Today it does, and is a major cause of aging.[17]

On the other hand, we can be thankful for this ozone layer in the upper atmosphere of the earth, according to the *Encyclopedia of Atmospheric Sciences* (p. 720). This very thin, protective layer does stop a tremendous amount of lethal solar radiation from reaching the earth's surface.[18] Scientists have definitely discovered that overdoses in radiation can contribute to premature aging. According to Dr.

Jacob D. Liedmann, an Israeli neurosurgeon, the human body is capable of living about 1,000 years if certain glands were to continue functioning. He agrees that increased radiation does play a role in shorter life spans, but believes God discontinued the functions of some human glands after the Flood.[19]

He explains that the pineal gland, located close to the third ventricle of the brain, just below the corpus callosum, has never functioned in modern man. The thymus gland, located in the breastbone area, stops functioning at puberty. A third group of glands, known as the parathyroids, located between the thyroid and thymus glands, undergoes functioning adjustments in puberty that can directly relate to the proper or improper action of other organs.

Dr. Liedmann says the function of the pineal gland is unknown, but is believed to have been connected with the renewal of cell structures. "Even though it doesn't appear to have any function today, its removal or the severing of connective tissue will result in death," Dr. Liedmann says.

Most medical specialists agree that the thymus is a remnant of an organ functional in our ancestors. Dr. Liedmann believes that when it did function, the thymus contributed to man's life span.

"The functioning changes in these three glands are most likely the major reason for our life span's reduction to about seventy years," he says. "The key to life spans like those mentioned in the Bible is within these glands. People who believe victories over disease and better nutrition will result in considerably longer life spans can only hope to add a few years to man's longevity. The expansion of our longevity is controlled by these glands."

According to Dr. David A. Kaufmann, a retired professor of human anatomy and physical education:

A commonly accepted but erroneous view is that man's life span is lengthening because of improvements in evolutionary development of human tissues helped along with so-called advances of evolutionary medicine and technology. The world human life expectancy, once one has survived infancy, has not improved since the "threescore and ten years" of King David as prophesied in Psalm 90:10.

The Bible actually states in Genesis 6:3 that our life span potential in the post-Flood world is 120 years. Human-aging research with mice in the early 1990s has clearly demonstrated that 120-year life spans are very achievable.

The Search for Immortality

The role of glandular functions, as described by Dr. Liedmann and others, may provide a scientific explanation of the mechanism God used to reset and shorten man's lifespan on earth after the Flood. As we will discuss in the closing of this book, God had better plans for man, than for man to live indefinitely in a fallen world. However, that was not how life for man was originally designed in the beginning. According to Bible expositor Chuck Missler:

Man was designed for immortality. In Genesis, there were two trees in the garden. The first tree was the Tree of Life. The second tree was the Tree of the Knowledge of Good and Evil. And God said to man, "If you eat of that tree then you shall surely die." As we know, Adam and Eve did eat its fruit, and death was introduced as a result of transgression.

Yet, even after he was expelled from the Garden of Eden, humankind continued to live life spans that averaged close to a thousand years, up until the time of the Flood, and then this lifespan decreased successively with each generation. According to Ancient Man researcher Arnold Mendez, "Many people believe that longevity decreased because of the wickedness of the pre-Flood world and that God was shortening man's lifespan. Now, considering that the lifespan was shortened, this implies that it once again can be lengthened, or that longevity may be able to be re-attained."

"Anti-aging Medicine" or "Longevity Medicine" is a new and developing field. One of its top proponents, Dr. Terry Grossman, a leading expert on anti-aging and life extension therapies, and coauthor of *Fantastic Voyage: The Science Behind Radical Life Extension*, shares his insights on life extension in a 2007 interview:

> We do not have the technology today to live forever or, in fact, to live much longer than 120 years or so, at least in our physical bodies. And the reason for that is due to some genetic codes that force us to live a rather restricted life span. When you think about longevity, we actually possess genes that are designed for us not to live for a very long time. In other words, genetically we have been programmed to live a shortened lifespan. In a more primitive world, in an era of scarcity, there was an advantage for people to live a shorter period of time.
>
> However, today we stand on the cusp of some cutting-edge technologies that are going to enable us to live longer than people have

been able to live in the past. These should occur within the next 20-40 years.

In anti-aging research, we're looking for processes that we can use to slow down, stop, and even reverse the aging process and damage that occurs within the passage of time; but this field is in its infancy of only a dozen years or so, and as of today, we still don't really have the ability to stop or even slow down the aging process very much, but we are very close to being able to do so. In the next few years, I anticipate that we'll be able to make some serious interventions to slow down, stop, and even reverse the aging process to a degree that was completely unprecedented until now.

Michael Fossel, editor of the *Journal of Anti-Aging Medicine*, and author of the academic textbook: *Cells, Aging, and Human Disease*, has done extensive research on the causes of aging at the cellular level. According to numerous studies, we can reverse aging at the level of cells and at the level of tissues; the next step is to find out if we can do it clinically.

At the 2004 International Conference on aging in Sydney, Australia, Dr. Fossel, in discussing the ability to reset the human lifespan, stated, "What we do is reset genes. The outcome of this is that we can probably extend the human lifespan to several centuries, perhaps as much as 300 to 500 years."

Perhaps because of man's original design for immortality, the inner quest to live forever continues to reside within us, and is not limited to the desire of simply extending our earthly lifespan. In the words of the writer of Ecclesiastes, "He has also set eternity in the hearts of men." Could this also mean that man's search for immortality is designed to help us find the very meaning of life itself, a life beyond this temporal world? In our search for answers, we will return to this topic in a latter part of this book. But we return our focus to man's modern-day efforts in pursuing longevity and immortality. In his recent interview, Dr. Grossman comments:

> The quest for immortality is as old as human history. The most ancient written text that we have, the story of Gilgamesh, tells of an individual who was seeking to achieve immortality. Human history goes on through the pharaohs who became mummies and were buried in pyramids and that was their attempt to achieve immortality. This quest continues even into the modern time and as recently as a few years ago, when the human genome project was 85 percent complete, President Clinton said that we might achieve to the point that our children will only know cancer as a constellation in the sky.
>
> Based on a new technique known as *enzymatic amplification,* scientists have been able to take fragments of DNA found in the mummies and analyze them to a degree that was unavailable even a few years ago. And the prospects for what we will be able to do in the years ahead are very exciting, and who knows where this might lead.

In Chapter 4 we highlighted a number of scientific studies and experiments that have resulted in increasing both the size and the lifespan of a number of organisms. Included was Dr. Carl Baugh's Hyperbaric Biosphere experiments simulating pre-Flood conditions and their relevance for longevity.

In additional work, done by Cynthia Kenyon with round worms, and by David Sinclair on yeast and mice, these experimenters have shown that it is possible to double the lifespan of these organisms. Since so much of our human DNA is identical to that of these other animals, these scientists claim applicable prospects for increasing our own human lifespan as well.

In review of the possibilities for longevity, in his recent interview Dr. Fossel concludes, "There have been claims throughout history that we could extend the human lifespan and live forever, essentially throughout human history....Well, we probably can extend the human lifespan by centuries, the healthy human lifespan. But it's not possible to live forever."

But as we will discuss in later chapter, the topic of "living forever" is where the mystery and the message of Noah and the ark will lead us.

Longevity Factors

Returning to Dr. Kaufman's earlier assertion, that man can easily attain the biblically apportioned 120-year lifespan after the Flood, he offers these guidelines:

There are three main factors that affect one's total health and longevity. First, the inherited, programmed aging process in one's cells. Secondly, one's total living environment at work, play, and at home, and thirdly, one's lifestyle. We have little control over the genetically controlled aging process, limited control over our living environment and much control over our lifestyle.[20]

Dr. Kaufmann also says that increasing pollution shortens life spans. Dr. Ethel Nelson, a pathologist and medical missionary from Tennessee, adds:

We note in the Bible that the Lord permitted the eating of flesh foods immediately after the Flood, and now we also know that eating large amounts of protein will shorten the life span considerably.

One of the most ancient civilizations was that of Egypt. Paleopathologist Dr. Marc Armand Ruffer and his associates, who have done over 36,000 autopsies on Egyptian mummies, concur that the arteries of the well-fed royal bodies reveal cholesterol deposits with narrowing of the artery lumens. Here is evidence that arterial disease (atherosclerosis) was shortening the life spans of humans enjoying flesh foods only ten to fifteen generations after the Flood.[21]

Dr. Kaufmann believes that modern man could maximize his own life span to potentially 120 years by adopting certain regimens.

He suggests following the seven known traits of centenarians: enjoyment of work, strong will to live, quiet independent lifestyles with contentment, eating a variety of natural foods, being devoted to family and faith, keeping mentally and physically active, and having no high ambitions, regrets, self-pity, or combativeness.[22]

"There are many theories about what causes humans to live for a long time. There also has been a broad variety of attempts throughout history to discover which factors lead to longevity. In the Middle Ages there were various theories. There are even more theories today," according to Arnold

Mendez, Ancient Man researcher and expositor, in a recent interview. "But what if the ancient patriarchs knew something that we don't know today?"

Mendez continued the prospect of what we might learn from the Ancients when it comes to longevity:

Discovering Noah's ark and finding it would probably be very important from the longevity aspect. We would probably learn a lot from the patriarchs and how they lived by examining the ark, and this would shed light on the longevity issue. Science has made great strides in analyzing DNA and various other living material. Consider the question: what would happen if Noah's ark was discovered and biological material was available for analyses? What would happen if we could analyze through DNA studies or various other material studies, living material, from the ark of Noah? The possibilities would be endless.

Repopulating the Earth

Men had large families in pre-Flood days and there is evidence of this practice after the Flood. The age of fathers at the birth of each of the *named* sons ranged from about 30 years in the case of some of Shem's descendants to 500 years in Noah's. Longevity declined after the Flood, but for centuries after the Flood, men still lived and procreated for hundreds of years at a time. Due to the combined effect of long lives and large families, mankind rapidly filled the earth (Genesis 1:28, 6:1, 11) before and after the Flood. The table of nations in Genesis, chapter ten, and the account of dispersion in chapter eleven also indicate large early post-Flood population explosions.[23]

Whitcomb and Morris estimate that the earth's population was as high as one billion at the time of the Flood, and this estimate has gained support in recent years. Others still estimate it at only a few million.[24]

Origin of Races

A question often heard from skeptics of the Noah's ark account is, how could all of the races and languages on earth today have possibly come from one family? We asked the late Dr. Richard Bliss, author of twenty-five professional scientific articles and books and the chairman of the Science Education Department at a California graduate school, if he could shed some light on racial and ethnic characteristics. His answer:

When it comes to the development of ethnic characteristics, the human genes allow for variations based upon natural selection, cultural preferences and isolated population groups. A geneticist named Punnett developed a mathematical or statistical formula called the Punnett Square which shows how, from brown-skinned males and females, you can easily and quickly get every racial color in the world.

Theoretically, all of the genetic changes that can be formulated for sexually reproducing species in the Punnett Square could happen in as little as one generation, as documented by the case of a family in Australia. This family, with one Nigerian black parent and one English white parent, produced twin boys who have

completely different ethnic characteristics—
one white son and one black son!

"Technically, the term 'race' should never have
been applied to humans, since there is only one
race—the human race," says Dr. Walter Brown,
author and former director of a U.S. Defense
Department laboratory.

"One should realize that the word 'race,'
referring to physical characteristics, hardly ever
occurs in the Bible. Instead, the word 'nation' is used
over 200 times. Common usage of the word 'race'
today refers to groups of people with distinguishing
physical characteristics such as skin color, physical
structure, shape of eyes and other facial features,
and type of hair."

According to Dr. Brown, to really appreciate
how minor these variations are in humans, consider
the large variations in the canine family. Most
varieties of domestic dogs were produced in the past
300 years. The sizes, colors, fur (or hairlessness),
bone structure, abilities, and temperaments of dogs
can vary tremendously. For example, look at the
differences between a Great Dane or a Chihuahua
or a St. Bernard. Since dogs can also interbreed with
the wolf, coyote, and the jackal, all are part of the
dog "kind."

"By comparison, human variations are relatively
few and minor," Dr. Brown says. "We must remember that in every kind of life, there are vast numbers
of genes that permit these variations, allowing
successive generations to adapt to environmental
changes. Without this design feature, extinctions
would be much more common."

The Tower of Confusion

After Noah and his family left the ark and established homes near the mountains of Ararat, their descendants populated the "land of Shinar," or the Mesopotamian region that has been called "the cradle of civilization." They continued to procreate, and their descendants are named in Genesis, chapter eleven, as building a great city with a tower "that reaches the heavens." According to the Bible, this displeased God, and he confused their languages so they couldn't understand one another. Then he dispersed them from the Tower of Babel in every direction throughout the world.

But the critics disagree. "Fundamentalist Christians have tried to teach that the confusion of the languages came as a result of the building of the Tower of Babel," claims J. David Davis, a U.S. representative of the Temple Institute in Jerusalem and leader of the B'nai Noah Community in Tennessee. "This cannot be proven from either historical data or archaeological evidence. The word Babel has its origin in a Semitic word, which is actually two words, 'ba' and 'bel,' meaning 'the gate to God.'"

The critics also disagree with the fundamental viewpoint on the purpose of the Tower. "Just exactly what the tower was for," says William Curtis, a college professor and former director of the Institute for Scientific and Biblical Research, "is open to much interpretation. The tower may have been an astronomical observatory or its purpose may have been as a central rallying point.[25]

"Whatever the tower's purpose was, it is clear from both secular and biblical history that such a tower existed. Ancient historians Herodotus and Eusebius wrote that the remains of such a tower existed in Babylon in their day, and many archaeologists today confirm that the tower ruins they have found in Babylon are that of the time era circa 2200 B.C.."[26]

Since linguistics is the study of languages and language origins, let us consider the position taken by Dr. John Oller, professor of linguistics and author of *Language and Experience* and nine other books in the field of linguistics.

Dr. Oller says, "Actually, as remarkable as it may seem, the biblical story of the Tower of Babel is completely consistent with all of the evidence. Anyone who denies this fact is simply engaging in fantasy or speculation.

"There are roughly 5,000 languages in the world today and fifty to sixty stocks. We can trace the best-known of those languages, the Indo-European system, back to about 3,000 B.C., roughly the time of Babel. There is simply no evidence that existing stock can be traced back further."

Dr. Steven Collins, a professor of Biblical Studies for Trinity Theological Seminary, offers further evidence for the credibility of the biblical story of Babel and the confusion of languages.

"It is common knowledge in anthropology that the growth of world populations began in the Near East, primarily between the Black Sea and the Caspian Sea. But it all started in the Middle East. The interesting thing about this is that we have a document in the Book of Genesis that describes this ancient process as having begun in and around the Tower of Babel. And, of course, this is exactly what modern anthropology knows by way of the evidence."

Dr. Jonathon Henry, professor of mathematics and science at Tennessee Temple University, explains:

Genesis, chapter ten, lists seventy ethnic groups which dispersed from the Tower of Babel and from which the earth's human population is descended. The fate of these groups is traceable from biblical statements and secular sources. These are said to be the progenitors of all the nations on earth after the Flood, and accordingly, Genesis, chapter ten, is often call the "Table of Nations."[27]

Noah had three sons—Shem, Ham, and Japheth. The descendants of Japheth experienced remarkable prosperity and dispersion, and their names make it clear that they inhabited vast portions of the earth, migrating westward into the Aegean, northward into Europe, and eastward into the Asian subcontinent. Japheth's descendants, then, are the Indo-Europeans. They are identified as the Gentiles in Genesis 10:5, and about 65 percent of Japhethite lines retain their identity today.[28]

The name of Japheth himself is found in ancient literature as Iapetos, the legendary father of the Greeks, and Iyapeti, the reputed ancestor of the Aryans in India. In Australian aboriginal legend, he was Yaperi.[29]

The descendants of Ham migrated mainly into Africa. However, it is incorrect simply to identify Hamites with Africans. Some Hamites eventually migrated to what are now the Oriental countries—China, Japan, and Korea. Still other of Ham's descendants ultimately crossed the Bering Strait which was then a land bridge into North and South America and became the native American peoples. In more recent millennia, other non-Hamitic peoples—the Muslims, a Semitic people—have conquered and settled huge portions of Africa. Of the thirty Hamite lines, only about 20 percent retain their identity today.[30]

Shem's descendants are the Semites, of which the Jews and Arabs are the only major Semite lines surviving today. They settled mainly in the Bible lands. None of the Semite family lines seems to have left any lasting mark on history except the descendants of Eber, ancestor of Abraham. Most lines seem to be extinct today. Approximately 5 percent of Semite lines can be traced in history.[31]

"In general", Dr. Henry says, "the fate of the families in Genesis, chapter ten, has included the following outcomes—retention of lineage or identity for some peoples such as the Jews, Greeks, and Armenians; apparent extinction with no mention later in the Bible or in history; and loss of identity now, but a re-emergence in later times as indicated by biblical prophecies."[32]

The Search is On

Today the search is on for Noah's ancient ark that preserved mankind and the animals. Some artifacts of this historic event have allegedly already been found. In 1943, the famous world traveler and "Believe It or Not" columnist Robert Ripley discovered enormously huge anchors in Kairouan, Tunisia (North Africa.) Ripley claimed that these were the anchors of Noah's ark, which no one disputed.

In addition, Ripley reported in 1941 that he had found the tomb of Noah in the Lebanon Mountains of Syria. Ripley went to great lengths to document the tomb, which is near Damascus. The tomb is 120 feet long and frequently has clothing—shawls and turbans—draped on it. The sick who often come to sleep by the tomb relate stories of miraculous healings as a result of their visits.

However, let's not settle for gigantic anchors, or a tomb visited by ailing pilgrims. Rather, let us journey to Mount Ararat where the ark is believed to be resting, buried under ice and snow—and where on rare occasions it is revealed to a few fortunate climbers.

Endnotes

1   Frederick A. Filby, *The Flood Reconsidered* (Grand Rapids: Zondervan Corp., 1971), pp. 107–108.

2   Balsiger and Sellier, *In Search of Noah's Ark*, p. 148.

3   Whitcomb and Morris, *The Genesis Flood*, p. 80.

4   Frank L. Marsh, *Evolution, Creation and Science* (Washington, DC: Review and Herald Publishing, 1947), p. 291.

5   Balsiger and Sellier, *In Search of Noah's Ark*, p. 149.

6   Rachel L. Carson, *The Sea Around Us* (New York: Oxford University Press, 1951), pp. 91–92.

7   Paul A. Moody, *Introduction to Evolution* (New York: Harper and Brothers, 1953), p. 262.

8   Whitcomb and Morris, *The Genesis Flood*, p. 87.

9 John C. Whitcomb, *Chart of the Period from the Creation to Abraham* (Hagerstown, MD: Whitcomb Ministries, n.d.).

10 Dave Balsiger and Charles E. Sellier, *In Search of Noah's Ark* (Los Angeles: Sun Classic Books, 1976), p. 140.

11 Henry M. Morris, *Scientific Creationism* (San Diego: Creation-Life Publishers, 1974), p. 213.

12 Balsiger and Sellier, *In Search of Noah's Ark*, p. 140.

13 Ibid., p. 141.

14 Ibid.

15 Ibid.

16 John C. Whitcomb, Jr., and Henry M. Morris, *The Genesis Flood* (Phillipsburg, NJ: Presbyterian and Reformed Publishing Co., 1961), p. 399.

17 Donald Patten, "Cataclysm from Space" filmstrip (American Media, 1971).

18 Balsiger and Sellier, *In Search of Noah's Ark*, p.142.

19 Dr. Jacob D. Liedmann, statements made during a March 1976 interview.

20 David Kaufmann, "Creation Medicine and the Aging Process," Twin Cities Creation Conference, Northwestern College, Roseville, MN, 1992, p. 36.

21 Ethel R. Nelson, "The Eden Diet and Modern Nutritional Research," Twin Cities Creation Conference, Northwestern College, Roseville, MN, 1992, p. 58.

22 Kaufmann, "Creation Medicine," p. 36.

23 Balsiger and Sellier, *In Search of Noah's Ark*, pp. 145–146.

24 Whitcomb and Morris, *The Genesis Flood*, p. 27.

25 William M. Curtis, "Babel: The Origin of Diverse Languages and Races," Twin Cities Creation Conference, Northwestern College, Roseville, MN, 1992, p. 178.

26 Ibid.

27 Jonathon F. Henry, "Fate of the Ethnic Groups in the Table of Nations," Twin Cities Creation Conference, Northwestern College, Roseville, MN, 1992, p. 91.

28 Ibid., pp. 91, 95.

29 Ibid., p. 91.

30 Ibid., pp. 92–93, 96.

31 Ibid., p. 95.

32 Ibid., pp. 97–98.

Seven

THE MOUNTAIN OF PAIN

At the end of the hundred and fifty days the
water had gone down and on the seventeenth day
of the seventh month the ark came to rest
on the mountains of Ararat
(Genesis 8:3–4, emphasis added).

MOUNT ARARAT is a unique mountain and perilous in many ways. It is fiercely rugged, always changing, dangerous and yet alluring with an unmistakable, resplendent beauty that is difficult to describe. Among the many wonders of Ararat, a rainbow appears almost daily over the northern parts of the mountain.

Mount Ararat is one of the largest landmasses of any single mountain on earth, and its peak is the highest point in Turkey. Its formidable terrain, however, hides many hazards from even the most expert climbers, with severe—and often fatal—consequences.

The mountain stands alone, with the peak called Big Ararat rising majestically 16,984 feet and an adjacent mountain peak known as Little Ararat rising 12,806 feet from the plain of Bayazit, which is itself 3,000 feet above sea level. Rising high into the clouds above the plain in eastern Turkey, climbers fortunate enough to reach the summit can glimpse through the clouds far into three countries—Russia, Iran, and, of course, Turkey.

Because Ararat is near the borders of these countries, it is a strategic location. Throughout history, Ararat has been claimed and fought over many times—not only by different countries, but also by ethnic groups in the area. Regional fighting still takes place on the mountain today with frequent gun battles between Turkish soldiers, terrorists, thieves, and local Kurdish people who want their independence from Turkey.

At its base, Mount Ararat is about twenty-five miles in diameter. Its magnificent, solid ice cap is more than 200 feet thick in many places and covers seventeen to twenty-two square miles of the upper slopes. Crevasses form when the ice and snow, slowly moving over the rough terrain, break into huge pieces. Some of these fissures fall over the Ahora Gorge. A misstep can send someone plummeting to his or her death hundreds or even thousands of feet below—swallowed up into the seemingly bottomless bowels of Ararat, never to be recovered.

Besides being an enormous area to search, the glaciers are slowly sliding and grinding the rocks of Ararat's upper slopes, creating avalanches that constantly change the shape of the mountain. A climber can easily set off an avalanche of rock or snow merely by talking to his companions. Even experienced climbers using maps and sophisticated equipment can get disoriented and lost. Ararat is an immense, inactive volcano that forever holds the bodies of many victims as proof of its lethal traps, creating many local legends regarding the mountain.

Dr. John Morris, geologist and an ark expedition team director, gives us his impression of Mount Ararat:

There are many obstacles to overcome in the search for Noah's ark. I've climbed Ararat thirteen times now and I've climbed mountains all over the world but, let me tell you, Mount Ararat is just brutal. It's the worst I've ever climbed.

Actually from the south side, Mount Ararat looks like a nice volcanic cone, but on the opposite side there's this incredible canyon called the Ahora Gorge. Lined by vertical rock walls, the gorge is about one and one-half times the height of the Grand Canyon. I'm convinced the walls are unclimbable—due to the nature of the rock. I know I can't climb them.

Mount Ararat is a volcanic mountain and it has erupted many times since the Flood. On top of that, the summit is covered by a 17-square-mile glacier, which descends to about 14,000 feet. Also, finger glaciers come down to maybe 11,000 feet.

As that glacier moves, it erodes the volcanic layers and produces avalanches. Climbing through that loose, crumbly rock to the glacier is very difficult. We have had to face and overcome all kinds of problems—some of them deadly, such as avalanches, the weather, wild animals, attacking dogs, and snakes.

Once we get up on the glacier, the bottomless crevasses pose an even greater danger. Many a time we've almost died up on the glacier.

The mountain, being 17,000 feet high and capped by a glacier, presents incredible weather problems. On the glacier the winds always blow hard, and any evaporation in the area condenses on the summit.

Every afternoon there's a storm—either wind, rain, or snow—even in the summertime. The winds often blow more than 100 miles per hour! I had a friend who got caught in one of these storms, and he actually had to bolt himself to the ice to keep from being blown away!

The coldest night we ever experienced was in August of 1972. The temperature got down to minus 40 degrees, and the wind blew at about 80 miles per hour. During the day, the temperatures rose to just above freezing. The weather alone made that a very difficult climb.

Because it's a volcanic mountain, toxic volcanic gases and the sulfur fumes ooze out in places creating breathing problems and severe nausea.

Many people also suffer at high elevations from what's called altitude sickness—or oxygen deprivation. We live up there sometimes for a week or more at a time, and it's very difficult to get your breath up there and feel normal in any sense of the word.

People who live near or on the mountain also pose a threat. We've been shot at a number of times—just by thieves mostly, but in recent years, terrorists have taken to the mountain and actually use Ararat as a staging ground for terrorism throughout the Middle East and against Turkey.

My groups have never encountered death, but we've had a lot of close calls and suffered a lot of injuries. A lot of people have died on that mountain searching for the ark. I know of one fellow that's buried in an avalanche up there, and I know of people trapped in crevasses whose bodies will never be recovered. There's just a lot of dangers that climbers face when they're on the upper slopes of the mountain.

Probably the worst thing that happened to my climbing group was when we were caught at the 14,000-foot level in an electrical storm. Before it was over, we were actually struck by lightning. Now, I'm convinced that God performed a miracle that day. No one was seriously hurt and we were able to complete our climb. We went up the mountain and spent about a week looking for Noah's ark.

There's just all kinds of dangers and problems faced by climbers who tackle Mount Ararat in their search for Noah's ark.

The Many Names of Ararat

Mount Ararat has several names among the different ethnic groups that allude to the ark landing on Ararat. The Turks call it *Aghri Dagh* (Ağrı Dağı), "the painful mountain." Its most common name means "the removal of the curse" or, in Hebrew, "the mountain of descent." The Armenians call the mountain *Masis*, which means "mother of the world." The ancient Armenian name was *Masis Leusar*, which means, "the mountain of the ark."

The Persians called Ararat *Kuhi-nuh*, "the mountain of Noah," or *Saad Dagh*, "the blessed mountain." *Urardhu* or *Urartü*, the Assyro-Babylonian name for the mountain as well as the area surrounding it and the peoples of Armenia, means "highlands," and the area was reportedly esteemed by the ancients as being the central part of the earth.[1]

Almost all of the names of the mountain and the towns surrounding it reflect the history of Noah's ark. *Arghuri* or *Ahora,* a town at the base of the Ahora Gorge, means "the planting of the vine," and this is presumably where Noah planted his vineyard. *Etchmiadzin,* where treasures from the ark were kept in the monastery, means "the place of descent." A village about eighteen miles from Mount Ararat is called Mahser, which means "doomsday."

There is also an ancient city called *Thamanin (Tshaminim* or *Temanin)* on the Iranian side, which means "the region of eight persons." The Armenian town of Nakhichevan was once called *Apobaterion,* which means "the disembarking or landing place." Its present name, *Nakhichevan,* means "the first place of lodging."

The ancient city of *Erivan* (or *Yerevan*) near Ararat means "the first appearance," while the town of *Sharnakh* means "village of Noah." The village of *Tabrīz* (or *Ta Baris*) means "the ship," while *Korhan* means "the first town." Since many of these names are thousands of years old, it seems logical to assume that Noah's ark landed right where the Bible says it landed—*on the mountains of Ararat,* composed of two lone volcanic summits, Big Ararat and Little Ararat.

Facing the Danger

The late astronaut Colonel James Irwin, who walked on the Moon, climbed "the painful mountain" five times looking for Noah's ark. "There is a strangeness about Ararat," he said. "You don't notice it at first, because of the novelty of just being there and because you are looking for the prow of the ark behind every rock. But then you notice it: there are no trees. The entire immensity of Ararat is absolutely devoid of a single tree."[2]

Often the sound of thunder can be heard on the mountain, but it's not thunder; it's a chain reaction of echoes created as winds blowing more than 100 miles per hour send gigantic boulders crashing down the Ararat slopes. According to recent accounts, climbers have been killed by such boulders, which they could hear but not see as they stood in the mist of clouds that dropped like thick fog over the mountain.

Colonel Irwin was one such victim. He was hit in the head and almost killed by an unseen rock or ice block that came flying down the mountain, knocking him unconscious. He lost several teeth, was badly injured, and lost a lot of blood. He was, however, miraculously found and rescued after spending the night alone. We'll be looking more closely at Irwin's frightening experiences in a later chapter.

In his book *More Than an Ark on Ararat,* Irwin said:

> We faced risk of physical danger, for Ararat is a crumbling mountain. Every few minutes we could hear rock slides and small avalanches. We slept in numbing cold, fell on loose rock, dodged tumbling boulders, grew exhausted from high-altitude climbing, had feet sore with blisters, had painfully cracked lips from sunburn, received various cuts and nicks, all in pursuit of a hidden and uncertain treasure.[3]

Ararat is an extinct volcano, and the north slope consists almost entirely of loose tailings of lava rock, which makes it much like walking on stacked bowling balls. There was no solid footing. Some rocks would roll away beneath us, starting small landslides. For hours almost every step would be on rocks that moved. This created extreme discomfort. Each step had to be calculated. You prepared yourself to slide, twist, and slip. Not only was it physically exhausting, the uncertainty of it all was mentally fatiguing.[4]

In addition to all of the other hazards on Mount Ararat, dangerous wild animals live at various altitudes. Near the base of the mountain, climbers encounter scorpions and deadly puff adder snakes. In the middle, vicious wolves and wild mad dogs prowl and will attack people, causing many explorers to carry guns for protection. On the higher parts of the mountain there are some bears that will generally leave climbers alone as long as they aren't disturbed or with their young.

Wild goats also populate the middle and upper reaches of the mountain, and while they are not dangerous in and of themselves, they trigger avalanches of crumbling volcanic rock and ash or snow in their efforts to get away from people.

The mountain claims lives on a regular basis. For example, Christopher Tease, a young college student from London, tried a solo climb in 1965. His parents sent search parties twice to try to find him, but his body was never recovered.

In 1985 two young women attempted to scale the mountain alone and were never seen again. The very next year, two Norwegians without permits attempted to climb the mountain. One went up one side with a guide, and the other one headed up in a different direction, alone. They were supposed to meet on the mountain, but the man and his guide were never seen again. The solitary climber was initially afraid to acknowledge his friend's disappearance since they were climbing without permits. Shocked and saddened, he went home alone.

John Libi, an experienced mountain climber who tackled Ararat eight different times in an effort to find the ark (the last time when he was seventy-three years old), saw two climbers killed. One, a Belgian, fell over 300 feet to his death. Libi himself fell off a cliff on Mount Ararat once, but was miraculously saved.

Altitude sickness was the most serious problem on Ararat for B. J. Corbin, a sociologist from Maryland and ark expeditioner. "I had the experience of flying on a helicopter that took us from 6,000 feet to 16,000 feet in about twenty minutes, and that's just too quick of a jump in altitude for your body," he says. "We were sick, nauseous, dizzy, and lost our appetites. We felt miserable and were ready to pass out. It was all we could do to put our tents up and then sleep."

Another hazard is the fog. The warm gases that vent from deep inside the volcano create fast-forming fog all over the mountain that can cause climbers to stumble into crevasses or lose their way.

Swiss climber Nicholas Van arkle, on an expedition to Ararat in 1966, broke through a thin crust of snow and fell about thirty feet into a bottomless crevasse. Only his rope and his quick-thinking Swiss companions saved him. Many other explorers haven't been as fortunate, and we will look at some of their stories in a later chapter.

Earthquakes are another natural phenomenon that can strike climbers without notice. In 1840 a devastating earthquake tore a huge chunk out of the mountain on the north side, completely burying the town of Ahora (also known as Arghuri) and the St. Jacob's Monastery. Underneath tons of rocks and dirt lie priceless treasures from Noah's ark in the monastery that will presumably never be seen again.

This incredible earthquake formed the almost two-mile deep Ahora Gorge that is not only deeper than the Grand Canyon but, according to many explorers, even more spectacular. The sheer cliffs of the gorge are two miles deep and a mile wide. Geologists say it was a more powerful earthquake than Mount St. Helens.

"That year, on July 2," says French explorer Fernand Navarra, describing the earthquake of 1840, "a little before sunset, the ground was shaken by undulating waves from the Great Ararat to the east. Fissures appeared on the sides of the mountain and gas fumes burst out, hurling stones. The ice cap was shattered. Witnesses heard a rumble for an hour within the mountain.

"The village of Ahora disappeared, also the monastery of St. Jacob which had stood for eight centuries. Of the 2,000 and some inhabitants, only a hundred survived—those outside the village itself when the quake struck."[5]

According to geologist Dr. John Morris, the volcanic rock and granite screen contain enormous boulders, some of which are the size of Volkswagens. Others are smaller, but fly down the mountain at deadly speeds as the result of avalanches and rock slides. It is a constant struggle for climbers not only to watch where they are going but also to look up frequently to see if any rocks are flying through the air toward them.[6]

Thieves and terrorists live and hide on the mountain, and many ark explorers have been robbed, barely escaping with their lives. It is also quite possible that some of the missing climbers have not been victims of the mountain at all, but victims of terrorists and thieves.

One of the extremely few female Ararat climbers, Debbie Redmer, a registered nurse from Las Vegas, describes the terrorist situation faced by her and other climbers:

> Two sides of the mountain face hostile neighbors—Iraq and Iran—and even the lower elevations of the mountain are occupied by terrorist groups of one type or another.
>
> With the civil war in neighboring Iraq and the unpredictable situation following the breakup of the Soviet Union, the entire area is a hotbed of instability and a jeopardy to the outside climber. Also, Kurdish terrorists have been known to give expeditioners a great deal of trouble—robbing them and even threatening them with death.
>
> My experience with terrorists has been that it's a constant pending situation no matter where you are on the mountain. You're always aware that they could be watching you. Many times, we've heard footsteps coming into the campgrounds. We never really know if they're Turkish authorities or terrorists. It's a constant situation of fear.
>
> On some occasions, climbers are even mistaken for terrorists. Many of the men that I've climbed with have been threatened at gunpoint by Turkish anti-terrorist squads thinking foreign climbers were terrorists.

They have robbers all over the mountain who come into your camp, and they don't care if they kill you or not. All they want is what you have—your camping equipment, your money—and your life is of no importance to them.

Following is an article from the Associated Press that appeared in numerous papers around the world in early September of 1992:

ANKARA, TURKEY—At least forty-three people, including Kurdish guerrillas and civilians, were killed Saturday in three separate incidents linked to the Kurdish insurgency in eastern Turkey.

The semi-official Anatolia news agency quoted the governor of the Agri province as saying at least twenty Kurdish guerrillas were *killed in fierce fighting on Mt. Ararat* [emphasis added].

Governor Ismet Metin told Anatolia that security forces could not get an accurate death toll because guerrillas took the bodies of their comrades.

Also Saturday, a group of guerrillas blocked a main highway in the southeastern province of Bingol and shot and killed seven travelers, Anatolia reported.

The illegal Kurdish Labor Party has been fighting for self-rule in the southeastern part of the country since 1984. More than 4,500 people, including guerrillas, civilians and soldiers, have died in the fighting, which has escalated recently.

Legal Entanglements

The Turkish government has also made it increasingly difficult for ark expeditioners to climb Mount Ararat. Due to changing policies within a frequently changing government, it's not unusual for an expeditionary group to have all of its permits in order and either be on or even halfway up the mountain when they are escorted back down by Turkish soldiers—sometimes without even an explanation. It is, of course, extremely frustrating for scientists and explorers who have traveled up to halfway around the world to be stopped from climbing Ararat for no apparent reason. Specific examples of recent difficulties with Turkish permits and regulations will be covered in another chapter.

The Turkish Embassy in Washington, D.C., informed us that according to Turkish law number 2863:

> As of May 13, 1988, foreign nationals can only be permitted to climb the tumulus [a possible alternative ark site advocated by a couple of Americans, as will be discussed in a later chapter] and Mount Ararat from the Dogubeyazit site, due to the danger of disrupting the area and for their own personal safety. Permission to scale the area must be obtained from the General Staff. The area is monitored from the air by the General Staff for both protection and rescue purposes.

In reality, this law means climbers are allowed to climb the south face of Mount Ararat but are prohibited from the north face, where all of the ark sightings have occurred.

Namik Tan, the First Secretary of the Turkish Embassy, says Ararat explorers must meet certain specific requirements to be granted a Mount Ararat "research permit." "They must meet an application deadline, justify their scholastic qualifications, and have contracted a professional Turkish guide. No visas are needed for U.S. citizens to visit Turkey, but to be on Mount Ararat, the research permit is required."

We learned that Turkish officials often deny Americans and other explorers research permits, and if they grant the permits, the officials frequently cancel them later, leaving expeditioners sitting in hotels at the base of Mount Ararat. To justify their actions, they cite bad climatic conditions, security considerations, attempted artifact smuggling, restrictions by local authorities, and attempts to research an area not covered by the permit (such as the north side of the mountain where the ark is located).

These reasons for research permit denials can be legitimate. However, even with valid permits things often function differently when in Turkey at Mount Ararat, as best illustrated by Bill Dodder, Colonel James Irwin's expedition administrator. "We had permission to fly around Mount Ararat, and Dutch National Television had permission to film. All of a sudden, we were arrested for what we were told was the failure to have a permit to film while flying."

One explorer explained all the problems this way: "It's almost like God doesn't want the ark discovered yet. How else could all of these frustrations and catastrophes dog the steps of so many expert mountaineers?"

Why Explorers Persist

Why, then, do explorers and ark expeditioners keep going back to Ararat when they have to face such insurmountable odds? The late Eryl Cummings, the "father of ark-aeologists," probably best summed it up in a 1986 interview (he was 81-years old at that time) with Dutch National Television when he said, "I've been on seventeen climbs on Mount Ararat. I know it's there. I've talked to seven people who've seen Noah's ark. I've talked to people who have stood on it, looked in the windows, been all around it. There's no question of it being there, but you're talking about a mountain with an ice cap covering twenty-two square miles varying in thickness from 80 to 800 feet in thickness. It's not an easy job finding it."

"I did an interesting man-on-the-street interview," says ark expeditioner B. J. Corbin, "asking as many of the locals as I could around the base of Mount Ararat where they thought the ark was located. I found it really interesting that every local thought the ark was under the ice. That also verifies for me that the locals really do believe the ark is on Mount Ararat.

"In my opinion," says Corbin, "the only way the ark could have survived almost 5,000 years would be if it was buried partially or completely under the ice cap. Ice is a natural preserver that would keep the ark intact."

Another ark expeditioner, Bob Garbo, has climbed Ararat multiple times and was the radar project technician on his climb with the Charles Willis Tiger Team Expedition out of Fresno, California.

"I used radar to survey the ice cap on Ararat," he says "and determined its depth. There are at least seventeen square miles of solid ice on Ararat year-round, and it's like a refrigerator freezer that is perpetually frozen. I've talked to glaciologists who study frozen artifacts at the South Pole, and they have indicated to me that a wooden boat can be preserved indefinitely in such surroundings.

"The ark needs to be resting in a caldera or a dome underneath the ice to survive," Garbo says. "If it's in an ice flow, it will be destroyed by the grinding action of the flowing glacier."

In an earlier chapter, in our discussion about the significance of "gopher wood," we saw that the ark was not only constructed from a particular type of treated wood, but was pitched both inside and out, giving the wood unique preservative properties.

In addition to the belief that the ark exists and has been preserved over time, there are additional motivations for some explorers who risk their lives time after time on the perilous Mount Ararat in the search for the ark. Explorer John McIntosh, President of SEARCH Foundation, who has already risked the dangers of the mountain on numerous expeditions over the past 20 years, shares in a 2007 interview the motivation behind many explorers' refusal to give up in this monumental search:

> Going back there to Mt. Ararat for many years was actually, in my opinion, a spiritual leading that we were supposed to be doing what we had been called to do, and that was to search for the ark, and with God's help, bring forth this witness.... Because if it can really be established that this structure, or part of it, is still on this mountain at a high elevation, it would be a powerful witness to the world ... which finds itself again ... in days like Noah's.

Discovering Ararat's Secrets

In their search for Noah's ark, Mount Ararat explorers have discovered some secrets about this foreboding mountain. The best time for exploring the mountain, they believe, is during the late summer months and in years when the melt back of snow is substantially above average.

John Wanvig, an ark expeditioner and attorney by profession says:

Mount Ararat is permanently covered year round with deep glacial ice and snow. There are, of course, some seasonal changes that cause the ice and snow to melt back heavily in August and September, increasing the chances of seeing the ark.

However, there are warmer weather cycles that occur every few years which cause increased meltback of the snow-covered summit. It must also be remembered that Mount Ararat is a volcanic mountain and there are fissures and vents through which steam and gases from the core of the mountain are released. Geologically speaking, it's quite possible that the heat released to the surface through these vents contributes to some of the periodic cycles of meltback.

Others have also studied the meltback cycles of the mountain and come up with some provocative conclusions of their own. Mary Irwin, widow of astronaut and ark expeditioner Jim Irwin, has searched for the ark on Ararat also and explains what she has learned about meltback:

Based on my own research of the meltback on Mount Ararat, it is not influenced by greater snows in the winter or warmer temperatures in the summer. Actually, it is influenced and depends a lot on whether the hot and powerful East winds come blowing off the desert in Iran. In fact, one local man told us that the way to stay out of these fierce winds is to stay on the trail that actually goes right up to Noah's ark.

This explanation may account for the view seen in some the declassified Air Force black-and-white reconnaissance photos obtained by Colonel Irwin before he died. These photos showed Mount Ararat in an extreme state of meltback on June 17, 1949. It may also account for some of the World War II Air Force sightings.

"At these particular meltback times, in the area where the ark is believed to be located, on the Western Plateau or above the Ahora Gorge," Wanvig says, "it is likely that the ark is only visible or accessible during these infrequent meltback periods. At other times, an expedition looking for the ark could walk directly over the ice-bound ship and never even know that it was there."

Mount Ararat is a deadly puzzle with mazes and traps that lure the adventurous to scale its unstable slopes and trek over its crevasse-covered glaciers, often with tragic results. ark explorers fortunate enough to even survive the treacherous climb frequently leave the mountain frustrated and discouraged. Why?

Maybe a clue can be found in this statement: "With no more than a half-dozen notable exceptions, all ark discoveries have been accidental and unplanned by 'novices with no special experience or qualification save curiosity and daring' who have stumbled upon the hiding place of Noah's old ship."[7]

Ararat entices and ensnares many, who pay dearly for a chance to see her exquisite treasures, but they are revealed to only a select few—usually those who aren't looking for the treasure in the first place. How ironic that the majestic Ararat is still carefully shrouding the 5,000-year-old mystery from some of the world's most experienced climbers using the most sophisticated equipment in the world.

What will it take to solve this mystery? Has the ark truly been found on Mount Ararat? Will it ever be found again? After viewing the evidence, you can decide for yourself.

Endnotes

1 Violet Cummings, *Noah's Ark Fact or Fable?* (San Diego: Creation-Science Research Center, 1972), pp. 44–45.

2 Jim Irwin, *More Than an Ark on Ararat* (Nashville: Broadman Press, 1985), p. 35.

3 Ibid., p. 46.

4 Ibid., p. 51.

5 Fernand Navarra with Dave Balsiger, *Noah's Ark: I Touched It* (Plainfield, NJ: Logos International, 1974), p. 121.

6 Violet Cummings, *Has Anybody Really Seen Noah's Ark?* (San Diego: Creation-Life Publishers, 1982), pp. 56–57.

7 Ibid., p. 6.

EIGHT

SIGHTINGS AND DISCOVERIES IN THE 1800s

By prevailing over all obstacles and distractions,
one may unfailingly arrive at his chosen goal
or destination.
— Christopher Columbus

THE DARK, STONE HALLWAY was cold with an almost eerie silence. The nervous traveler stood alone in the long, narrow hallway of the old St. Jacob's Monastery at Ahora Village on the slopes of Mount Ararat. He was wondering if his visit—pilgrimage is what the monk had called it—was such a good idea after all.

Still, the lure of seeing treasures from Noah's ark rumored to be locked away there had compelled him to write several letters explaining his reasons, desires, and academic credentials, and then travel in 1829 to the monastery.

The trip had taken more than two months and now, instead of being thrilled with what might be one of the greatest discoveries of his life, he was uncomfortable to the point that he would have run out of the monastery and back into the fresh air if he'd only known how to find his way back to the front door.

St. Jacob's Monastery, built in 1088, was a dark, quiet labyrinth of hallways and small rooms made mostly out of smooth polished stones. It had a stale, musty smell and was obviously very old—eight centuries old according to his research. It had almost no windows that he could see and very little natural light. There were oil lamps on the walls, but they were spaced too far apart to illuminate the place effectively. They just created small halos of light surrounded by deep, mysterious shadows.

To the monks, the dark, dank silence of the monastery presumably felt serene and perfect for contemplation, but the gloom sent chills up and down the traveler's spine, and he couldn't wait to get out of there.

The monk who had met him at the door was un-communicative, soft-spoken and solemn-looking, covered from head to toe in a dull, dark brown, hooded robe. Everything about him was dull, brown, and quiet. Only his eyes sparkled with the faintest glimmer of life. After the introductions, the traveler was led inside to wait for the monk who had corresponded with him for the past six months.

Within a few minutes, the monk appeared. He was short and round with dimples and a ruddy complexion. As uncommunicative as the first monk, he led the explorer down the hallway to the office of the Holy See. The monks all wore cloth slippers that were silent as they plodded through the halls of the monastery. The traveler's boots were the only shoes that had made any noise, and he felt self-conscious as he clumped along behind the short monk.

He had traveled thousands of miles for the sole purpose of seeing the rumored Noachian relics and a manuscript hidden among the stone walls of this monastery. He also knew that the Holy See could easily refuse his request, making the entire effort futile.

The rotund monk, who waddled more than he walked, went into the office alone, closing the heavy wooden door behind him without a sound, leaving the traveler in the hallway, alone again.

Standing there by the stone wall outside the Holy See's office, he felt odd and totally out of place. The time of waiting and wondering felt awkward—almost painful—and he could hear himself breathing heavily in the stuffy, oppressive silence.

Monks would suddenly appear in a pool of light and then pass him in the hallway without saying a word—just nodding a solemn greeting as they went by. If they had not been moving, one would have thought them dead, they seemed so lifeless. They were all covered with the same long, brown robes that almost made them blend in with the color of the stone walls. The soft rustling of their robes was the only sound they made in passing before they were swallowed up once again by the darkness.

The explorer peered nervously first in one direction, then in another so as to not be startled by a silent monk walking by. Waiting in the hallway seemed like an eternity before the thick wooden door of the Holy See's office creaked open.

"The Holy See will speak with you now," the monk smiled. "Come with me."

They went into a spartan room and bowed reverently in the Eastern style instead of shaking hands.

"I understand that you have come a long way to see the ancient relics of Noah's ark entrusted to us," the Holy See inquired softly. An old man with no hair visible on his head, he had piercing, intelligent eyes and a gray and white beard covering his gaunt, wrinkled face. He appeared serious, yet kind; thin but not feeble.

"Yes, your Holiness. I have traveled thousands of miles to see what God has entrusted to you from Noah's ark."

The Holy See nodded. "Well, the brothers have assured me that your motives are pure, and we will grant your request." With that he turned and went back to his desk. The visitor and the monk bowed, and then the monk led his guest from the room, silently closing the door behind them.

The monk took him through an impossible maze of narrow hallways to a tiny chapel containing a couple of wooden benches, a wooden altar, and two ornate chests. The monk told him to sit on one of the benches and he would show him the holy artifacts. So begins the 1829 story of the search for the ark by the Russian-born German physician Dr. J. J. Friedrich W. Parrot.

Explorer Achieves Amazing Goals

Dr. Parrot, professor at the University of Dorpat in Russia, was the first modern ark explorer to leave a record of his Ararat adventures with the 1846 publication of his book, *Journey to Ararat*.

The physician achieved three amazing goals in 1829 when he conquered Mount Ararat. He visited the Armenian Etchmiadzin Cathedral where he saw a cross made from the wood of Noah's ark, he visited the St. Jacob's Monastery at Ahora where ancient ark relics and manuscripts were kept, and he scaled the treacherous mountain, reaching the summit in late September. The Parrot Glacier on the northwest side of the grueling mountain is named after him.

At the Etchmiadzin Cathedral, located in what until recently was Soviet Armenia, Dr. Parrot was the first Westerner to ever view a piece of wood said to be from Noah's ark. He described it this way: "A fragment of the ark of Noah [hangs] by a little chain: it is a small, dark-coloured, quadrangular piece of wood, in good preservation, and carved upon one surface."[1]

From the time of Parrot's account, we hear very little of the relic until it is shown again to the American traveler and Los Angeles radio commentator, Carveth Wells, in 1932. Wells captured the occasion by taking a picture of Archbishop Mesrob, acting head of Etchmiadzin Cathedral, holding the large ornate casket containing the wooden cross.

"I opened the last casket, which looked very much like an ordinary icon from the outside, but on opening the two doors of the casket, instead of finding the usual painting of Jesus, there was a piece of reddish-colored petrified wood, measuring about 12 by 9 inches and about an inch thick," says Wells, describing the moment in his book. "It was obviously petrified wood, as the grain was clearly visible."[2]

In 1989 Texan Bill Crouse, founder of the *Ararat Report*, a newsletter that chronicles modern-day ark expeditions, visited the Etchmiadzin Cathedral. This cathedral is still the current seat of the Armenian Apostolic faith, and it is said that the stones used in the building of the cathedral came from Mount Ararat forty miles away.

In a newsletter, Crouse reported:

They say the ark relic was brought to Armenia by Saint Jacob in A.D. 318, and finally found its way to the Etchmiadzin Cathedral in A.D. 678, where it has been kept locked in an elaborate silver case since 1698.

I was only the second Westerner this century allowed to view and examine the bejeweled cross up close. The relic looked like petrified wood. It was grayish brown with some dark markings. To me, its size was about 8 by 5 inches—it seemed smaller than Wells's estimate.

When I noticed one of the corners was broken off, I was told that in the eighteenth century a piece was sent as a gift to Catherine the Great of Russia.

Dr. Parrot left Etchmiadzin and proceeded to St. Jacob's Monastery at the 2,000-foot level of Mount Ararat. Here at the monastery in the village of Ahora, he viewed ancient Noachian relics and a manuscript. Although he never said what he actually saw, scholars surmise he probably saw household items and pottery from the ark. The manuscript could have been the ship's log or the story of Noah and the Flood written by priestly scribes. However, Dr. Parrot did tell us the small facility included a chapel, a walled enclosure, a garden, an orchard, and a small residence area.[3]

Dr. Parrot's recorded adventures gave the world valuable information about the St. Jacob Monastery and the village of Ahora, once located on the slopes of Mount Ararat. Eleven years after his visit, the village of Ahora was destroyed by the devastating earthquake of 1840, a cataclysmic disaster somewhat akin to the Mount St. Helens eruption in 1980. Explorer James Bryce wrote about the destruction in 1840 that killed 2,000 people:

There formerly stood a pleasant little Armenian village of some 200 houses, named Arghuri, or Aghurri. Not far above the village

... stood the little monastery of St. Jacob, eight centuries old. Towards sunset in the evening of the June 20, 1840, the sudden shock of an earthquake, accompanied by a subterranean roar, and followed by a terrific blast of wind, threw down the houses of Arghuri, and at the same moment detached enormous masses of rock with their superjacent ice from the cliffs that surround the chasm.

A shower of falling rocks overwhelmed in an instant the village, the monastery, and a Kurdish encampment on the pastures above. Not a soul survived to tell the tale.

The little monastery, where Parrot lived so happily among the few old monks is gone forever.[4]

Dr. Parrot's group left St. Jacob's Monastery and proceeded to the Ararat summit, where he describes what he saw:

I pressed forward round a projecting mound of snow, and behold! Before my eyes, now intoxicated with joy, lay the extreme cone, the highest pinnacle of Ararat. Still, a last effort was required of us to ascend a tract of ice by means of steps, and that accomplished, we stood on the top of Ararat.

[The summit] formed of eternal ice, without rock or stone to interrupt its continuity, it was the austere, silvery head of Old Ararat. Towards the east, this summit extended more uniformly than elsewhere, and in this direction it was connected by means of a flattish depression, covered in like manner with perpetual ice, with a second and somewhat lower summit, only 397 yards, or less than a quarter of a mile [away].

The gentle depression between the two eminences presents a plain of snow moderately inclined towards the south, over which it would he easy to go from the one to the other, and which may be supposed to be the very spot on which Noah's ark rested, if the summit itself be assumed as the scene of that event.[5]

In Violet Cummings's book *Noah's Ark: Fact or Fable?* there is an amusing account taken from Dr. Parrot's book:

[Dr. Parrot's] first attempt to scale the peak met with minor disaster when he and his climbing companion lost their footing and rolled a considerable distance down the mountainside. When they arrived back at camp, at the Armenian monastery ... with bruises and sore, they took "special care" not to let a moan escape them while among the Armenians, since they would certainly have taken the tumble as an evidence of divine punishment for their rash attempt to reach the top, "access to which," explains Parrot, "has been forbidden by a divine decree."[6]

Dr. Parrot never did see the ark himself, but he wrote, "They are all firmly persuaded that the ark remains to this day on the top of Mount Ararat, and that in order to ensure its preservation no human being is allowed to approach it."[7]

Further Expeditions

At the summit, Dr. Parrot is reported to have planted a cross to mark his accomplishment. After he returned home, news of his climb inspired scores of others to attempt to conquer Mount Ararat, many with the goal of finding—or disproving the existence of—Noah's ark.

In 1835 Karl Behrens reached the summit and confirmed seeing the cross planted by Dr. Parrot, but he also failed to locate the ark. His ascent was attested to by the Imperial Russian Geographical Society.

Dr. Hermann von Abich, a German geologist and professor of mineralogy also from the University of Dorpat, finally reached the summit on July 29, 1845, after three frustrating and unsuccessful attempts. The eastern summit is named after him as well as two of the mountain's glaciers—Abich I and Abich II.

Dr. Abich apparently wasn't looking for the ark at first but rather climbed Ararat to see whether or not the stars and the other planets were visible during the day from extremely high mountaintops.[8]

In 1850 a Russian Army officer, Colonel Khodzko, reached the summit with a well-organized team of sixty persons. Their goal was to systematically search the mountain until the ark was found. However, due to severe weather, they were forced to leave the summit and abandon their plans for an extensive search.

According to Ararat explorer Fernand Navarra, Napoleon III sent an expedition to Mount Ararat sometime between 1852 and 1870 specifically to search for the ark. A Frenchman reported to Navarra that his grandfather had participated in that expedition and that a piece of wood had been recovered. However, no one knows where the wood is today.[9]

In 1856 British Major Robert Stuart led an expedition of four other British climbers that successfully reached the summit of Mount Ararat and created quite a sensation with the local Kurds. The group's original goal was apparently just to reach the summit, but the accounts of several members of the expedition show how they also became intrigued with the idea of finding the ark. These accounts give us some fascinating insights into the post-earthquake mountain and the beliefs of the local Kurds, which have changed very little in the past century.

Ark Legend Part of Kurdish Faith

Major Stuart wrote:

The Kurdish tribes who dwell on the slopes and at the base of Aghri Dagh, and whose forefathers have been there since the earliest dawn of history, the native Christians of Georgia and Armenia—all indeed who preserve the traditions of the land—are familiar with the story of the Deluge. Their account of that great event varies but slightly from that which has been transmitted to us by Moses, and they hold it as part of their faith that Noah's ark rested on Aghri Dagh, that the hull still remains on the summit, deeply buried out of sight.[10]

The Kurds firmly believed that the summit was the "second cradle of the human race" and that it was not only impossible to reach the summit, but that any attempt to do so would be followed by serious repercussions and, as Major Stuart put it, "the immediate displeasure of Heaven."

Another member of the Stuart expedition, John Evans, wrote:

The Kurds were quite superstitious about the mountain, saying that it was a holy mountain, and no one was allowed to set his foot on it; that several attempts had been made, but that the parties had either given up the attempt, or that their bones had been found afterward at the foot of the mountain.[11]

According to Major Stuart:

The Kurdish attendants came to a stop and refused to proceed any further alleging in justification [their] ancestral traditions and the fear of treading on hallowed ground. Their superstitious companions abandoned them without further ceremony, leaving the foolhardy climbers to spend the night as best they could, alone in the lee of the rocks, while they retired to a safer position below!"[12]

When Major Stuart's party reached the summit, they could be seen by the Kurdish chief waiting below, who reportedly said, "Mashallah! God is great. We have always thought, and our fathers before us thought, that God had made that holy mountain inaccessible to man. Many have tried to ascend it, but no one ever succeeded until you came. [He presumably wasn't aware of the successful climbs of two previous groups.] Allah be praised!"

Violet Cummings reports:

As the members of Stuart's party returned from their strenuous climb, "They found horses awaiting them at the nearest possible spot. The Kurdish messengers held their stirrups with profound reverence as they mounted, and as they approached the upper encampment, its occupants—old, young, and middle aged—turned out to look at these strange English Beys, who, as they had all seen with their own eyes, had scaled the forbidden mountain.

Until a late hour the door of the tent was blocked up by Kurds, old and young, who were anxious to see with their eyes and hear with their ears the wonderful Beys of the mountain, for they no longer looked upon them as ordinary men, but as beings of a superior order, who could not be affected by the religious restrictions imposed upon themselves, and who were not subject to the physical infirmities of other men.[13]

Incredible Discovery

In the late 1870s, Viscount James Bryce, a respected British statesman and author, conducted extensive field and library research and became thoroughly convinced of the historical accuracy of the Bible. Persuaded that the ark was still on Mount Ararat, he set out to disprove the prevailing winds of atheism that Charles Darwin had set in motion at that time.

In 1876 Bryce successfully climbed the mountain, reaching the summit of Mount Ararat alone after his guides left him at the ice cap. He then wrote an intriguing and well-researched book about his experiences called *Transcaucasia and Ararat* as well as an article for the *Journal of the Royal Geographical Society* in London titled "The Ascent of Mount Ararat in 1876."

The highlight of Bryce's trip was not conquering the summit but rather being the first person in modern times to discover hand-tooled lumber on Ararat. Following is an excerpt from his book regarding his wood find:

> Mounting steadily along the same ridge, I saw at a height of over 13,000 feet, lying on the loose blocks, a piece of wood about four feet long and five inches thick, evidently cut by some tool, and so far above the limit of trees that it could by no possibility be a natural fragment of one.
>
> Whether it was really gopher wood, of which material the ark was built, I will not undertake to say, but am willing to submit to the inspection of the curious the bit which I cut off with my ice-axe and brought away. Anyhow, it will be hard to prove that it is not gopher wood.
>
> And if there are any remains of the ark on Ararat at all, this wood suits all the requirements of the case. In fact, the argument is exceptionally strong.[14]

It's impossible to say whether or not the wood that Bryce found came from Noah's ark, as no scientific dating tests were available in his time—but it is a distinct possibility given the circumstantial evidence.

Amazing Nineteenth-Century Sightings

Probably the most significant nineteenth-century eyewitness sighting of the ark occurred somewhere between 1850 and 1880. It is the story of Haji Yearam, an Armenian who lived his final days in America. His story was told in 1952 by Pastor Harold H. Williams of Logansport, Indiana. Here are excerpts of this most amazing story, published by Violet Cummings in her book, *Noah's Ark: Fact or Fable?*:

Haji Yearam's parents and family lived at the foot of Greater Mount Ararat in Armenia. According to their traditions, they were descended directly from those who had come out of the ark, but who had never migrated from that country. Haji's forebears had always remained near the mount where the ark came to rest in a little valley surrounded by some small peaks.

For several hundreds of years after the Flood, his forebears had made yearly pilgrimages up to the ark to make sacrifices and to worship there. They had a good trail and steps to the steep places. Finally the enemies of God undertook to go to Ararat and destroy the ark, but as they neared the location there came a terrible storm that washed away the trail, and lightning blasted the rocks. From that time on, even the pilgrimages ceased, because they feared to betray the way to the ungodly, and they feared God's wrath.

When Haji was a large boy, but not yet a man fully grown, there came to his home some strangers. There were three vile men who did not believe in the Bible and did not believe in the existence of a personal God. They were scientists. They were on this expedition specifically to prove the legend of Noah's ark to be a fraud and a fake.

They hired the father of young Haji Yearam as their official guide. They hired the boy to assist his father as guide.

It was an unusually hot summer, so the snow and glaciers had melted more than usual. After extreme hardship and peril the party came to the little valley way up on Greater Ararat, not on the very top but a little way down from the top. This little valley is surrounded by a number of small peaks. There the ark came to rest in a little lake, and the peaks protected it from the tidal waves that rushed back and forth as the Flood subsided. On one side of the valley the water from the melting snows and glacier spills over in a little river that runs down the mountain. As they reached this spot, there they found the prow of a mighty ship protruding out of the ice.

They went inside the ark and did considerable exploring. The whole structure was covered with a varnish or lacquer that was very thick and strong, both outside and inside the ship. The ship was built more like a great arid mighty house on the hull of a ship, but without any windows. There was a great doorway of immense size, but the door was missing.

The scientists were appalled and dumbfounded and went into a rage at finding what they had hoped to prove non-existent. They were so angry and mad that they said they would destroy the ship, but the wood was more like stone than any wood we have now. They did not have the tools or means to wreck so mighty a ship and had to give up. They did tear out some timbers and tried to burn the wood, but it was so hard it was almost impossible to burn it.

They held a council, and then took a solemn and fearful death oath. Any man present who would ever breathe a word about what they had found would be tortured and murdered.

They told their guide and his son that they would keep tabs on them and that if they ever told anyone and they found it out they would surely be tortured and murdered. For fear of their lives, Haji and his father had never told what they found except to their best trusted and closest relatives.[15]

According to Pastor Williams, Haji's story was confirmed by an elderly scientist on his deathbed in London. His report continues:

One evening (I am pretty sure it was in 1918) I sat reading the daily paper in our apartment in Brockton. Suddenly I saw in a very small print a short story of a dying man's confession. It was a news item one column wide and, as I remembered it, not more than two inches deep. It stated that an elderly scientist on his deathbed in London was afraid to die before making a terrible confession. It gave briefly the very date and facts that Haji Yearam had related to us in his story.

Haji Yearam had died in my parents' home in Oakland, California, about the same time that the old scientist had died in London. We had never for a moment doubted Haji's story, but when this scientist on his deathbed on the other side of the world confessed the same story in every detail, we knew positively that the story was true in every detail.[16]

In 1883 a surprising turn of events affected every subsequent expedition searching for the ark of Noah.

On May 2 another devastating earthquake encompassed Mount Ararat, causing destructive avalanches of rocks and ice that once again buried villages on the slopes of the mountain. While not as severe as the 1840 earthquake, it did shake the mountain to its very foundations and the devastation was reported around the world.

Later that year, the Turkish government sent an expedition of commissioners to survey the mountain to determine the extent of the damage of this earth-quake-prone region.

Captain Gascoyne, an Englishman and attaché of the British Embassy in Constantinople (now called Istanbul), went with the Turkish surveying team. The explorers actually stumbled upon the ark and, once informed of the historical significance of the find by Mr. Gascoyne, the surveying team took detailed measurements and notes on the great, wooden ship. Part of the ark was protruding from a glacier, but they were unable to determine the exact length because much of it was still completely submerged in glacial ice. The surveyors were able to go inside.

The local people also told the surveying team that the ship had been partially exposed for the previous six years and that it had been the topic of much discussion by those living near the mountain.

Elated with their historic find, the Turkish commissioners informed the world's press and were totally unprepared for and shocked at the response. The original press release from Constantinople has never been found, but the article supposedly closest to the original story was located in the British *Prophetic Messenger*, published in the summer of 1883. The following is an excerpt from the article:

We have received from our correspondent in Trebizond news of the return of the

Commissioners appointed by the Turkish Government to inquire into the reported destruction of Mosul, Ashak, and Bayazid by avalanches, and to render relief to the distressed villages in the glens of the Ararat ranges, who had suffered so severely from the unusual inclemency of the season.

The expedition was fortunate in making a discovery that cannot fail to be of interest to the whole civilized world, for among the vastnesses of one of the glens of Mount Ararat, they came upon a gigantic structure of very dark wood, embedded at the foot of one of the glaciers, with one end protruding, and which they believe to be none other than the old ark in which Noah and his family navigated the waters of the deluge. The place where the discovery is made is about five days' journey from Trebizond, in the Department of Van, in Armenia, about four leagues from the Persian frontier.

At last they were rewarded by the sight of a huge dark mass, protruding twenty or thirty feet from the glacier, on the left side of the ravine. They found it was formed of wood not grown in these elevated districts, not nearer than the hot valleys of the Euphrates, where it is known by the natives as "izim," said to be the gopher wood of the Scriptures. It was in a good state of preservation, being painted on the outside with a dark brown pigment, and constructed of great strength.

The projected portion seemed about forty or fifty feet in height, but to what length it penetrated into the glacier they could not estimate.

Effecting an entrance through one of the broken corners, the explorers found it filled for the greater part with ice, the interior being partitioned off into compartments about twelve or fifteen feet high, into three of which only they were able to make their way, owing to the mass of frozen substance with which these were filled, and also because of their fear of the structure collapsing with the overhanging mass of the huge glacier.[17]

Widespread Ridicule

Rather than inspiring scores of scientists, archaeologists, and journalists to journey to see the ark for themselves, the report received widespread ridicule and disbelief of the sort usually reserved today for tales of alien abductions and UFOs. Anyone who dared to express any belief in the report was humiliated for his or her naïveté.

Following is a brief excerpt from the August 10, 1883, edition of the *New York Herald:*

Now let the heathen rage and the free-thinkers call on their respective beer cellars to hide them, for has not Noah's ark been discovered? If arks were the fashion 4,400 years ago, why may not dozens of them have drifted from their moorings during the great November freshet of 2616 B.C. and gone ashore on Mount Ararat?[18]

And from the August 13, 1883, issue of the *New York World* comes the following ridicule:

At this point archaeology could afford to rest at any ordinary period of the world and we should expect the luckiest finders to form a syndicate and open a bazaar for the sale of relics.

We must not forget that the planting of the Cardiff Giant was not so much to make money as to establish the missing link. The Noah's ark syndicate are only following the tactics of the antiquary who recently offered to sell an original manuscript of the Mosaic Law signed by Moses to the British Museum.

With these principles in view, the reader must not be surprised to learn by the latest dispatches from our representative ... that the engineers have broken through the third compartment of the ark, and in the true spirit of the age have discovered the original log kept by Noah and his sons.[19]

Embarrassed and irritated by the reaction of the world's press, the Turkish government did not follow up the amazing find with another expedition, and apparently, the snows that year covered the ark and hid it once again from view.

Prince Nouri's Notable Discovery

The next notable discovery of the ark was by Prince John Joseph Nonni.[20] The prince, who spoke ten languages, claimed to have climbed Ararat three times and to have finally found the ark on his third climb on April 25, 1887, when he was in his early twenties. His account gave support to the 1883 account of the Turkish surveying team.

Prince Nouri's account of finding Noah's ark was published in the *Zion's Watch Tower* of August 15, 1894:

The bow and stern were clearly in view, but the center was buried in snow, and one end of it had fallen off and decayed.

It stood more than 100 feet high and was over 300 yards long [an estimate; without any ability to measure the vessel, Nouri has overestimated the size compared to biblical dimensions]. The wood was peculiar, dark reddish in color, almost iron colored in fact, and seemed very thick. I think the cold has preserved the wood. I am very positive that we saw the real ark, though it is over 4,000 years old!

Though within rifle shot, they could not reach it, the slope from the bench on which it rested being a glare of ice and snow, and they could not remain till the midsummer thaw.[21]

To no avail, he tried desperately to find help and financial support to recover the ark before it froze over again or before it fell deeper into a crevasse. His dream was to take the ark to the Chicago Exhibition, the 1893 World's Fair. But his dream, obviously, never came true. He died suddenly of pneumonia a few years after the World's Fair without leaving a map or any written record of the ark's location.

Flamboyant Prince Nouri's report wrapped up the expeditions and ark sightings of the nineteenth century—a most significant century for studiers of Noah's ark. Many climbers achieved the conquest of Mount Ararat's summit during that century. Hand-tooled wood believed to be from the ark was recovered at the 13,000-foot elevation. Also, the first official recognition by the Turkish government of the discovery of Noah's ark occurred during this century. Finally, the attempt by disbelieving scientists to destroy the ark made the 1800s a particularly intriguing era.

Were Stories of Sightings Credible?

The question which must be asked about ancient and even modern Noah's ark sightings is, are the claims and stories about actually seeing the ark on Mount Ararat really credible? Richard Bright, a retired commercial airline pilot and author of *The Ark, a Reality?* has been on more than twenty expeditions to Mount Ararat and has done an extensive comparison of ark sightings:

I have studied virtually every historical sighting account of the ark on Mount Ararat. They are pretty close to always being consistent in what is being described by eyewitnesses.

Over the past 200 years many accounts of these sightings have gone into considerable detail. I have compared in detail thirty-two of these sightings and have found there's tremendous consistency between eyewitnesses even though they never knew each other, and may have seen the ark many, many years from each other.

For instance, there are four reports of the ark with the door off. There are seven reports of one end broken off, and eighteen reports of it sticking out of the ice and snow. There are nine reports of a melt-water pond, eight reports of a ledge, and ten reports of a ravine, valley, gully, or some such place which the ark sitting on a ledge could be in. There are three reports of a very difficult or hazardous climb to reach the ship.

There are at least two reports of the ark leaning against a rock or ridge, and two reports of it sitting in a north-south direction. There are three reports of a stream down the mountain and two reports of the ark having openings around the top.

We can choose to believe that all of these reports are based upon lies, or based on the information presented, we can choose to believe the ark or a large wooden barge is on Mount Ararat—if just one of the reports is true.

From all the eyewitness reports, Bright says in his book, it's possible to reconstruct the ark site at about 13,000 to 14,000 feet and show what modern-day searchers will find regarding the condition of the ark:

The ark is located on a ledge, in some sort of a ravine, leaning against a rock or ridge, and is in the ice and snow. When there is melting, the melt-waters form a small pond, that when full to its banks overflow and run down the hill. The ends of the ark point generally in a north-south direction, with at least the exposed end broken, or broken off, and the door is missing.[22]

The nineteenth century unveiled incredible evidence of the existence of Noah's ark on Mount Ararat. But the twentieth and twenty-first centuries are proving to be even more rewarding in its disclosures. Not only has the scientific knowledge and space technology of our time confirmed the ancient sightings, but the hidden secrets of this historic vessel have been unlocked as well.

Endnotes

1 Friedrich Parrot, *Journey to Ararat* (New York: Harper and Brothers Publishers, 1846), p. 113.

2 Carveth Wells, *Kapoot* (New York: Robert M. McBride and Company, 1934), p. 228.

3 Tim LaHaye and John Morris, *The Ark on Ararat* (Nashville: Thomas Nelson Publishers, 1976), p. 30.

4 John Warwick Montgomery, *The Quest for Noah's Ark* (Minneapolis: Bethany Fellowship, 1972), p. 140. Cited from Sir James Bryce, *Transcaucasia and Ararat* (1877), pp. 239-241.

5 John Warwick Montgomery, *The Quest for Noah's Ark*, pp. 137138. Cited from Friedrich Parrot, *Journey to Ararat* (1846), p. 176.

6 Violet M. Cummings, *Noah's Ark: Fact or Fable?* (San Diego: Creation-Science Research Center, 1972), p. 52.

7 Charles Berlitz, *The Lost Ship of Noah* (New York: G. P. Putnam's Sons, 1987), pp. 20-21.

8 Ibid., p. 21.

9 Cummings, *Noah's Ark: Fact or Fable?* p. 196.

10 Montgomery, p. 166. Cited in Proceedings of the Royal Geographical Society (1877), pp. 77–92.

11 Cummings, *Noah's Ark: Fact or Fable?* p. 54.

12 Ibid., p. 52.

13 Ibid., p. 53.

14 LaHaye and Morris, *The Ark on Ararat*, pp. 53–54. Cited from James Bryce, *Transcaucasia and Ararat* (1877), pp. 264–265.

15 Cummings, *Noah's Ark: Fact or Fable?* pp. 189–192.

16 Ibid., pp. 192–193

17 LaHaye and Morris, *The Ark on Ararat,* pp. 56–57.

18 Ibid., pp. 59–60

19 Ibid., pp. 60–61

20 Prince Nonni's full name and title as listed in one account are as follows: His Pontifical Eminence, the Most Venerable Prelate, Monseignior, the Zamorrin Nonni, John Joseph, Prince of Nonni, DD., LL.D. (by Divine Providence), Chaldean Patriarchal Archdeacon of Babylon and Jerusalem, Grand Apostolic Ambassador of Malabar, India, and Persia. The discoverer of Noah's ark, and the Golden Mountains of the Moon [who was soon to be coronated as] Patriarch of the Chaldean (Nestorian) Church. He was also called the "Sacred Crown's Supreme Representative-General of the Holy Orthodox Patriarchal Imperiality" as well as "The First Universal Exploring Traveler" of a million miles. Another publication in 1894 listed his titles as follows: The Rev. Dr. John Joseph Nonni, DD., LL.D., Chaldean Archdeacon of Babylon and Jerusalem, Pontifical Delegate General of Malabar and Ex-grand Secretary of the Metropolitan Archdiocese of India and Persia. (See Cummings, *Noah's Ark: Fact or Fable?* pp. 119–120, 122; Richard Bright, *The Ark, a Reality?* (Humble, TX: Ranger Associates, 1984), p. 57.)

21 Ibid., p. 58.

22 Ibid., pp. 405–406.

NINE

GROUND AND AERIAL SIGHTINGS IN THE EARLY 1900s

Every man without passions has within him no principle of action, nor motive to act.
—Claude Adrien Helvetius (1715-1771)

TEN-YEAR-OLD George Hagopian visited Noah's ark in 1902. Here is what he had to relate:

My grandfather was the minister of the big Armenian Orthodox Church in Van (near Lake Van), and he always told me stories about the holy ship on the holy mountain.

And then one day my uncle said, "Georgie, I'm going to take you to see the holy ark." We packed supplies on his donkey, and together we started our trek toward Mount Ararat.

My feet were getting sore, and the donkey kept wanting to go in the wrong direction, but we continued climbing until we got about halfway up. Then uncle took both supplies and me on his back, and we climbed and climbed.

It took us almost eight days from the time we left Van to the moment we got to the place on the holy mountain where both my grandfather and my uncle had said the holy ship had come to rest.

I guess my uncle took me there that year because it was a year without much snow—a "smooth year" we called it. There's one of those about every twenty years.

And then we got to the ark. It was getting dark and misty around us. My uncle dropped his pack, and together we began to haul stones to the side of the ship. Within a short time we had stacked a high pile of rocks against the side of the ship.

"Georgie, come here," he said, grabbing me by my arm. "You are going on top of the holy ark." He lifted me up and put me on his shoulders, and together we climbed the pile of rocks. When he had reached the top, his hands grabbed my ankles and he began to push me up.

"Reach for the top, Georgie," he yelled. "Grab the edge and pull yourself up!"

I stood up straight and looked all over the ship. It was long. The height was about forty feet.

"Look inside the ark," my uncle called up to me. "Look for the holes. Look for the big one. Look inside and tell me what you see."

I shivered from the cold and from fear and glanced around me. Yes, there was the hole, big and gaping. I peeked into the blackness of the hole, but saw nothing. Then I knelt down and kissed the holy ark.

When we were there, the top of the ark was covered with a very thin coat of fresh fallen snow. But when I brushed some of it away I could see a green moss growing right on top. When I pulled a piece off, it was made of wood. The grain was right there. This green moss made the ark feel soft and moldy.

On the roof, besides one large hole, I remember small holes running all the way from the front to the back. I don't know exactly how many, but there must have been at least fifty of them running down the middle with small intervals in between. My uncle told me these holes were for air.

That roof was flat with the exception of that narrow raised section running all the way from the bow to the stern with all those holes in it.

I remember, my uncle took his gun and shot into the side of the ark, but the bullet wouldn't penetrate. Uncle then pulled his long hunting knife from his belt, and with the heavy handle he chipped a piece from the side of the ark. Then we went down the mountainside and returned to Van.[1]

Artist Sketches Ark from Description

George Hagopian was an eighty-year-old Armenian when he related this account to artist-illustrator Elfred Lee and ark researcher-explorer Eryl Cummings in Easton, Maryland, in 1970. Following several additional interviews with Hagopian, Lee was able to sketch the very first likeness of Noah's ark, including where the windows were placed. Lee's illustration of the ancient vessel has since been published in biblical reference books throughout the world. In addition, Elfred Lee is the last living person to have worked with explorers who claimed to have actually seen Noah's ark on Mount Ararat.

Hagopian again went back to the ark in 1904 while on a pilgrimage for "holy" flowers. He gave Dr. Lee additional details regarding the ark's features:

I saw the ark a second time. I think it was in 1904. We were on the mountain looking for holy flowers, and I went back to the ark and it still looked the same. Nothing had changed. I didn't get to the top that time, but I stayed at the side, and really got a good look at it.

It was resting on a steep ledge of bluish-green rock about 3,000 feet wide.

Another thing I noticed was that I didn't see any nails at all. It seemed that the whole ship was made of one piece of petrified wood.

There was definitely no door in the side of the ship that I could see. No opening of any kind. There may have been one in the part I couldn't see, but that I don't know. That side was practically inaccessible. I could only see my side and part of the bow.

The sides were slanting outward to the top and the front was flat. I didn't see any real curves. It was unlike any other boat I have ever seen. It looked more like a flat-bottomed barge.[2]

Paul Meier, a renowned medical doctor and psychiatrist, author and co-founder of the Minirth-Meier New Life Clinics across the United States, is an expert in analyzing the behavioral patterns of people. Dr. Meier was asked to analyze the audio tapes and video interviews of George Hagopian and two of the ark eyewitnesses discussed in Chapter 14. He is particularly well suited for the task, having been the medical officer on a 1985 ark-Ararat expedition led by John McIntosh from California. He reported:

As a psychiatrist, I've authored forty books on personality types and traits, and human behavior, and can determine whether or not people are telling the truth and whether or not they are in touch with reality. By studying audio and video tapes for several hours over several days, I was able to make an analysis of George Hagopian's eyewitness account as well as those of other eyewitnesses.

I found George Hagopian to be a very interesting Armenian in his seventies who actually grew up and lived in the Mount Ararat area. He claims that he and his friends made treks up the mountain to Noah's ark. These types of things have been reported by a number of Armenians who live in the United States, Russia, and in other parts of the world. [Seeing the ark] was a tradition of the Armenian culture.

When George got up there, his father told him, "You are a holy man now." He traveled to the ark when he was only ten years old and then again when he was thirteen years old. Now, his description of the ark and some of the details were not accurate, but he was describing them from a ten-year-old's perspective and a thirteen-year-old's perspective.

George said that the ark seemed like it was 1,000 feet long and we know from the Bible and reconnaissance photos that it's only about 450 feet long. His descriptions of the width and height were much closer. He said that the cliff it was up against was 3,000 feet high and

3,000 feet wide and we know that that was a gross exaggeration, but again, he was a young, ten-year-old child and a thirteen-year-old child when he saw the ark.

When asked about windows, he said, "No, I didn't see any windows, but I saw fifty holes along the top." Well, that's exactly what others have described—a series of windows on a top piece along the top of the ark. He mentioned that it was on a northeast corner of the mountain.

I found George Hagopian to have a very normal personality. He has broken English so it's hard to understand him at times, but he did not brag about himself. He did not brag about his exploits. He seemed very humble. He had a lot of what we call obsessive-compulsive features. He was a perfectionist in his description of the details. He had some normal, healthy, human emotions and concern for the interviewer. I found Mr. Hagopian, in spite of some of the discrepancies from his childlike perspective when he climbed the ark, to be extremely credible and I believe his account.

Goat Path Led to Ark

Another Armenian to see the ark in the early 1900s was Jacob Chuchian, who lived in the village of Ortulu on the southwest side of Ararat. Chuchian saw the ark a number of times between the ages of nine and nineteen. Information concerning Jacob's visit to the ark comes from his son, Arthur, who was an engineer at Channel Two television in St. Louis, Missouri at the time he was interviewed.

In a 1975 interview with Rev. Stuart Brassie, Arthur related what his father Jacob told him regarding the path to the ark and what his father reportedly saw at the site:

To reach the site where the ark is, one must follow a narrow goat trail, approximately four feet wide, which starts out of nowhere and runs for about three miles. It is an obvious, worn trail and ends at a solid mountain wall overlooking the ark, which is positioned about one hundred feet below the trail.

The ark rests in a large body of water about three to four times the size of the boat, and except for one time when the front third of the boat was plainly visible, the boat was completely covered by a shimmering, very clear covering of ice, so that only the huge, but clear outline, of the ark could be seen.

The boat has a reddish brown wood appearance and is similar to a houseboat with a flat deck surface. The ark rests on a type of cleft or ledge and is accessible only by the goat's trail. The ledge on which the ark rests drops off very rapidly from the front side, and is surrounded on the other three sides by walls of rock.[3]

Chuchian's account of how one reaches the ark is almost identical to other mid-twentieth-century sightings in which the guides were Armenian. These Armenians all say that by staying on the Great Trail, climbers avoid the tremendous winds in reaching the ark site, which they indicate is about two thirds of the way up the mountain. They also claim that around the turn of the century, the Armenian people used to take entire villages by groups up to visit the ark. They said the climb was not that difficult.

In 1982 astronaut James Irwin and veteran ark hunter Eryl Cummings used a map drawn with the help of Arthur Chuchian. They located the old goat trail and followed it for a time, but it branched off in several directions at various places. Armenians knew which path to take to the ark because of a special insignia marking the path. Unable to locate the insignia, Irwin's group abandoned the effort in favor of other approaches.

Turkish Soldiers See Ark

Many others in this century have also reported seeing the ark. In 1916 six Turkish soldiers, returning home after serving in World War I in the Baghdad area (approximately 450 miles south of Mount Ararat), claimed that they had climbed Mount Ararat and had seen the ark. Since none of the men could read or write, they told their story to a learned friend, Duran Ayranci of Adana, Turkey. In 1946 the men asked him to write a letter to the American Embassy in Turkey offering their services as guides to any Americans looking for the ark.

The letter affirmed, "We saw Noah's ark leaning against the mountain. I measured the length of the boat. It was 150 paces long. It had three stories."

Little is known about these men because none of them were still alive by the time researchers became aware of their letter and story in 1966—twenty years later! All that researchers now know is what they've been able to learn from Mr. Ayranci, the man who wrote the letter and knew the soldiers, but unfortunately did not know the route to the ark.[4]

Russian Pilots Sight Ark

Also in 1916, another report surfaced about a Russian pilot who allegedly saw the ark while flying around Ararat testing a high-altitude engine. The story of Vladimir Roskovitsky's sighting of the ark was vividly described in a 1940 issue of *The New Eden* magazine. It generated thousands of inquiries before the editor admitted that the article was ninety-nine percent fiction. However, it was based on the single fact that a Russian aviator had seen a boat like structure on Mount Ararat.

If the Roskovitsky account was false, what do we know about the real Russian aviator who actually saw the ark? The answer came on October 6, 1945, in a detailed article in the White Russian publication, *Rosseya*. Russian General Alexander Jacob Elshin and Colonel Alexander A. Koor not only confirmed that there was a Russian aviator sighting but also an expedition sent by the Russian czar to investigate the wooden boat on Mount Ararat.

Colonel Koor, an officer in the czar's White Russian Army, was a friend of some of the solders involved in the aerial expedition that spotted the ark on Mount Ararat. Ark researcher Eryl Cummings obtained the following communication from Colonel Koor in 1946:

> Some enlightening data comes from the official records of the Russian Caucasian Army, 1914-1917, by General E. B. Mavlovsky. In 1916, the 3-D Caucasian Aviation Detachment, under the command of 1st Lt. Zabolotsky, served air duty over the region at Mount Ararat, Lake Van and Lake Urmia. This aviation detachment served the 4th Caucasian Corps, and the Army Aviation Inspector was Captain Koorbatoff. I hope 1st

Lt. Zabolotsky is the man you are looking for, for he, from an airplane, sighted the ark and started the investigation. Captain Koorbatoff was his supervisor.

I understand that the discovery of Noah's ark was in the end of 1916, with the scouting parties having to wait until the summer of 1917.

About July or August 1921, I and Lt. [Peter Nicolovich] Leslin met 1st Lt. [Paul Vasilivich] Rujansky in Harbin. During one of our conversations, 1st Lt. Rujansky told me about the details because he was wounded and sent to Russia, but he knew because his brother, Boris Vasilivich Rujansky, Sergeant of the Military Railroad Battalion, was a member of the investigating party which was sent to Mount Ararat to corroborate the discovery of Noah's ark.

Lt. Leslin admitted he had also heard about the discovery of Noah's ark, not as a rumor, but as news, from the Senior Adjutant of his division, who had told him that Noah's ark was found in the saddle of two peaks of Mount Ararat. This is all I heard from these two officers, and I am sure both told me the truth.[5]

"I personally talked to Colonel Koor," says Dr. Elfred Lee, "and he told me Noah's ark was very much like George Hagopian described it. He also confirmed that the czar's expedition did indeed take photographs and measurements of the ark."

Mrs. Gladys Evans of El Cajon, California remembered that three of the White Russian airmen who had flown over the ark in 1916 and had been on the 1917 foot-reconnaissance expedition spent a week in her father's San Bernardino, California, home as houseguests in the fall of 1940. In the late 1970s, Mrs. Evans vividly shared some of the details described by the airmen to her father and brother:

They told how the ark was "half in and half out of a lake like a log floating in water. It was an immense thing, and it had cages—some with metal on them. It had a catwalk on top and the door was off. The door was nearby and had apparently been struck by lightning because it was partly burnt. The ark was pitched within and without with some kind of lacquer. It was just as good as the day it was built." The wood reminded them of oleander.

When they first saw the ark from the air, they thought it was a submarine, but couldn't figure out why someone would be building it on a mountain. On the later reconnaissance expedition, these three airmen actually got inside the ark where they took pictures and measurements. The film was turned over to the Russian government.[6]

The Russian airmen who stayed at the home of Mrs. Evans's father were not the same airmen who first spotted the ark while testing their airplane. Mrs. Evans said that these airmen also flew around the site, but the original discoverers were other Russian airmen, whose names, mentioned at the time, had since been forgotten by Mrs. Evans.

Czar Sends Expedition to Ararat

In the summer of 1917, the czar sent two research divisions with a total of 150 infantrymen, army engineers, and scientists on a ground expedition to find the ark. It took them a month to reach the site due to all of the difficulties they experienced—including incredibly harsh weather.

The hardships were worth it, however, when they finally reached their goal. "As the huge ship at last loomed before them, an awed silence descended, and 'without a word of command everyone took off his hat, looking reverently toward the ark; everybody knew, feeling it in his heart and soul,' that they were in the actual presence of the ark. Many 'crossed themselves and whispered a prayer,' said an eyewitness account. It was like being in a church, and the hands of the archaeologist trembled as he snapped the shutter of the camera and took a picture of the old boat as if she were 'on parade.'"[7]

The Russian investigators took measurements and found that the ark was about 500 feet long, about 83 feet wide at the widest place, and about 50 feet high.[8] These measurements correspond more closely to the 20-inch cubit rather than the 18-inch cubit most frequently cited by Bible scholars.

The results of the ground investigation and photographs of Noah's ark were sent back to Czar Nicholas II, who many say never received them due to the outbreak of the Bolshevik Communist Revolution in 1917.

The results of the investigation have either never been found or never been reported. A rumor exists that the results of the investigation and the pictures of the ark came to the attention of Leon Trotsky, who either destroyed them or placed them in a file destined to be kept permanently secret. According to the same rumor, the special courier's silence on the matter was also permanently secured by his execution.[9]

An exhaustive effort to locate the 1917 czarist expedition photographs and report on Noah's ark has been made both past and present without success. A Moscow radio commentator was hired to go through the Kremlin archives and museums looking for these items. Christie's and Sotheby's auction houses in London were contacted and asked to review the czarist family collections to determine if these items might be hidden among the czarist papers and artifacts. Weeks of searching did not produce the report or photos, but did reveal that both had reached the czar at his palace.

Minnesota resident Alvin Holderbecker, nephew of a czarist expedition eyewitness, reported the following:

My Aunt Eva worked in the czar's palace as a housemaid during World War I when she was about nineteen or twenty years old. Her father was a medical officer in the White Russian Army and a highly respected friend of the czar and his family. He was the chief medical officer on the expedition that found Noah's ark. When he came back from the expedition, he showed my Aunt Eva the photographs and reports.

Then, the Bolshevicks took over, confiscated all of the photographs and reports, and killed as many of the men from the expedition as they could find. My Aunt Eva was the only one from her family who escaped. She was sent by the czar to Kaiser Wilhelm in Germany.

My aunt, having seen the pictures, told me the ark was three decks high, and on top of the roof there was a catwalk that was about knee-high with openings underneath to provide ventilation or light.

She said that the czar and his family were not killed, but rather, it was a rumor they started to hide their escape. She said they actually escaped into Poland, and my Aunt Eva escaped from Germany to Canada, and then later came into the United States.

Megan Butler, managing editor of Regnery Gateway Publishers in Washington, D.C., commented in a past interview:

There's been controversy surrounding the czarist expedition that took place in 1917. Our author of *Anastasia: The Last Expedition* spent twenty years researching Anastasia, the last surviving member of the Russian royal family. During one of his personal interviews with her, he was shocked when she started talking about the expedition her father, the czar, had commissioned to go to Ararat to measure and photograph Noah's ark. She told him that she'd actually seen the photographs and report from the expedition. She then told him that she wore a cross made of wood from Noah's ark.

Noah's ark archivist Elfred Lee, talked to Alexi Nicholi Romanov, the son of Czar Nicholas Romanov, and reported the following:

He told me that when he was a boy in the palace, there was much talk about the discovery of Noah's ark. He said there was much excitement about the photographs and the measurements. But he said when the Revolution broke out, there was a lot of confusion, and "we don't know what happened to everything. We were in fear of our lives."

Radio Celebrity Smuggles Piece of Ark

As stated in an earlier chapter, Carveth Wells, once well-known radio personality from KFI Radio in Los Angeles, set out in 1933 to find Noah's ark on Mount Ararat. He visited the Etchmiadzin Cathedral, where he viewed the cross made of wood from Noah's ark. He was allegedly prevented from climbing Ararat on the Russian side, but apparently slipped across the border, visited the ark, and brought back a piece of reddish-colored wood.

One of Carveth Wells' friends wrote Eryl Cummings the following note:

I am very interested in the ark and about thirty years ago, Carveth Wells was at the ark and smuggled a piece of it out, and I examined it and it is of very hard wood. The piece he brought out was by bribing a government inspector. The piece was about 2 feet long and 8 inches wide and 1-1/2 inch thick.[10]

American Flyers Spot Ark

Many sightings over the years have been by pilots who either specifically went looking for the ark or just happened to see the great ship while flying over or around Mount Ararat. During World War II, American flyers flew hundreds of flights over Mount Ararat in an effort to keep the Russian Army supplied with war materiel. These flights took off from Allied bases in Tunisia en route to the Soviet Air Base in Erivan.

Reports frequently surfaced about American, Australian, and Russian airmen seeing the ark locked in Ararat's icy snow. One of these sightings was reported in the military *Stars and Stripes* newspaper.

"Since the early 1800s, there have been dozens of newspaper articles concerning the ark on Mount Ararat," says Noah's ark researcher, Cliff Moody. "The *Stars and Stripes* alone published forty-nine articles dealing with Noah's ark from September 1949, through August 1984. Unfortunately, the particular European issue containing actual photos of the ark has not yet been located."

However, Vence Will, a pastor, who saw the photographs while serving in the Air Force as a TEC Sergeant during World War II, recalled:

In World War II, I was stationed in North Africa with the signal installation battalion that was attached to the Army Air Force. We put up electronic beacons on which these airplanes would fly. These beacons stretched from North Africa and India on up into Europe. At the time, I was working in Tunisia, Algeria and in Italy.

One time, I was in the airport in Naples, Italy, with a buddy of mine and we went over to the officer's mess to have a cup of coffee. Our guys had been flying supplies over Turkey to the back part of Russia, and one of the pilots had taken some pictures. Three officers were looking at the pictures of Mount Ararat and a boat-like object on it, and we looked too.

Some of them thought that it was Noah's ark. Two of the pictures were hazy, but one of them was clear. A section of the ark was sticking out of the snow forty to fifty feet without anything underneath it. The wood was darker than the rocks around it. The ark itself was in pretty good shape. I couldn't see any holes on the top. There was a hole on the right side where you could see the different levels and structural beams. I could see two decks through the hole.

As we looked at these photos, there was no question in the minds of these flyers that this was Noah's ark. I'm convinced that I was looking at Noah's ark, and a similar picture was put into the *Stars and Stripes* in about 1944. It was a front-page photo that looked just like the one I saw in the officer's mess.

Another interesting World War II sighting of the ark involved Lester Walton of Spring Valley, California. He was in the Army Air Force, assigned to testing a new Fairchild camera that was supposed to give better resolution of bomb sites during bombing missions. They were flying in a seven-plane squadron of B-24s from their base in North Africa to a target in Eastern Europe when they flew over Mount Ararat and accidentally photographed Noah's ark.

"The on-board cameras were designed to take movies of the bombing mission. When we flew over Mount Ararat, a structure was seen and the speculation was that it was the ark," remembers Walton. "The pilot of the plane banked sharply to position the camera to get a good shot, and then proceeded on to our objective."

Walton recalls a major canyon on the north side of the mountain. He remembers "a box-shaped structure protruding out from the ice or rock debris. The north end of the structure was higher than the south end and the entire thing was tilted about thirty degrees. It was darker than the surrounding rock.

"At the time, an expeditionary effort was proposed to document the object, but was ruled out due to the lingering instability of the area," says Walton. "Soon, word came that the documentation would be carried out by the National Geographic Society as soon as hostilities cooled." Mr. Walton never heard the results of any such expedition.

Ark Photos Disappear Mysteriously

Many passengers aboard aircraft also claim to have seen Noah's ark. George Jefferson Greene was an American oil and pipeline engineer working in the Middle East in the early 1950s. In the late summer of 1953, he was on a helicopter flying over the northeastern flanks of Mount Ararat on business when he was suddenly shocked to see a wooden ship protruding from the ice and rocks below.

Greene directed the pilot to fly as close to the ship as possible, and he took pictures with the superb photographic equipment he had on board that belonged to his employer. Some of the incredible photos were shot from just 90 feet away. He was thrilled with his unbelievable archaeological discovery and couldn't wait to see the proof in his priceless photographs.[11]

He showed the developed eight-by-ten-inch black-and-white photos to friends both in the Middle East and in the United States in an apparently futile attempt to find financial backing for an expedition to recover his historic find. Incredibly, even with clear photographs that were seen by a number of people, he was unable to generate any interest in the project.

Disheartened by the lack of interest, he went to British Guyana, where he hoped to make a fortune in a placer mining operation. On December 27, 1962, George Greene was murdered, and his body was found floating in the hotel pool.

Frank Neff, a friend of Greene's, was one of the many people in Texas who had seen the photos of the ark on Mount Ararat. When he found out that researchers were looking for copies of the photos, he remarked that he thought Greene had kept duplicates in a manila envelope in a storage unit he had rented there in Texas. Ark researcher Eryl Cummings went to the storage unit with Neff only to find that it had been broken into and ransacked just ten days before.

"As he opened the door [of the storage unit], Cummings stared in dismay. The contents of the once well-organized shelves had been unceremoniously dumped into a great scattered heap in the middle of the floor.

"For what had the vandals been searching? Had a certain large—and vitally important—manila envelope been among the items the robbers had carried away?"[12]

The copies of the photos were never found, but Eryl Cummings tracked down a total of thirty individuals who readily recalled seeing Greene's high quality photos of the ark. With so many witnesses, the fact that the explicit, eight-by-ten-inch black-and-white photos existed cannot be questioned. But where are they now?

"He was probably murdered for his gold," says Dr. Elfred Lee, ark researcher-illustrator, whose friend tracked down the final demise of Greene. "The contents of his briefcase were stolen, which included both the gold and the six precious photographs."

Did the murderer or murderers want the gold that he supposedly had in his briefcase, or did they want his maps and photos of the ark? Was the robbery of the gold just a "bonus" for the killer's main objective?

Fighter Pilots Describe Ark

In the late 1950s, a number of American pilots based in Adana, Turkey, with the 428th Tactical Flight Squadron under the command of the NATO Military Assistance Pact, reported seeing an enormous ship on Mount Ararat, but none of them were able to take any photographs because of their close proximity to the Russian border.

One fighter pilot, Captain Gregor Schwinghammer (then a Second Lieutenant) saw the ark from his F-100 cockpit.

In 1959 we were flying fighters over Mount Ararat when we spotted what looked like a large, rectangular, barge-like structure sticking out of the side of the mountain. It was in kind of a horseshoe-like depression and it definitely appeared to be man-made. I didn't think of Noah's ark at the time because, frankly, I wasn't aware of a biblical story placing Noah's ark on Mount Ararat.

Lieutenant Colonel Ben Bowthorp, the deputy base commander at the time Captain Schwinghammer saw the ark, told author Charles Berlitz, "It was about two thirds of the way up the mountain, made of wood, and it looked like a boat or a wooden boat-shaped wall. I don't know who first said it was Noah's ark. Most of us felt it could be."[13]

Secret Photo Mission Over Ararat

In 1974 Dr. Walter Brown, a retired U.S. Air Force colonel, was summoned to the Central

Intelligence Agency headquarters in Langley, Virginia. There he was debriefed by the highest CIA officials on all he knew about Noah's ark on Mount Ararat. The CIA indicated they were making a study of the ark, but did not disclose the reason behind the study.

It's believed that the Brown CIA debriefing had something to do with a mysterious top-secret photographing of the ark by the Air Force in the same year. Al Sipple (real name being withheld to protect pilot's identity) flew on that secret Air Force mission and provides these details:

Something happened in 1974 when I was in the service. Another pilot and I were assigned a mission from the higher ups to fly a highly secret mission over Mount Ararat to photograph something that they thought might be a Soviet-made defense installation.

I had experience in aerial photography, so I was taken along on an F-4 fighter to take pictures of the object. We flew over it at a low altitude—less than 1,000 feet from the surface of the mountain while I took pictures.

The film was turned over to the Air Force and classified "Top Secret." I don't know what they did with it, but I can tell you what I saw with my own eyes. It was a dark, black foreign object about two thirds of the way up the mountain near a gorge. It was oblong and partially buried in ice, overhanging a cliff. To me, it certainly looked like a boat like object—definitely manmade. It also appeared as though it didn't belong on the mountain. It was just totally out of place.

U-2 Pilots Photographed Ark

This would not have been the only secret mission flown over Ararat for the U.S. military and the CIA. It's been reported that pictures of Noah's ark were taken by U-2 pilots before the unexpectedly sudden ending of the U-2 program when American Gary Powers was shot down by the Soviet Union.

Apache Jim Wilson of Oden, Arkansas, had a client whose son was a U-2 pilot. The father was a Bible believer, so his son had obtained from secret military files a couple of photos of the ark on Ararat. The father is now dead and his sons told Wilson they destroyed the photos on their father's death because they didn't want classified photos in their possession. However, Wilson saw the photos in 1973 and described what he saw in the pictures.

> The object looked as though it was broken into two pieces—the ends were jagged. The pieces were separated, being some distance apart and partially covered with ice and snow. The parts sticking out of the snow looked to be twenty to fifty feet long. I saw six to eight windows on the top. I don't know where it was on the mountain, but the enlarged pictures were very clear.

Also in the early 1960s, the Air Force was dropping freight for the CIA in eastern Turkey and doing aerial electronic eavesdropping on the Soviets. In preparation for this book, one of the Air Force technicians aboard the DC-3s on secret Air Force–CIA flights agreed to talk—providing we didn't mention his name.

> We flew over Ararat at a low altitude several times and I saw Noah's ark. It was near the gorge and half sunk in ice, [lying] in

a north-south direction with the lower side tilted slightly to the west. It was large and long—like a narrow barge. It had blunt ends that were kind of rounded. You could see it was made of wood; it stood out as plain as day. There was no doubt what it was in my mind.

These are just two of the accounts of dozens of pilots who say they have seen Noah's ark while flying over Mount Ararat.

Ark Sighted From Air Force One

Probably the most interesting aerial sighting of the ark during the late 1970s involved a U.S. president and a UPI White House photographer. Ronald Bennett, was a UPI White House photographer who saw Noah's ark while flying aboard Air Force One (AF One Plane 2700) with then-President Jimmy Carter.

The Bennett sighting took place on a flight that departed from Washington, D.C., going to Warsaw, Poland, on December 29, 1977, and then on to Tehran (or Teheran), Iran, on December 31, for a New Year's Eve party being hosted by the shah of Iran at his winter palace. It was en route to Tehran that Bennett and other journalists aboard Air Force One saw Noah's ark on Mount Ararat. Bennett says:

During the terms of four U.S. presidents— from Nixon through Reagan—I was the UPI photojournalist covering the White House. I always flew aboard Air Force One, reporting the activities of the president. On this particular occasion, with then-President Jimmy Carter, we were en route from Poland to Teheran to attend a New Year's Day celebration given by the shah.

During the flight, while we were flying over eastern Turkey, our attention was called to the window. It was a dramatic moment as Soviet Mig fighter jets were escorting us wing-on-wing. At the same time, someone also told us that if we looked down we would see Noah's ark. We looked and there was a mountain with snow and glaciers on it.

There, maybe halfway up the mountain, clearly visible, was a large, dark boat. It was partially covered with snow or ice. I'm convinced, based on what I saw there, that it was Noah's ark. It's my opinion that the president probably had Air Force One routed over Mount Ararat and most likely saw the ark too.

Carter has not confirmed whether he also saw the ark.

The ark of Noah has also been photographed by U.S. and foreign spy satellites—but more about that in a later chapter.

The ark has been seen by literally hundreds of people in this century alone—many just by accident. It's been seen by people from every walk of life and from many different cultures. It's been viewed by peasants and possibly even a U.S. president, and by people who were totally unaware of the biblical story.

Just think how bizarre the sight of Noah's ark must be to many people—a wooden ship, almost the size of a modern aircraft carrier, near the top of a mountain? It's almost impossible to believe—except for the people who have seen it.

Endnotes

1   Elfred Lee, George Hagopian interview, July 1990, in Easton, MD.

2   Ibid.

3   Interview with Arthur Chuchian conducted in St. Louis, MO, on June 24, 1975, by Rev. Stuart Brassie and Thomas Sass of the arkfact Research Association.

4   Tim LaHaye and John Morris, *The Ark on Ararat* (Nashville: Thomas Nelson Publishers, 1976), pp. 90-91.

5   lbid., pp. 84–85. Cited material from Violet M. Cummings, *Noah's Ark: Fact or Fable?* (San Diego: Creation-Science Research Center, 1972), pp. 143–145.

6   Dave Balsiger and Charles E. Sellier, *In Search of Noah's Ark* (Los Angeles: Sun Classic Books, 1976), pp. 108–109. Cited interview with Gladys Evans in February, 1976, El Cajon, CA.

7   Cummings, *Noah's Ark: Fact or Fable?* p. 136.

8   Ibid.

9   Charles Berlitz, *The Lost Ship of Noah* (New York: G. P. Putnam's Sons, 1987), p. 33.

10   LaHaye and Morris, *The Ark on Ararat,* p. 97.

11   Cummings, *Noah's Ark: Fact or Fable?* p. 215; and LaHaye and Morris, *The ark on Ararat,* pp. 135–137.

12   Cummings, *Noah's Ark Fact or Fable?* p. 222.

13   "Berlitz, *The Lost Ship of Noah,* p. 45.

TEN

THE NAVARRA AND OTHER
GROUND EXPEDITIONS

There was never any doubt in my mind ...
that it could only be the ark.
—French Explorer Fernand Navarra

The following is an account by Fernand Navara:

In 1937 I served in the French military forces in the Middle East. During my days off, I took long walks in the hills above Damascus, accompanied by an Armenian friend, Alim.

"I was born in 1907 on the island in Lake Van," Alim said. "As a child, I lived there happy with my mother, father, and sister, until 1920. Then my parents moved to Damascus. Before I left Armenia, I went to visit my grandfather in the town of Bayazid at the foot of Mount Ararat. The old man assured me that Noah's ark was still on the mountain. 'When I was young,' he told me, 'I once tried to reach it. But I wasn't strong enough in the high altitude and had to give up. I never found it.'

"I promised granddad that I would try, too," continued Alim. "But you are the one who should go, Navarra. Mountain climbing does not wear you out the way it does me. I am sure you would bring back a fragment of the ark."

The idea intrigued me, and I determined to give it a try. But it was 1952 before I was able to take my first expedition, which included a friend, two motion-picture cameramen, and a retired staff officer who had studied at the French Museum of Natural History.

It was the middle of August before we began our ascent, plagued by mosquitoes, 120-degree temperatures, and thunderstorms. Our goal was to reach the summit and then look at a lower elevation for the ark.

We followed our guide along a goat trail, then through névés [fields of snow at the head of a glacier], pastures, and rocky terrain. The mosquitoes disappeared at the higher elevations, but clouds with intermittent showers and hail—up to 13,450 feet— hindered our climb over and around numerous blocks of lava.

We set up camp on a plateau and were up before dawn. Clouds heavy with snow were gathering and a strong icy wind whipped our faces. The snow that had fallen during the night was wet, and our footprints filled with water that froze immediately.

By 9 A.M. we reached 15,400 feet. A half-hour later, the altimeter read 15,850 feet. Here we stopped.

It was not good at such a height to make prolonged halts. We realized this when we set forth again. Our cooled joints rebelled when we started to move. Breathing was difficult. The rarefied air, the lower pressure, made us gasp. Just lifting an arm was painful, and throwing a pickaxe forward to catch a block seemed impossible.

A sharp wind kept us awake. Above our heads, a cover of dark clouds gathered; underneath us, a sea of lighter clouds. Between the two, as between two shrouds, we were rowing in a moonlike scene, hallucinating, wondering if we were losing our minds.

The altimeter read 16,934 feet. A few steps more and the team would reach the summit of Noah's mountain. But the most important part of all was yet to be accomplished. Now I wanted to find the remains of the ark.

After returning to Bayazid for fresh supplies, we set out for this new adventure.

On August 17, at two o'clock in the afternoon, I was alone on the cap of ice, which in this place was clear of snow. I felt no fatigue, but a great anxiety. In the sky, an eagle circled, carried by the wind.

I crossed an arm of the glacier and climbed to the top of the moraine. On one side, I could see a mountain of ice lined with crevasses, on the other, sheer wall. At the bottom, I saw a dark mass.

This mass was clearly outlined, its lines straight and curved. The general shape, I thought, resembled that of a ship, at least fragments of one.

At that altitude, in that desert of ice, what could it be? The ruins of a building, church, refuge, or house never mentioned in any account, or tradition, never seen by any of these who came to this place? The wreckage of an airplane? No one ever used beams of that size to build a fuselage.

Those remains, I thought, must be what's left of the ark. Perhaps this is the flat bottom of the biblical vessel, the top structures of which must have been scattered.

The structure was really there, but out of reach, and I lacked the necessary equipment to go down to the site. All I could do was to locate it as accurately as possible and rejoin my companions, promising myself that I would come back again.

Our expedition had been a success from an alpinist's point of view, for we had scaled the fabled mountain. But as regards the discovery of the ark, it was an apparent failure. We brought back neither fragment nor photograph.

In July 1953, I made a second attempt, accompanied by a Turkish photographer. I found my way fairly easily, climbing to within a hundred yards of the site of the timbers. But boulders, perched precariously above, rolled down at the sound of my voice. Photographer Alaedin Seker had already stopped his climb, and I was on my own.

I was able to get about twenty yards closer, when I suddenly felt faint. My head felt as if it was caught in a vise and about to burst. I could not coordinate my movements, and could think of only one thing—to go back down!

My own interest kept on growing, becoming an obsession. Night and day, I recalled the dusty Turkish roads, the glaciers, the moraines of disintegrated rocks, and the big shadow of the ark. At night, I dreamed of extraordinary ways by which I could pull off a fragment of the wreck and triumphantly bring it back.

Months went by. In September 1954, I learned that the American, John Libi, had come within thirty yards of the ark, and that he planned another expedition in 1955. Then, I made up my mind: I would go a third time.

The Libi story reinforced my conviction that the glaciers had receded. What had not been possible in 1952 and 1953 might be possible in 1955. If the winter was mild, my chances of reaching the ark would be better.

To explore Mount Ararat, a forbidden military zone, I needed to obtain a pass, which the Turkish authorities were reluctant to give. They most likely would refuse if I applied before leaving France. Yet, requesting a permit in Turkey, as we had done in 1952 and 1953, posed the risk of being told every day for a month or two: "Come back tomorrow." And I had no time to lose.

My knowledge of the area enabled me to plan an itinerary along Lake Van, avoiding the main roads which are more closely watched. But even after having taken this precaution, I might meet up with a police patrol. Any foreigner in a border area is suspected of spying. However, a family on vacation would hardly arouse suspicion. That is why I decided to take my wife and three sons—Fernand, thirteen; Raphael, eleven; and Jose, nine. We set our departure for June 1955.

It was in late June the road to Mount Ararat opened up before us! Now, I decided, we would go to Karakose, fifty miles from Mount Ararat. There, my wife would stay in a hotel with Fernand and Jose, while Raphael and I attempted the ascent.

On July 5, at 7:30 A.M., we stood at the bottom of the mountain of ice which separated us from the site where the ark rested.

We attached our crampons, roped ourselves together, and began to climb. I stopped at times to film this awesome fairylike scene. In some places, the ice was a light blue; in others, it resembled transparent lace.

When a gust of icy snow fell on us, we took shelter behind a wall of ice. It was rather precarious; the temperature had suddenly dropped twenty degrees—to zero—and we were frozen.

When we set forth again after the storm, we still had to cross a maze bordered with deep crevasses. Two hours later, we had climbed the last thirty yards, reaching the top at noon.

The first problem was solved. Now for the second one. The other side ended in a sheer wall, and we could not see what lay at its foot. If I walked too close to the edge, I feared the ice would break under my feet. How could we have a look into this hollow without falling into it?

Raphael found the solution. "Take a good hold of me with the rope. I'll get close to the edge and try to see what's at the bottom."

I hesitated a moment, then agreed. I braced myself carefully and propped my back against the rock. He leaned over.

"A little bit more," he called. "More—a bit more ..."

I played out a little more rope.

"There, I can see now. Yes, the boat is there, papa. I can see it distinctly."

I almost fainted with joy, but this was no time to let Raphael go! I gave him the camera, and he took the scene in movies.

Still, the problem was to reach the basin bottom. We had to lower ourselves down a bank about as high as the one we had just climbed.

We took from our sacks tools to cut wood from the ark. Just then, the snow started falling heavily. Fortunately, a few steps away, there was a little hollow where we took refuge. It was a real ice cave, almost square, five yards deep and two yards high—a perfect shelter for a few minutes.

An hour passed, and still the snow fell thickly. To go out was impossible. We were really imprisoned. We could not keep on with the search, nor could we return to camp. At three in the afternoon, the sky was almost as dark as night. We could only hope that the whimsical temper of Mount Ararat would change, and the weather would clear up soon.

After emptying his knapsack, Raphael sat on it to avoid direct contact with the ice. Our eyes were getting accustomed to the near obscurity, and we examined our abode more closely. It was hollowed out like the inside of an igloo.

Still, we sat enclosed in a refrigerator, and I began to think about spending the night there. Even if the snow had stopped falling and the weather had cleared, we could not have returned to camp in less than two hours. The snow, hiding the crevasses, would have turned them into death traps.

At six in the evening, the curtain of snow lightened, but night had come for good. My principal concern was not to get frozen. I had heard about the sense of wellbeing one feels when freezing. I felt comfortable, and that worried me; wasn't this the first symptom of the freezing process?

About 5 A.M., Raphael went out, took a few steps in the snow, and threw some snowballs. "Come out—it's warm." His voice sounded cheerful.

I joined him. The snow lay soft and white under the clear sky. We lost no time in gathering our equipment, attaching crampons, and heading toward the crevasse in foot-deep snow.

Once on the edge of the crevasse, I lowered the equipment on a rope. Then I secured the ladder and climbed down myself, assuring Raphael I would not be long.

Passing through the corridor, I found the sloping terrace and started clearing off the snow to uncover the dark strips I had seen the day before.

Soon the strips appeared, but—this was the worst disappointment of my life. These shapes were not wood, but frozen moraine dust! It was easy to be fooled; from a distance, the mass looked like a ship's carcass. I cleared off the snow along another fifty yards. Everywhere it was the same.

At that moment Raphael's voice, distorted by the echo, came to me.

"Well, Papa, have you cut off a piece of wood?"

"No, it isn't wood, it's only moraine dust."

"Have you tried to dig in?"

In my dismay, I had not thought of it! Attacking the ice shell with my pickaxe, I could feel something hard. When I had dug a hole one and one half feet square by eight inches deep, I broke through a vaulted ceiling, and cleared off as much icy dust as possible.

There, immersed in water, I saw a black piece of wood!

My throat felt tight. I felt like crying and kneeling there to thank God. After the cruelest disappointment, the greatest joy! I checked my tears of happiness to shout to Raphael, "I've found wood!"

"Hurry up and come back—I'm cold," he responded.

I tried to pull out the whole beam, but couldn't. It must have been very long, and perhaps still attached to other parts of the ship's framework. I could only cut along the grain until I split off a piece about five feet long. Obviously, it had been hand-hewn. The wood, once out of the water, proved surprisingly heavy. Its density was remarkable after its long stay in the water, and the fibers had not distended as much as one might expect.

I took snapshots and movies, then carried my wooden prize to the foot of the ladder. I attached it to the rope and left it there, for I wanted to give Raphael the joy of hauling it up himself. At last I climbed up the ladder.

Back on the edge of the crevasse, I took movies of Raphael hoisting up this ancient piece of wreckage.

It was 7 A.M., July 6, 1955.[1]

So goes the account of how French explorer Fernand Navarra and his son found the ark in 1955.

Was Navarra's Wood Actually from the Ark?

Navarra was sure the wood was from the ark. "There was never any doubt in my mind. I had done so much research and had so many documents that proved that it could only be the ark."

He had to cut the wood into pieces to keep the weight of it across his knapsack from making him lose his balance on their descent. "I regretted having to cut up such a venerable relic, but felt better about it later on when I split it up in smaller pieces to submit to various experts."[2]

Then, in 1969, the famous French explorer agreed to join the Scientific Exploration and Archaeological Research team known as SEARCH. Navarra would prove for the first time since 1955 that he could lead an expedition back to the same glacial ice pack on Ararat and, it was hoped, recover more wood.

After retracing his way up the treacherous mountain, the SEARCH team struggled to locate wood in the same crevasses where Navarra had found it. But the crevasses were not melted as deep as they were in 1955. No wood could be found in them.

Navarra then decided to probe the bottom of a small pond adjacent to the ice pack. Since the team's probing poles would not reach to the bottom, he began to probe a small runoff stream from the pond.

At 11:15 A.M. on July 31, 1969, Navarra and the SEARCH team struck paydirt—five pieces of wood resembling planking, the longest piece nearly 17 inches long.[3]

Navarra, being the only person bringing back wood from Mount Ararat in modern times and declaring it to be from Noah's ark, created quite a stir in both scientific and religious circles. Critics also raised three significant questions: Was the wood actually from Noah's ark? What kind of wood was this that came from a totally treeless mountain? Did the wood date old enough to be from Noah's ark?

The late Dr. Richard Bliss, former Science Department head at a California graduate science institution in San Diego, examined the Navarra wood and the age-dating reports acquired by Navarra. He reported:

The Navarra wood sample is a structural beam and impregnated with bituminous pitch. It has mortise and tenon joints. And it's definitely hand-hewn and squared. These observable features square with the biblical account and pre-dynastic ship building methods.

The corroded and cracked surface indicates deterioration by freezing and thawing as well as water soaking. The wood will no longer float on water because of its gain in density. The elongated cells in the specimen most likely resulted from glacial pressure on the wood.

The heartwood of 50 centimeters [indicated in the wood] means Navarra's sample came from a tree about 5 feet in diameter with a height of about 150 feet. Also, the particular Quercus variety is a white oak and grows only in the Mediterranean region where Noah is believed to have built the ark.[4]

Although much has been learned about the Navarra wood sample, additional testing has raised some peculiar findings. The late astronaut James Irwin had a sample of the Navarra wood tested in 1985 at the University of Georgia in its Center for Applied Isotope Studies. Dr. John Noakes reported these findings back to Colonel Irwin:

A second portion of wood was submitted to pretreatment cleaning prior to dating. The dark bituminous-like coating turned out not to be just surface coating but distributed throughout the wood. This was very surprising as we have only encountered this before in dealing with pressure pretreated woods.

The bituminous-like material associated with the wood sample was very much of an intrigue to us. How a modern-age coating material could be associated with a wood sample at least 1,500 years old is a perplexing problem to explain. Still further of a mystery is how this material could be impregnated so deeply within the wood fibers without the use of present-day technology.[5]

[The answer may be earlier in this book, where Dr. Don Shockey explained that "gopherwood" was the term for a treating and sealing process rather than for a species of wood.]

How Old Was Navarra's Wood?

Just how old was the wood brought back by Navarra? In 1956—prior to the popularity of Carbon-14 testing—Navarra had four different archaeological tests conducted on the wood. His test methods determined the degree of lignite, or coal, formation, gain in wood density, cell modification, and the degree of fossilization.

The following explanation provides a better understanding of the tests used by Navarra in dating his 1955 wood sample:[6]

The degree of lignite formation is assessed to determine the present stage of conversion of wood to coal. A very thin section of the wood is mounted on a slide and examined by using a petrographic microscope that measures the angle of reflection of the X-rays off the wood.

Another method to determine degree of lignite formation is to treat the wood sample with alcohol or organic solvents to destroy the cell material, leaving only the coal or carbon. If it dissolves very little cell material, the sample is highly coalified; and if it dissolves a lot of cell material, it is only slightly coalified.

The degree of fossilization is assessed by determining the amount of water salts contained in a wood sample. This test is performed by treating the wood samples with acids or alcohols, then examining the specimen under microscope for traces of calcium carbonate or silica. The fuller the cells are with these minerals, the greater the degree of fossilization.

The gain in wood density tells us how compact the wood is and whether the wood will float or sink in water. To determine the gain in density, the sample is weighed in the air using a Metler analytical balance. Compression or contraction can cause a sample to sink. Also, a piece of wood that has undergone any degree of fossilization will show a gain in wood density.

Cell-modification tests determine the degree of cell collapse and cell-wall chemical change: Wood cells may become elongated or may combine with each other. This modification can be charted for age.

A slide of the wood sample is examined under a microscope for cell changes. The key factor in this test is the interpretation of what is seen through the microscope; that is, determining what caused the cells to change shape, to combine with other cells, or to collapse.

The Navarra tests were conducted at the National Museum of Natural History in Paris, the National Center of Scientific Research in Paris, the Forestry Institute of Research in Madrid, the Center for Forestry Research and Analysis in Paris, the Department of Anthropology & Prehistoric Studies at the University of Bordeaux, and at the Cairo Museum in Egypt.

All the tests performed by these distinguished institutions placed the age of the wood at around 5,000 years old, give or take 500 years. But what did American ark illustrator Dr. Elfred Lee discover when he had both the 1955 and 1969 Navarra wood samples dated by Dr. Willard Libby's Carbon-14 process? The results of the Carbon-14 tests conducted at the University of Pennsylvania obtained dates ranging between 1,250 and 1,700 years old. Similar results were obtained on the 1955 sample at the University of California, with the Center for Applied Isotope Studies in Athens, Georgia, setting the Carbon-14 dates at 862 and 1,557 years old—far short of the 5,000 years given by the biblical account, and a rather extreme fluctuation between tests on the same piece of wood.

Although many have assumed that Carbon-14 dating is always the final word in age dating, the method is plagued with some serious flaws, as stated in the McGraw-Hill publication, *Encyclopedia of Science and Technology*:

A measurement of the Carbon-14 content of an organic sample will provide an accurate determination of the sample's age if it is assumed that (1) the production of Carbon-14 by cosmic rays has remained essentially constant long enough to establish a steady state in the Carbon-14/Carbon-12 ratio in the atmosphere, (2) there has been a complete and rapid mixing of Carbon-14 throughout the various carbon reservoirs, (3) the carbon isotope ratio in the sample has not been altered except by Carbon-14 decay, and (4) the total amount of carbon in any reservoir has not been altered. In addition, the half-life of Carbon-14 must be known with sufficient accuracy, and it must be possible to measure natural levels of Carbon-14 to appropriate levels of accuracy and precision. Studies have shown that the primary assumptions on which the method rests have been violated both systematically and to varying degrees for particular sample types.[7]

Dr. Melvin A. Cook, former professor of metallurgy at the University of Utah and the 1968 Nitro-Nobel Gold Medal winner for his invention of slurry explosives, says Carbon-14 results indicating an extremely young age on Navarra's wood are "inaccurate because the assumptions on which Carbon-14 is based are not applicable to this piece of wood." He explains,

Living mollusks are sometimes found deficient in Carbon-14 to such an extent as to appear to have been dead as long as 3,000 years. This is due to carbonate-ion exchange in salt water in contact with old calcite and dolomite deposits. These mollusks are in an environment of old carbonates, and during their life cycle, they assimilate those carbonates that have no radiocarbon in them, rather than [being] in steady state with the atmosphere.

The reverse (dates that are too low) will also happen by involving carbonate-ion exchange in freshwater lakes, which become high in alkalinity and thus tend to absorb carbon dioxide from the air to form new calcites and dolomites—which explains the discrepancies in dating of bristlecone pine.

The bristlecone pine is always dated by tree-ring dates as older—as much as 2,000 or 3,000 years older—than the date obtained by radiocarbon dating. It's due to the contamination of the bristlecone pine with newer material … diffusion of new carbon into the cells of the bristlecone pine.

We can't really use the Carbon-14 dating method to date the Navarra wood. It can't be used unless we know exactly the conditions that the wood has been under during its existence.

That's a volcanic mountain, and the wood has been taken from water subjected to the gasses and the solutions from volcanism. It also shows fossilization, which means there has been an ion exchange within the wood.

All it would take for this test to be completely off would be to have excess carbonate-ion exchange, and the carbonate-ion in this case would be from freshwater deposits where the wood was found submerged. Carbon-14 dating would make it appear younger than it really is. And I think this is probably the explanation of the fact that the dating on this wood is only 1,300 to 1,700 years.

Also, just contamination of the wood sample alone would make it impossible to really date it by the radiocarbon method. The sample has undergone a lot of different environments that would promote the possibility of ion exchange.[8]

Dr. Libby, the inventor of the Carbon-14 procedure, says the Navarra wood cannot be accurately dated using his method. According to Dr. Elfred Lee, "A group of our men talked to Dr. Libby, and he stated that his method is unreliable, especially during certain time periods. This wood brought back from this mountain, he said, has been soaking in meltwater at a very high altitude and bombarded by carbon of a more recent vintage, and the date would be thrown off. He said we should try another dating method."

With Carbon-14 not being a suitable method for dating Navarra's wood, the four tests performed by Navarra and widely used by archaeologists remains the best evidence that the wood is 5,000 years old and probably from Noah's ark. We'll leave the final conclusion up to you.

Mystery in a Box

Another mid-twentieth-century ark account nearly as dramatic as the Navarra wood recovery on Ararat unfolded in the life of David Duckworth, a former Smithsonian employee. This unsolved mystery started in 1968, as Duckworth relates the story in his own words:

I was working at the Smithsonian Institution in Washington, D.C. in 1968 as a volunteer in the vertebrate paleontology section. When I went to get some acetone to clean up a specimen I was working on one day, I noticed my immediate supervisor with a visiting scientist named Dr. Robert Geist. They were both bending over a magnification tripod viewer looking at some photographs. I wandered over there and just asked what they were doing. They told me to take a look myself, so I did.

What I saw was a composition picture of like four photographs put together to make one whole picture. In the picture, there was an oblong object resembling a ship that wasn't under the ice and snow but was semi-covered with it. This object appeared to be broken in the middle with several feet separating the two halves, and one end definitely appeared to be smashed.

I asked my supervisor some more questions and he said the photos had been taken on a mountain named Ararat in Turkey and that the photos had been taken from a balloon suspended by cables with an airborne camera package. You could see the shadow of the balloon on some of the pictures.

He said the film that I was looking at was a composite of infrared photographs. So I looked at it and browsed through the pile of pictures next to it. Some of them were just taken from different angles at different altitudes and some showed people on the ground looking at the ship.

There were also some pieces of fossilized wood. It was heavy wood, like stone, but it was wood. You could see where it had been chopped and drilled—where it had been worked and the remains of wooden-like pegs in it.

Then, the next day, a friend of mine and I took a shortcut to the cafeteria. You can either cut through the underground loading docks or through the visitors' center, and we cut through the loading docks. Anyhow, there were some boxes and crates on the loading dock. My friend mentioned that they were from Ararat and they were going into his section, which was physical anthropology.

One of these was an oblong, sacrophagus-like box that I was told later was made out of alabaster. It had a sliding panel on one end that slid down into grooves and locked with stone pins on the side. It was on a pallet, and it was lashed down.

Later on, this same fellow told me that they found the body of some fairly important personage from the Bible in it covered with resin. They said they had reason to believe—and I don't know why—but reason to believe it was Noah.

Now, there never was a gag order from the Smithsonian, indicating, "Don't discuss this with anyone under penalty of law." It was just an understood thing at the time that, "What you see here, what you say here, what you hear here, you leave here," and that was the understood thing.

So I didn't tell anyone about it at the time except my parents. I told them because they had some interest in Noah's ark after a pilot friend of theirs said he saw something in the ice over there during the Korean War years.

Frankly, I didn't think much more about it until I came out to Farmington, New Mexico, where a fellow named Eryl Cummings called me about his book, *Noah's Ark: Fact or Fable?* I said, "Fable? Well, that's a strange title for the book since I'd seen it [the ark] four years before."

That's really about all I remember.

In Cummings's second book, *Has Anybody Really Seen Noah's Ark?*, Duckworth comments, "It [the ark] *does* exist, and it *did* happen. If the government itself is covering it up–the people will be mad, or if the museum is covering it up–then the people and the government will be mad."

Duckworth said he later again questioned his friend about who was really in the coffin box. "Noah," was the friend's response. "They found him in the wreck, preserved, and a tablet with him."

When Duckworth asked Dr. Geist about the "man in the box," he was told it was "none of his concern. If the religious fanatics ever found out who was in that box it would really cause trouble." Duckworth, being nineteen at the time, asked no further questions.

Elfred Lee, the respected explorer and Archaeological illustrator who interviewed eyewitnesses Ed Davis and George Hagopian for his ark sketches, had a first-hand opportunity to interview David Duckworth. He shares his assessment of Duckworth's credibility in a recent 2007 interview:

By the time I had heard of David Duckworth I had already been on the mountain where we had found wood on the Parrot Glacier. It was one night after our ark-a-thon in Farmington, New Mexico in 1986; I was staying at the home of Eryl and Violet Cummings. They said, "David Duckworth lives right near here. Would you like to meet him?" I had heard about him, so I say "Fantastic." He came over, sat down at the table and we talked about the Ed Davis experience and all of the drawings that I had put together from Davis' personal experience. Violet said, "Show David your drawings." I said, "No, wait." And I handed a piece of blank paper to David Duckworth. I said, "I want you to show me what you saw at the Smithsonian from all of those photos from the expedition that came in from Mt. Ararat." And he drew on a paper what he had seen, and then I showed him what I had drawn. And they were both the same! There's no way David could have manufactured this. The coincidence is just too great.

Now there is some controversy about David Duckworth. Some people do not believe what he said, but I do. I found him to be an honest, humble person, had no agenda, and didn't want fame, fortune or anything. All he wanted was to help us find the ark of Noah.

Some skeptics do not believe that Dr. Robert Geist even existed, that he was a figment of the imagination of David Duckworth. I beg to differ. I have met Dr. Geist personally in San Diego in his home at least once ... fine man, but I don't agree with him. I believe he has a vested interest in not really supporting publicly the story of David Duckworth. But I do know that Dr. Geist exists, I've met him. But I personally believe the story of David Duckworth, as a very fine and honest witness to what he saw coming into the Smithsonian.

Whether there was an expedition with undisclosed findings at the Smithsonian, or a preserved and coffined body aboard the ark, the possibility that it could be Noah is speculative, but intriguing. For one thing, although disputed by other claims of burial locations, there is an allegedly authentic tomb of Noah in the Lebanon Mountains near the ancient city of Damascus. And unless there was a clay or stone tablet found within the alabaster coffin, (as already indicated), that was able to specifically tie the identity to Noah, then the preserved body, if it exists, could as readily be presumed to be that of another ancient personage found in or near the ark.

An even greater conjecture comes from hints found in an apocryphal book–that the preserved body might be that of Adam. Classified as "Apocrypha," these books were not accepted as part of the Old Testament canon, (Jewish or Christian), and were considered primarily for their theological rather than historical value. In addition, they were not considered as genuine prophetic records. (In other words, rather than advance predictions, they were written years after the events.)

Keeping this in mind, in the apocryphal book of Second Adam, (2 Adam 8:9-18; 2 Adam 21: 7-11), Adam not only prophesied about the future Flood, but directed that his body be taken aboard the ark, and that after the Flood his remains be laid in the "middle of the earth," the location where "God shall come thence and save all our kindred." These apocryphal passages suggest that Adam's body could have been taken aboard the ark for preservation from the Flood, but the question of their historical value remains.

The previous discussion on pre-Flood longevity, in Chapter 6, introduced the prospect of what we may be able to discover from DNA studies if biological material from the ark of Noah's time were available. The possibility that the freezing ice through the centuries might have preserved some form of biological material for our analyses, awaits discovery.

Cover Up?

To check out Duckworth's story, Cummings's daughter, Phyllis Watson, contacted S. Dillon Ripley, secretary of the Smithsonian Institution, who had this to say in a letter dated December 12, 1976:

> I want to assure you that the Smithsonian Institution has never been involved in a search for the remains of Noah's ark in any manner. None of our staff has participated in such an expedition, nor have we solely or jointly been involved in supporting or financing such a project, nor have any artifacts recovered from such an enterprise been seen by our staff.

Still further emphasizing Secretary Ripley's firm insistence that "the Smithsonian Institution has never been involved in such a search" was an almost identical statement by Dr. Henry Setzer, curator of mammals at the Smithsonian. He said that he had even gone so far as to question "the Research Committee of the National Geographic Society" on the subject and had, in turn, been assured that "the Society has never mounted an expedition to search for the ark, nor had they even contributed toward such an expedition."

In spite of these official denials, it was later learned through Ralph Crawford, president and founder of the SEARCH organization, that the National Geographic Society had, after all, contributed to "an expedition to search for the ark;" that, in fact, in 1969, they had "contributed" to an expedition they themselves had not "mounted" by supplying "thousands upon thousands of dollars' worth of free (and the finest type of) film" to the Navarra-SEARCH expedition to Ararat to search for the ark!

Rene Noorbergen, a hard-hitting veteran newsman, war correspondent, and author of *The Ark File*, at that time was the public relations director of

SEARCH, and he confirmed Crawford's statement. "The National Geographic," he said, "had reserved first rights to the photographs in the event of a possible discovery."

Also, Noorbergen related that he met a "man at a legal meeting who mentioned to him that he had been involved in an expedition to Mount Ararat in 1968, at which time they had, among other activities, shot infrared photographs of an object they believed to be Noah's ark. 'Can't talk about it any further though,' the spokesman apologized. 'I've already said too much.'"

"During the course of Noorbergen's personal sleuthing (as reported to Cummings in April 1972), he had learned of a man who had 'sat in' on some kind of meeting in 1970 in which these two institutions (Smithsonian Institution and National Geographic Society) allegedly discussed a 'joint expedition' and its discovery—and decided *not to reveal it!*"[9]

Additional corroborating information came from two chaplains in the U.S. Air Force in Turkey and three other officers. Sometime during autumn of 1964, a group reportedly "identifying themselves as members of a National Geographic expedition returning from Mount Ararat" stopped at the U.S. Air Force base in Trabzon, Turkey. This significant event is carefully recounted in a letter dated November 12, 1973, from Chaplain (Lt. Col.) Roger H. Pearson, in response to a letter from Dr. Charles Willis, an ark expeditioner from Fresno, California. Excerpts from Chaplain Pearson's letter are as follows:

> Sometime in late 1964, a group of people stopped at Trabzon [Turkey] and asked for overnight lodging. They drove a Land Rover and I believe there were four individuals

in the group. I could be mistaken, but my recollection is that one of them was a woman, the wife of one of the men in the party. They identified themselves as members of a National Geographic expedition from Mount Ararat.

When I asked him almost jokingly if they had discovered the ark, he said, "Chaplain, you wouldn't believe what we found!" He went on to explain that he couldn't talk about what they had found, but gave the impression that they had made a discovery of tremendous significance. I was impressed so much that for about a year I kept checking issues of *National Geographic* for information. When I saw nothing about it, I assumed they hadn't discovered anything, and stopped looking for an article about it.[10]

In another letter noted by Cummings from Chaplain (Capt.) Clair Shaffer to Dr. Willis dated September 4, 1973, he writes:

A team had stopped and spent the night at our base [Samsun, Turkey]. This was a National Geographic expedition which had been to eastern Turkey and to Mount Ararat and was on their way home. When asked the expected question, "Did you find the ark?" they answered, "We cannot answer that question now, but may we say that we have made the greatest discovery in the history of man!"

Three other substantiating letters were received by Dr. Willis, reinforcing statements of both Pearson and Shaffer that a group identifying themselves as affiliated with the National Geographic Society did stop at both Trabzon and Samsun en route from Mount Ararat, where they admittedly had been interested in a search for the ark.[11]

So, the plot thickens. Who is lying about the National Geographic Society and Smithsonian involvement in an ark expedition—and why?

We do know from the last chapter that military man Lester Walton was informed in 1946 by the "higher ups" that the National Geographic Society was going to undertake an expedition to investigate the boatlike object photographed by them while testing the Fairchild bombsite camera. According to the testimonies of eyewitnesses, the National Geographic Society conducted expeditions to Mount Ararat in 1958, 1964, and 1968, and the Smithsonian was involved in the analysis of the Ararat findings.

Navarra's wood finds in the 1950s spawned a surge of interest and a renewed search for the ark in the 1960s and 1970s.

Amazing Discoveries

In recent years, it's been determined rather conclusively that the ark is not located in the Cehennem Dere of Mount Ararat but that the canyon cited by Hewitt and Bishop, near the Ahora Gorge on the north side of Ararat, is in the target area. However, the late Ray Anderson, former ark expeditioner and aerospace engineer and photo analyst, made some amazing discoveries while studying Dr. Hewitt's slides of Mount Ararat taken over several expeditions:

I found one slide that had a very interesting object in it. When I looked at this particular object under the microscope, it appeared to me that it could be the north end of the long piece located in the horseshoe above the Ahora Gorge at about 15,500 feet.

Now the ark is broken in two—we have conclusive evidence on that from many witnesses. During an earthquake, the south end of the ark, about one hundred feet or more of it, slid down the slope and lodged in a crevasse at about the 14,500-foot elevation.

So I examined this lower, shorter object which is only shown in one picture of the many hundreds that I have examined, and under the microscope, I could quite clearly see what appeared to be a section of the roof of what we call the superstructure.

I then examined the slides of the upper north end. You can see a rectangular shape of the north end with decks faintly exposed.

I took this slide and used a millimeter micrometer to determine the size of the object. I measured the width and height and came up with seventy-five feet wide by roughly forty-five feet high. Using the same procedure, I found this long piece to be approximately 350 feet in length. Now eyewitnesses have estimated the shorter piece to be approximately one hundred feet in length.

You have 350 feet in the long, north-end piece and one hundred feet in the short, south-end piece, equaling 450 feet in total length.

Coincidentally, if you go to the Bible and check the measurements that Noah was instructed to use, he should have built the ark to be 450 feet long, seventy-five feet wide, and forty-five feet high—that's precisely what we got from the measurements of these two pieces.

Interest in finding the ark had reached an almost feverish pitch in the 1970s, and groups from around the world with and without official permission tackled Mount Ararat in search of the ark. The expeditions ranged from groups of highly qualified scientists to bizarre religious fanatics clumsily combing the mountain for clues. But little was achieved on any of the expeditions.

The 1980s ushered in a decade of Ararat exploration that saw many high-tech innovations brought into the ark search and a considerable amount of public attention when astronaut James B. Irwin joined the search. Colonel Irwin led his first expedition to Ararat in 1982, which ended in a nearly fatal fall to be discussed in a later chapter.

Most Significant Expeditions

Although during any given summer, about a half dozen groups attempt Ararat expeditions, the following is a recap of the most significant expeditions and their achievements:

• 1986—Colonel Irwin returned to Ararat on his fifth expedition, having obtained a much sought after permit to fly a light plane over the mountain. His expedition ended suddenly when his team was put under house arrest for allegedly spying. However, before the arrest, a Dutch National Television crew headed by Jan Van den Bosch went with Irwin and shot a documentary while Irwin's team shot twenty-two rolls of film of the Ahora Gorge area in their search for the ark. One of these Dutch TV photos will be discussed later as possibly a photo of Noah's ark.

• 1987—Colonel Irwin of the High Flight team and Dr. John Morris, geologist and Author of *Noah's Ark and the Ararat Adventure*, of the Project Ararat team, hoped to fly both a helicopter and a fixed-wing aircraft in and around the Ahora Gorge. Again, the Dutch Television crew was along to document the event. However, the Turkish governor of Dogubayazit forbade them to fly over the gorge and suggested that the team publicly promote an alternative location fifteen miles away called the Durupinar site as the "real" location of Noah's ark—more about this so-called Durupinar-Wyatt-Fasold site in a later chapter.

Both Irwin and Morris eventually received permission to fly around the southwestern side of the mountain, but not over the massive Ahora Gorge, which is larger than the Grand Canyon.

• 1988—This was a year of unprecedented and significant activity by new ark expeditioners. Colonel Irwin did not participate this year, but San Diego commodities trader Larry Williams and former police officer Bob Cornuke represented him, making four flights to photograph obscure areas of the Ahora Gorge.

Dr. Charles Willis, a prison physician-psychiatrist from Fresno, California, whose most famous client is Charles Manson, fielded the sixteen-member Snow Tiger Team to study the ice cap of the eastern plateau of Mount Ararat. This was Willis's fourth Ararat expedition, having used ice drills and chain saws in 1983 and 1986 to cut large trenches in the plateau ice cap, where he had believed the ark to be hidden. With the use of ice-penetrating radar, the Snow Tiger Team was able to determine that the eastern plateau was merely an 80-foot-deep ice-filled saddle depression—without Noah's ark encased in it! They came to the conclusion that the ark would have landed at a lower elevation.

• 1989—Scott Van Dyke of the Houston-based Mount Ararat Research Foundation succeeded in hiring a professional Turkish mapping company to completely map the Mount Ararat area with a high-resolution camera. Four types of film were used, including infrared. In all, 910 overlapping photos (in stereo pairs) were made, covering approximately fifty square miles and all of the mountain above 10,000 feet. Van Dyke says the resolution is so good that sheep on the mountain are clearly visible. They say it will take years to analyze all the photos—with anticipation of maybe finding a clue of the ark under the icy surface.

Dr. Don Shockey's expedition from Albuquerque, New Mexico, returned again to follow up on an ark location pinpointed by satellite on the north side of Ararat above the Ahora Gorge in the Abich II glacier area. It was on this trip that Shockey's guide obtained a clear photo of a snow-covered object with sharply marked symmetrical lines at the site where military satellite imagery indicates there is a wooden structure.

• 1990—The Don Shockey expedition spent well into the six figures using a Russian-made M18 helicopter, which was flown in from Istanbul complete with six crew members and space for up to twenty-four passengers. Numerous flights were made to get aerial video footage and still photographs of the site pinpointed by satellite and photographed from 300 yards away by Dr. Arslan in 1989. An attempt to reach the site by ground failed when the three members of the ground team came down with severe mountain sickness.

- 1991—The Kurdish insurgency and the Desert Storm operations kept ark searchers home with the exception of explorer Chuck Aaron, who in July made ten quick flights around the mountain in a fixed-wing aircraft. No new discoveries were made.

- 1992—Heavy fighting between Turkish soldiers trying to put down Kurdish insurgents and terrorists kept ark climbers and aerial observers away from Mount Ararat. The Ararat slopes were the site of several deadly confrontations between Turkish soldiers and terrorists.

- 1993—A nine-member Search for Truth Expedition headed by airline pilot Dick Bright and assisted by Explorer/ark Expeditioner and current President of SEARCH Foundation (Scientific Exploratory Archaeological Research), John McIntosh, made another attempt to search Mount Ararat. They were granted a permit in Ankara to fly a helicopter around Ararat. However, their permit was later canceled by the regional governor of Kars, headquartered fifty miles from Mount Ararat. The governor cited a secret military operation that was taking place on Mount Ararat as the reason for canceling their permit.

Within a couple of hours, after the expeditioners departed their hotel, PKK guerrillas attacked the hotel and killed two Turkish policemen that were involved in security measures for the hotel and the expeditioners.

Also in 1993, twenty-three year-old New Zealander Paul Thomsen, who was looking for the ark on Ararat, was captured by the PKK and held for five weeks. The PKK was also holding other Ararat climbers—two Italians, two Germans, and two Swiss —as hostages in an attempt to persuade the Turkish military not to bomb their strongholds for fear of killing the foreign hostages.

• 1994—No ark-Ararat expeditions were attempted due to the heavy shelling and bombing on Ararat slopes.

During the period of 1988 to 2004, American expedition teams were denied official research access to Mt. Ararat. Americans were again allowed on the mountain in 2005.

Secret, small groups continued to do research on Ararat every summer. These groups include Italian, Swiss, Hong Kong Chinese, American, New Zealand and Australian.

• 2004—The Hong Kong Chinese claimed to have made a discovery on the Southwest face of Mt. Ararat, which appears to be a volcanic cave, but their claim was that it was a hole in the side of a petrified, fossilized ark. The claim was never substantiated.

• 2007—A team of scientists and ark researchers from Hong Kong and Turkey reported that they had discovered a "wood structure" more than three-quarters of the way up Mount Ararat.

The expedition, sponsored by Noah's Ark Ministries International, was investigating a report that Ahmet Ertugrul, a Kurdish mountaineer, had found a substance that was suspected to be wood. Subsequent laboratory tests of the collected sample, performed by the Applied Geoscience Centre of the Department of Earth Sciences at the University of Hong Kong, confirmed that the object consisted of petrified wood.

Encouraged by the documented corroboration of a wooden substance, the expedition was organized. After several false starts due to bad weather, the exploration team succeeded in finding the cave discovered by Ertugrul two years earlier. Inside, they reportedly encountered a massive wall of petrified wood measuring 11.5 meters (nearly 38 feet) in width by 2.6 meters (about 8 ½ feet) in height.

Since Mount Ararat is a dormant volcano, it was not surprising that the wall was covered in volcanic ash. Careful removal of the ash revealed that the base structure had a white wooden texture, leading to speculation that the search for the ark may finally be reaching fruition.

Noah's Ark Ministries International was cautious about declaring the finding definitively as part of the ark, but expressed the possibility that it may eventually prove to be the first tangible proof of the ark's existence and survival.

One fact that has excited researchers is that, according to Professor Oktay Belli of the University of Istanbul, it is unlikely that indigenous wood would be found at that elevation—4,000 meters (over 13,000 feet.) Belli points out that the harsh climate of the higher altitudes of the mountain has not sustained significant vegetation since 2000 BC.

According to one report, many Mount Ararat natives believed Noah's ark broke into three parts during an 1840 earthquake, and as a result the parts of the ark became scattered.

Any conjecture that the wood may have come from an ancient settlement has been dismissed by Dr. Ozlem Cevik of Trakya University, who points out that the inhospitable environment of the mountain has historically discouraged human habitation.

Also noteworthy is that no sign of a manmade settlement has ever been uncovered in the area. A team of archaeologists has explained that houses in that part of the world were commonly made of mud brick, with very little use of timber. They added that no ceramic artifacts have ever been found on the slopes of Mt. Ararat higher than 3000 meters—9800 feet.

One skeptic has argued that Noah and his family would have disassembled the ark in order to build shelter in the timber-less post-Flood earth. That theory, however, conflicts with the Biblical account where Noah is described as living in a tent. *"When he drank some of its wine, he became drunk and lay uncovered inside his tent."* (Genesis 9:21)

Given the size and weight of the artifact, it seems unlikely that anyone would carry it up the mountain. Scientists have speculated that, while ice may have pushed the structure down from the top of the mountain, there was no credible scenario where volcanic activity could somehow push the wood up from below.

While it appears likely that the wood structure found on Mt. Ararat is part of an archaic man-made artifact, further research is required before it can be declared part of Noah's ark.

Both the hopeful and the doubtful await confirmation. But even the speculation spurs plans for continuing expeditions and research.

This treacherous and deadly mountain called Ararat, and Agri Dagh, "the painful mountain," has exacted a heavy price from almost every expedition that has set out to search for its hidden treasures. In the next chapter, we'll tell you the stories of three modern-day ark eyewitnesses who survived terrorist attacks and near-death experiences with the mountain itself to get a look at Noah's ark.

Endnotes

1   Fernand Navarra with Dave Balsiger, *Noah's Ark: I Touched It* (Plainfield, NJ: Logos International, 1974), pp. xiii, xiv, 31–39, 40–63. Reprinted by special permission.

2   Dave Balsiger and Charles E. Sellier, *In Search of Noah's Ark* (Los Angeles: Sun Classic' Books, 1976), p. 176. Cited interview with Fernand Navarra by Robert Guenette of Sun Classic Pictures, February 9, 1976.

3   Balsiger and Sellier, *In Search of Noah's Ark*, p. 177.

4   Ibid., pp. 180, 185. Cited interview with Richard Bliss, March 1976.

5   Letter to James Irwin of the High Flight Foundation from John Noakes of the Center for Applied Isotope Studies, University of Georgia, Athens, GA, February 12, 1985.

6   Balsiger and Sellier, *In Search of Noah's Ark*, pp. 182–183.

7   R. E. Taylor and R. A. Muller, "Radiocarbon Dating," *Encyclopedia of Science and Technology* (New York: McGraw-Hill, 1987), p. 124.

8   Melvin A. Cook interviews, Salt Lake City, UT, February, 1976, and June 16,1992. The 1976 interview cited in Balsiger and Sellier, *In Search of Noah's Ark*, pp. 188-189.

9   Violet Cummings, *Has Anybody Really Seen Noah's Ark?* (San Diego: Creation-Life Publishers, 1982), pp. 201-203.

10 Ibid., pp. 206–207.

11 Tim LaHaye and John Morris, *The Ark on Ararat* (Nashville, TN: Thomas Nelson Publishers, 1976), p. 147.

ELEVEN

THREE MODERN-DAY ARK EYEWITNESSES

The only thing worse than being blind is having sight but no vision.

—Helen Keller

MODERN EYEWITNESSES OF THE ARK on Mount Ararat cover the human spectrum—young, old, rich, poor, and everyone from firm believers in God, to apathetic agnostics, to atheists. Their stories have many similarities even though their sightings may have been many years apart.

The eyewitnesses have never met, but many of their experiences are so similar that at times you feel that they must have seen the ark together. For some, locating the ark was a true paradox: what they found was not necessarily what they were looking for.

Maybe it's ironic, or perhaps fitting, that those in recent years who have seen the ark are the most average of people—humble individuals who have no exalted point to prove, no book to sell, no doctrine to foist upon the world—just simple people, like many in the Bible.

We chose three modern-day eyewitness accounts to examine in this chapter. All are men—two were soldiers stationed in the Middle East who just happened to become friends with some of the local people. The third man accidentally stumbled on the ark after a near-fatal fall on the slopes of the mountain. All three cases are unique because all of the eyewitnesses are still alive and all three had close ground encounters with the ark. In each fascinating account, the explorer's experience of seeing the ark was very moving, intriguing, and highly personal.

Ed Davis

In 1943 a young serviceman named Ed Davis was stationed in Northern Iran and became friends with a young Kurdish man. In his military position, Davis did some significant favors for his friend, and in return, the man's Kurdish family adopted Davis and gave him their most valuable "possession"—the rare experience of a visit to Noah's ark.

When they asked Davis if he would like to see the ark, he wasn't even aware that the ark was on Mount Ararat or what agreeing to see it would entail. It was the adventure of his life, and in his late eighties Davis still spoke about seeing the ark with awe and wonder. Here is the story in his words:

I was Master Sergeant in charge of construction in the Army Engineer's Special Service Group in northern Iran in 1943. I was hauling rock from a rock quarry. I had a crew of men building, and this boy was driving for me, and one day when the atmosphere was just right, we saw Mount Ararat.

He smiled and said, "Yes, that's where my folks live—where the ark is, and my dad knows where the ark is."

I said, "Boy, I sure would like to see that." He said that when his dad came to visit, he would bring him over and introduce him.

One day, his dad came to see him. He brought him over to introduce him to us. His name was Abas.

At that particular time [of his visit], you couldn't see the ark. He said that when it got where you could see it, he would come back and get me.

A couple of months later, Abas came back. He said, "We can see it, let's go."

There were six or eight of us who went up, and I've never been so cold or so wet or so tired in all my life. If I'd known it was going to be that bad, I don't know that I would've even gone.

As we went up the mountain, we stopped at Jacob's Well. It was a tradition there before traveling on to make a prayer on a small stone and place it on a large pile of other stones that folks before you had lain down.

We left Jacob's Well and traveled a distance, and we crossed from the main trail to what they call the back door. There are easier routes, but this was the shortest. The climb up went on for a few days and we were all roped together. They gave us two staffs and a long rope with a noose tied in it. Also, we were all roped together. I was fifth in the line.

Two Kurds walked behind me at all times. I guess they were like my bodyguards. Abas had lost two sons before they tied themselves together, and he was real careful now.

I could tell this group of climbers had made this trip many times. They knew exactly where they were going even in the dark. I felt more than a little strange being the only American on the trail.

I didn't have any really special equipment other than my G.I. issue. The Kurds and Abas had good equipment. They acquired it from raids or it was found on the mountains. All of the climbers were given an aviator-type goggle by Abas. We wore them most of the time.

Abas gave me a piece of shiny metal that we could signal with. I never once had a chance to use mine. There wasn't enough sun for it to work. Abas also gave each of us a hand-operated flashlight we used in the caves. They never yelled or used loud voices at any time. I was given a small whistle to blow if I needed to get their attention.

We slept in four to six caves on the way up and ate out of one big stew pot. I don't know what was in it, meat, vegetables, and stuff. There were pictographs on the cave walls and Abas knew what they meant.

They kept everybody roped together for safety and even when nature calls, you didn't go off alone. There were always two or three together no matter where you went.

There wasn't any good weather on the trip. It was all bad—wind and rain. You could be walking along and go around a corner and bam—it would be completely different weather. We walked in snow, ice, and rain with rocks rolling all around us. That's one of the reasons why we had to use staffs. There were so many dangers. We all got skinned up falling, slipping, and sliding.

They said they never bring a body down when someone gets killed on the mountain. You can see bones and stuff sticking out of the ice. They leave people that die up there. I don't know why.

Abas was the caretaker of the ark just like his father and grandfather were before him, all the way clear back to Noah. Abas told me he hated anyone that went up exploring and searching for the ark. He said everyone wants to get a piece, chop it up, and carry it off. They made sure that the ark wasn't molested.

When the ark broke in two, they found some lamps and some pots and tools, hammers, wedges, and other things. The pots were about 2 1/2-feet high. The workmanship on the tools, the metal, was quite primitive. And Abas will tell you right quick that they didn't take those things out of the ark. They came out when the ark broke up.

Abas and his family have found what looked like the pantry or kitchen area in the front of the ark. Here they have found everything from beans, honeycombs, nuts and shells, to dried fish bones. I saw some of the things in Abas' home—pottery vessels that were about seven or eight inches long, kind of like the shape of a boat and opened in the middle. They said I could look but I couldn't touch them. They told me they even found some honey in one of the jars and sent it to Switzerland to be tested and it was pure honey.

Abas described a small opening or door that opened to the outside of the ark. I don't recall his telling me where it was, but he called it by the same name they use for toilet hole. He said the people on the ark used it to dump and remove the animal waste into the water.

I wish I had asked him more about it, but I didn't at the time.

Abas described to me the method Noah used to water the animals. They used animal stomachs sewn together. Abas says there are many, many of these on board the ark. They are still there. I didn't see any of these because they have never carried them down off the mountain.

When we walked from Doomsday Point to the spot where we viewed the ark, there was whispered talking. There was a reverence and awe. You could feel like someone was watching your every step, every minute.

The first time I saw the ark, I was on a ledge above it, and it looked like a big blue rock. As we got closer, I saw it wasn't a rock at all. It was the end of the ark that had broken off. It was big and had different levels to it. Different decks, I guess you'd say. The only word I can think of to describe what it was like to see the ark is "awesome." We saw the ark in snow but both pieces were in water too.

Looking at it, you felt like someone was standing behind you or watching you. You didn't dare move hardly. I don't know how to explain the feeling except to say there was a mighty power present.

I was very disappointed that I couldn't walk and explore inside this biblical treasure. I had an overwhelming desire to touch it, something I can't explain.

I have a picture of the village and camp that Abas gave me. I wish he had given me a photo of the ark, but he never showed me one or offered one even though he told me where two are located. I wish I could go back and visit just one more time.

They say there's a curse on the ark. Some people got stuck in it one time and they died right away with a lung infection or fungus in their lungs. Anyway, that's what they told me.

Seeing the ark made a big difference in my life. I joined the church. I never thought I'd see the ark when I was growing up. I never thought about it at all. When I did see it though, it made me begin to think about the future, and I sure don't want to die and go to hell.

The people with me were very proud of the ark. You could see it in their faces. It was a big honor.

There's no question in my mind what I saw on that mountain. I saw Noah's ark. I won't argue with nobody if they disagree, but I know I saw Noah's ark.

Dr. Paul Meier, co-founder of the Minirth-Meier New Life Clinics and author of numerous books on human behavior, reports on his analysis of Ed Davis's testimony:

I analyzed several hours of Ed Davis's audio and video interviews. I found him to be a very normal, well-rounded personality. He was concerned about others and he did not brag about himself. Usually when people are confabulating or making up stories they talk excessively about themselves. He didn't do that. He was very reverent. He respected the Muslim faith of his Kurdish friends and guides. He's also intelligent.

He knew that his friend Abas had lost two sons in previous treks, which is something only someone who has actually been on the mountain would know specifically—that many people have died from all the dangerous crevasses and rock slides and glaciers in that area.

He based his descriptions of the ark totally on his own experience rather than on what he had read in the Bible. At times it seemed like the interviewer was planting words or remembrances in his mind and Ed would say, "No, that's not how I saw it." He gave very clear details.

A grateful father of two Kurdish soldiers took him up there in gratitude for something he had done that he didn't brag about—in fact, he won't even talk about it. Ed knew the customs of the Kurdish people very well. He knew the towns. He knew about Jacob's Well and the buildings around it in the Ahora Gorge. He knew about the religious practices of the Kurds. He knew about the glaciers, the rockslides, the walking sticks, and being tied together on the climb, which is very necessary. He talked about the ledge, the cliff wall where the ark was sticking out of the ice.

The reason why this is important is that I have personal knowledge of some secret U.S. Government reconnaissance photos that the government has taken of the ark above the Ahora Gorge on the northeast corner of Mount Ararat. This is exactly where Ed describes that he went, and his description of what he saw is what I have personally known to be true from those reconnaissance photos.

I firmly believe that Ed Davis is telling the truth.

Dr. Meier wasn't the only expert who carefully examined the Ed Davis account. Larry Williams of San Diego, an internationally known commodity-trading advisor, author of two books, and publisher of the *Treasure Hunter Confidential* newsletter, also decided to check out Davis's story:

I publish a newsletter for treasure hunters and archaeologists throughout the world. I've investigated archaeological sites throughout North America and Europe and when I heard the Ed Davis story, I was fascinated, but I've found that you simply can't trust a lot of stories. So, I decided to personally investigate not only the story, but also Ed Davis himself.

To investigate most stories, archaeologists try to investigate the secondary data, but I think you can use high technology to investigate stories, and there's no better way to do this than with a polygraph or lie detector test.

I asked Ed Davis if he would be willing to take a polygraph test to find out if he was telling the truth or not. To do that, I went to Albuquerque, New Mexico, and found the most competent polygraph expert not only in Albuquerque, but also in the entire state of New Mexico, with fifteen years of experience on the New York City police force.

This man was aware of the Ed Davis story and he frankly didn't believe it. He told me, "Larry, I'll talk to this guy for an hour or so and I'll literally eat him up and spit him out of here. Give me an hour and I guarantee I'll break this man."

After two intense hours with Ed, the polygraph expert came out and said, "Larry, I can't tell you what mountain Ed was on or where the boat is, or even whether or not it was Noah's ark, but I can tell you this— he's not lying and he did see a boat on that mountain."

Ed Behling

In 1973 another American soldier became an unlikely eyewitness of the ark. Ed Behling was in the Air Force assigned to a defense installation at Diaberker, about 100 miles southwest of Mount Ararat. He became friends with a Turkish soldier, a Kurdish man named Mustafa. Behling is a family therapist in Colorado.

This is his own story from articles and two appearances on the "Prophecy in the News" television show:

His name was Mustafa and he was in the army at that time, and I probably never would have met him. However, I wanted to see how the people operated, who the people were, what feelings they had since this was a rare experience for me to be in a foreign country.

I met Mustafa and I told him how privileged he was to live in a country where all these artifacts of the Bible existed. He said he had a great-uncle who had been to the ark, and he'd ask him to take us to see it. Mustafa had never seen it before either.

It was the last weekend of May when we took off to go see the ark. It was exciting. I asked him if I could take a camera. He said, "I would prefer you not take a camera because Ararat is close to the Russian border, and you're American, I'm Turkish, and it's not going to look good. It would mean trouble if we were stopped by soldiers." I didn't have a very good camera at that time anyway, so that was fine with me.

We got our gear together and took off to see his uncle. Three to four hours later, we were at this old tent, this old camp of three shepherds plus Mustafa's great-uncle. He was like the master shepherd. He looked like he had been dead three years and just didn't know enough to drop over.

His uncle seemed rather reluctant to take us up there. Locals are very suspicious of outsiders. "I convinced him you're okay," Mustafa said. Mustafa made it possible for me to go up there and if it wasn't for him, they wouldn't have taken me up there at all.

I had the impression that most of the shepherds around the mountain know where the ark is located—at least the older ones do anyway.

It's amazing so many groups have gone to the mountain in recent years looking for the ark of Noah, and none of them have been able to find it. All of their guides seem to be taking them off into another part of the mountain. Some of the younger men might want to take them to it. But the older ones won't allow it and you better believe that those young men won't go against the ruling of the older men. Nobody goes near that ark without the elders' permission.

We got up early. Basically, my night was spent battling the cold; it was chilly that night. I had no idea how high we were because I really wasn't paying attention to specifics.

[Mustafa's great-uncle] took us right up the side of the mountain. We were going around rocks and above cliffs and below cliffs—it was like a trail. There was a lot of snow on the mountain at this time, but it wasn't that uncomfortable. It was hard snow; it wasn't very slippery. He was like a guide; he knew exactly where he was going.

I was incredibly worn out. I half hoped they'd decide to go back down. Suddenly, Mustafa turned to me and motioned.

I looked over the side of a ledge and fifty feet below us was a gigantic black structure. It was so large and awesome I was overwhelmed—completely amazed by its size.

The snow had melted quite a bit off the ark so there wasn't very much on top, and there was nothing on the sides.

The front end of the ark is broken off, with a gaping hole. It is hard to give you a mental picture of just how wide and how tall it is. I saw no doors at all, nothing that looked manufactured. I have no idea how something that large came to rest that high on Mount Ararat. I can't explain it. It was kind of eerie, especially when I looked down over the cliff and saw the ark. I didn't have any direct sun any time I was there, so the gaping hole that I saw was dark. The whole ark was black.

I don't know how long it was; but looking into the mouth where it was broken off on the edge of the shelf, I saw it was basically square. The walls were straight up and down on each side and the base, which I couldn't see because of the angle, looked fairly flat.

From where I was standing, you could tell the roof sloped very gradually, maybe a 10-degree slope, 15-degree slope to it. Then it had a wide spot in the center of it that went the length of it. Now this was maybe ten feet wide—like a catwalk. It was about ten to fifteen inches high with a roof over it. I guess they walked on that or maybe it was used for windows, but that's the way it looked to me.

Basically, it was a big box that was very long. I could only see 150 to 200 feet of it and then it tapered off into the snow. I noticed from where I was standing that the front was chopped off or broken off or something. How much of the front was broken off, I had no idea, but it was broken off. The ark was forty to fifty feet high and about sixty feet wide. The walls must have been eighteen inches thick.

After we looked at it a little bit, Mustafa's uncle motioned for us to come on. We couldn't jump down on it because it was too far to jump. We didn't have any ropes or anything. I kind of wanted to walk on it, but I never got a chance. But we walked down below it. There was about a 100-foot cliff—the shelf that it was on, a big table.

When I was up there, the clouds were low on the mountain. We could see at the maximum maybe 100 or 200 yards because of the fog around us. It was so dark and overcast late in the afternoon that we left the next morning.

We spent the night underneath it [the ledge] and went back down the mountain.

Dr. Meier analyzed Ed Behling's account, and this is what he had to say:

Ed Behling is a therapist in Colorado who, at the age of twenty-three, was in the Air Force in the Middle East and made friends with a Kurdish soldier by the name of Mustafa. Like Ed Davis, Ed Behling was befriended by local people, which led to his encounter with the ark. They had been friends for about five months when Mustafa took Ed to see his great-uncle who was a sage on Mount Ararat.

The people have great respect for these sages, and you don't do anything without their permission. I was there and I talked to the Kurdish people and analyzed what their personalities were like. Ed describes their customs and behavior very accurately.

Ed's trip to the ark after he went to where the sage was, which was about halfway up the mountain, took one day. Now, the things that make his testimony credible are that Ed had good eye contact with his interviewer. He did not seem dramatic. He did not brag about himself. He seemed to have a well-rounded personality.

In general, usually therapists are quite honest so I tended to believe his story about the ark and especially since his description fits the U.S. reconnaissance photos of the ark above the Ahora Gorge. The only thing that made me question Ed's story slightly is that he said he made it up [the mountain] in one day.

Now, with good weather, that can be done, and I know that my own team made it down in half a day because we were being chased down by Kurds with guns! Usually, a team will take several days to get up and several days to get back down. But it made me question him somewhat—although he did say that it was one day from the location of the sage.

Another questionable aspect is that Ed didn't know where he was. He thought it was on the northwest corner [of Mount Ararat], and we know that it is more towards the northeast corner.

His description of the customs, the climate, and the ark being near the Ahora Gorge is in agreement with what we know from secret U.S. reconnaissance photos. His description was accurate enough. His personality traits and body language were satisfactory to me.... I believe Ed was telling the truth.

Ahmet Ali Arslan

Fate played a big part in the eyewitness account of Dr. Ahmet Ali Arslan. Dr. Arslan is the Washington Bureau Chief for Turkiye, a major Turkish newspaper, and a former broadcaster for the Voice of America radio network. He is also a senior researcher for the International Science and Technology Institute in Washington, D.C. But he knows Mount Ararat like few other people.

My family is from Aralik at the base of Mount Ararat toward the Soviet side. That's where I grew up. I've gone up on the mountain maybe fifty times—including expeditions with Fernand Navarra, Don Shockey, and the late James Irwin.

I was accompanying a scientific group [the 1989 Shockey expedition] in exploring a site on the Ahora Gorge side of the mountain, a very treacherous place, covered with crevasses.

Because I was a Turkish national, only I was allowed to investigate certain sections of the mountain. I was sent off to check out a particular site identified by satellite as one that could possibly be the location of the ark.

As I was nearing that site, the ice and snow I was standing on began to give away. I ended up sliding a couple hundred feet down the slope. Fortunately for me, I did not fall into a crevasse.

When I regained my footing, I noticed about 100 to 200 feet away what appeared to be a building-type structure—definitely made of wood. It was something that shouldn't be there—just a few thousand feet below the summit.

It almost looked like kind of a captain's cabin. You could look in and see beams and things like that. I immediately took my camera and shot three pictures—one wide-angle, one regular, and one close-up. In the pictures, you can see flat beams and such, in what appears to definitely be a man-made structure. My belief is that what I saw and what is in the photographs I took was without question Noah's ark.

The photographs taken by Dr. Arslan while on Don Shockey's 1989 FIBER Foundation expedition will be discussed further in the next chapter along with 1990 photographs taken of the same site from helicopter and by U.S. and foreign satellites.

So far we have recounted a number of twentieth-century civilian and military aerial sightings of Noah's ark. We've also presented the modern eyewitness accounts of Ed Davis, Ed Behling, and Ahmet Ali Arslan. But is there one single factor that all these accounts have in common that would help us solve the Noah's ark mystery? Is there something to help us actually find the ark for the world to see?

The answer is yes. The one single factor common to all these accounts is the ark's location on Mount Ararat. All reliable sightings have been on the north side of Mount Ararat above the Ahora Gorge. Furthermore, satellite imagery also helps pinpoint the area where the ark could be located. The question is, why do the military and CIA keep these photos top secret?

TWELVE

COMPELLING
NEW EVIDENCE

*The lot of critics is to be remembered by
what they failed to understand.*
—George Moore (1852-1933)

CONTINUING NEW EVIDENCE places Noah's
ark on Mt. Ararat in Eastern Turkey. The following
is a report by Dr. Paul Meier, former Medical Officer
on a 1985 Noah Ark-Ararat Expedition:

In 1985, I decided to become the team
physician for an expedition to Mount Ararat
to search for Noah's ark with Jim Irwin and
his team. But before I put my life in danger I
wanted to be sure that the ark was up there
so I talked to a close friend who is a former
reconnaissance pilot for the Strategic Air
Command in Omaha, Nebraska. He told me
that right now at the Strategic Air Command
there are secret documents—including
photographs—confirming the existence and
location of Noah's ark. In fact, the photographs
are even labeled "Noah's Ark" and match the
description of the ark given in the Bible. The
ark is buried in ice but, periodically, the glacier

melts enough for the ark to be revealed and it looks like it's sticking out of a lake.

The classified secret reconnaissance photos were seen by my close friend and by several close friends of Jim Irwin. They clearly reveal that the ark is above the Ahora Gorge on the northeast corner of Mount Ararat facing Russia at, or a little below, the 16,000-foot level.

When Jim Irwin went to the moon he took a Turkish flag with him—partially so that he could ask the Turkish authorities for a favor when he got back. He asked them if he could go and find Noah's ark on Mount Ararat and they gave him permission.

Jim went to Turkey faithfully year after year. Each year, however, the authorities would give him permission, but when he went near the site on the northeast corner of Mount Ararat, the Turkish soldiers would turn him away and say, "No, you can't go any further." They used different excuses each time, such as, "This, is too close to the Russian border and it's going to create tension with the Russians."

Tragically, he never actually got to the site on the northeast corner of Ararat, and two weeks before he died, in 1991, Jim told a very close friend of mine that a general and several other senior officials in the United States Air Force had given him up-to-date information on the reconnaissance photos confirming the ark's location. So, Jim knew for a fact where the ark is and desperately wanted to go there but was always prevented from doing so.

The search for Noah's ark is rapidly reaching a climax as eyewitnesses, aerial observers, military reconnaissance pilots, and spy satellites have pinpointed a specific location above the Ahora Gorge.

Our mystery would be solved if the U.S. Central Intelligence Agency and Defense Department would release all of their reconnaissance photos and spy satellite imagery of Mount Ararat. The obvious question is why won't they?

Government Cover-Up

Seeking answers to these questions, we hired the late Dr. Ray Smith, a top government relations consultant who had been highly successful in the past in obtaining cooperation from the Defense Department, CIA, and Secret Service for television and film producers. For example, he received nothing short of miraculous cooperation from these agencies for movies such as *Patriot Games, Top Gun, The Hunt for Red October, A Few Good Men, For the Boys, In the Line of Fire,* and many others.

Dr. Smith was supplied with seven solidly documented military/CIA-related sightings of the ark on Mount Ararat. Our request to government agencies—communicated through Dr. Smith and our own personal visits to high-level Defense Department officials—was threefold: (1) to gain access to their Mount Ararat/Noah's Ark files and search for evidence establishing the fact that the ark is still on Ararat, (2) to obtain permission to use old and current photographs or footage of the ark taken by military or intelligence personnel, and (3) to gain use of Defense/CIA high-resolution aerial/satellite photos and radar-penetrating imagery of the ark on Ararat.

To Dr. Smith's surprise, the Pentagon, Defense Department, various service branches of the military, and the CIA quickly denied even having any information or photos of the ark in their files. Typical was the Department of the Air Force response stating, "We checked with the offices most likely to have the information you requested and none was found." Talk about being stonewalled by a government agency! The CIA response probably reflects it the best:

I have made an informal inquiry of the appropriate offices in the Agency about the availability of such materials. They have informed me that there are no current records bearing directly on the subject of your inquiry. Further, they advise that any systematic review of general Agency records for such material would be a daunting task requiring many man-years of work and in all likelihood unproductive.

Peter Earnest
Chief, Media Relations

This was a most interesting denial by the CIA since we provided the agency with the exact Mount Ararat coordinates to pinpoint the satellite photos and radar-penetrating imagery. In addition, we gave them the name of a former high-level CIA official who was conducting a formal investigation of Noah's ark on Mount Ararat.

Retired USAF fighter pilot Captain Gregor Schwinghammer made this observation:

The government probably does have surveillance photos and satellite imagery of Noah's ark on Mount Ararat. They won't declassify or release these pictures, however, because it would disclose just how good our spy technology is and the fact that we have spied on a friendly nation—Turkey—while monitoring military activities in the former Soviet Union.

It seems puzzling that any agency of the U.S. government that happened to have information concerning the existence of Noah's ark would withhold even a sanitized version of that information.

Intelligence Investigation

Since the U.S. government would not cooperate with our search for Noah's ark on Mount Ararat and provide copies of clear photos of the ark that we believe with certainty exist, we decided to conduct our own intelligence investigation. We acquired the satellite imagery of Mount Ararat from two foreign governments, France and the former Soviet Union. We also uncovered some significant military and CIA ark accounts—some of which were related to us on the condition that we not use the informants' real names.

One incident still classified as "top secret" that occurred around 1980 involved U.S. military personnel from various branches who made an on-the-ground survey of the ark on Mount Ararat. Their original objective was to check out reports of objects foreign to the terrain that might have military implications.

Members of this secret military expedition boarded the vessel, measured it, and took both black-and-white photographs and color slides. They did not remove any major pieces or harm the ship. Their report on the location and description of the ark is consistent with sightings described by Ed

Davis and George Hagopian as well as the Shockey FIBER expedition sightings and photographs.

The following CIA-related account is quoted directly from a confidential Air Force colonel's memorandum dated August 4, 1978. The document relates to a couple who were stationed at Maxwell Air Force base but working for the CIA:

Betty Plum [all names in this account have been changed], who worked in the CIA headquarters for Mr. Roland Rhodes from 1973 to 1974, saw a file in her office labeled Noah's ark, Eyes Only—Mr. Roland Rhodes. Betty described Mr. Rhodes, chairman of the Visual Requirements Committee, as a Christian gentleman who probably would not be inclined to suppress any concrete evidence of Noah's ark. However, both Betty and her husband, Leonard Plum (the CIA advisor to the Air War College), said that it wouldn't do any good to contact Mr. Rhodes about this file.

Betty at first thought the title "Noah's Ark" was a code name and stated that to Mr. Rhodes. He told her that it was not a code name and that she was not to open the file. Betty said that she "was a good girl and never looked in that file; it was the only file that I couldn't see." Betty has no reason to believe that the file contained a photo, but it could have. Furthermore, there is no reason to believe that the file contained direct evidence of the ark. It could have contained only sensitive information that was illegally obtained from another government.

Years later, on March 11, 1993, a CIA agent, after making a speech to 400 people at the Palm Beach Round Table, answered a question from the audience regarding the 1973 CIA expeditions to Mt. Ararat. The CIA agent was the late Dr. George A. Carver, considered as "America's foremost authority on intelligence and security." He served as Deputy of national Intelligence to former Directors of the CIA George Bush and William Colby and as the senior intelligence officer in NATO. A Yale graduate, with a doctorate from Oxford University, he is the only person in the history of the CIA to twice be awarded the Distinguished Intelligence Medal. His speech that evening, in the context of National Security Requirements for the 1990s was entitled, "We Cannot Afford Surprises—We Must Be Prepared To Prevent Them." Following is an excerpt from the transcribed question and answer session that followed the speech:

Porcher L. Taylor, III: "Dr. Carver, I'm a West Point graduate, and while I was a cadet at the Academy in 1973, there was a strong rumor going around, that one of our military spy satellites was flying down the Russian/Turkish corridor taking photographs of a Soviet missile site and apparently, accidentally took photographs on the Turkish side, of a large wooden object which appeared to be a ship stuck in a glacier about 14,000 feet on Mount Ararat. Strong rumor going around the Academy at that time was that apparently our intelligence people at the CIA might have classified photographs of Noah's ark, and I was wondering if you had any comments about that."

[Laughter from Audience]

Dr. Carver: "Well, I don't recall CIA working on Noah's ark, but I do remember that at the time there were some pictures taken, and there were clear indications that there was something up on Mount Ararat which was rather strange. There were various archaeological expeditions that were mounted. The Turkish government was not too thrilled about supporting them, because it was getting into an area that was politically dicey from the Turks' point of view. But that is but one of the indications, you know, I haven't been up there, I don't think anyone has, but it certainly was eyebrow lifting and it was certainly another indication that despite its splendor as a work of poetry, the Pentateuch, the first five books of the Bible, might not be all that bad as history also."

The same Air Force colonel who wrote the confidential 1978 memorandum documenting "Betty Plum" and "Roland Rhodes," wrote an earlier confidential memorandum, dated June 24, 1975, that cites an Air Force account of U-2 photos of the ark:

About five or six years ago, Lieutenant Colonel Walter Hunter saw two photos of what allegedly was Noah's ark. These photos (either 5 by 7 inches or 8 by 11 inches) were in the possession of "two guys" who were standing in Base Operations at Beale Air Force Base in California.

An object in the photos, which looked like a boat, was enclosed in a glacier on an unrecognizable mountain. Lt. Col. Hunter did not know who took the photos or where they were taken but felt that they probably were taken from a U-2 aircraft. He thought they may have been taken in November but did not say why. He also recalled that the photos were oblique shots.

In further describing the photo(s), he said, "It looked like a glacier with an object buried in it—obviously underneath ice. The photo had red caliper marks on it, which were used in determining its length of 450 feet. The first photo was a pan shot of a large glacier."

Lt. Col. Hunter described this experience in Base Operations as a "passing thing," lasting no more than ten minutes while he filed his flight plan.

After reviewing these two memos, we concluded that both the U.S. Air Force and the CIA had more than a passive interest in Noah's ark, despite their official denials and "know nothing" policy expressed to the public.

An even more interesting CIA-related report comes from retired USAF Colonel Walter T. Brown of Phoenix, Arizona. In 1974, he was summoned to CIA headquarters in Virginia and debriefed about Noah's ark by the special assistant to CIA Director William Colby. They wanted to know everything Colonel Brown could possibly tell them about Noah's ark. No piece of information was considered trivial. Colonel Brown suspects that as a result of the meeting, a later top-secret photography mission to Mount Ararat was conducted by the U.S. Air Force. Al Shappell, a military reconnaissance photographer (whose account was given in an earlier chapter), participated in the mission.

The next break in exposing military/CIA involvement in the reconnaissance of Noah's ark came in
1988 when inventor-satellite analyst George Stephen
met Dr. Don Shockey of the FIBER Foundation
expedition group. Stephen was developing top-
secret high-tech equipment for a government
contractor that would aid the military and the CIA
in enhancing satellite imagery as well as improve the
interpretation of imagery from radar-penetration
satellites.

Although Stephen said he could not show Dr.
Shockey the imagery or the processing equipment,
he did tell him that the military satellite imagery
revealed a large, wooden, rectangular structure under the Ararat snow and ice. It was at an elevation of
about 15,800 feet with an additional large portion of
the structure at about the 14,900-foot level. According to the satellite data, the location was above the
Ahora Gorge and not only matched the eyewitness
sightings but was, in fact, where Dr. Ahmet Ali
Arslan (1989) and the Shockey FIBER Foundation
expedition had photographed the structure from
helicopters in 1990.

Stephen did not go public with the information
until the television show "Unsolved Mysteries"
featured an investigative report on Noah's ark in
1992. On the program, Stephen confirmed what he
knew but refused to be identified, allow his face to
be shown, demonstrate the processing equipment,
or show the imagery. Frankly, many thought the
reason for the secrecy was that Stephen had no
evidence for his claims. When asked to do the same
interview for the television special related to this
book, Stephen first agreed and then declined, telling
us that his employers had forbidden him to proceed
with the interview.

It was later learned from other sources, and confirmed by Stephen, that he had been severely reprimanded for doing the "Unsolved Mysteries" interview. His use of the military/CIA satellite imagery and the secret, high-tech equipment he was developing had not been authorized.

From several other sources we were able to confirm and learn more about the secret satellite imagery that Stephen was using and the capability of the processing-enhancing equipment. Both the Russians and the United States have microwave radar-penetrating satellites. However, these satellites do not penetrate very far below the surface—as will be discussed later when we examine the use of the Russian ALMAZ, radar-penetrating satellite imagery in the search for Noah's ark.

From what experts were willing to say off the record, Stephen had apparently made a significant breakthrough. His processing equipment could identify structures buried up to 600 feet under water, ice, or snow. The ark was sixty feet under the ice when he discovered it. In 1990, when Shockey's expedition flew over the site, the ark was twenty-eight feet under the ice, with a portion partially exposed. The upper piece of the ark is reportedly 200 feet long.

Military and scientific analysts can determine the atomic elements composing an object using a combination of satellite infrared and radar imagery high-tech processing equipment. They can conclude whether it is organic or inorganic and whether or not it is a man-made object. The technicians involved performed a spectrographic atomic analysis where each element gives off a different level of energy. The analysts were able to determine quite easily that the structure under the ice on Ararat is made of wood.

Since the U.S. government would not cooperate in providing photographic, infrared, or radar-penetrating satellite imagery, we approached the French SPOT Corporation to obtain photographic imagery and we approached the Russians for radar-penetrating imagery as well as their spy satellite photos.

We already knew that the Russian imagery was very good from a 1984 interview with Dr. Bulent Atalay in the *Washington Post*. Dr. Atalay, the son of a Turkish general who served as a military attache to Washington, relates this story regarding the Russian surveillance of astronaut James Irwin:

> Turkish officers and their Russian counterparts have protocol meetings at the border to talk about the weather and small things. In this instance, they told the Russians that the American astronaut was going on the mountain for an expedition. There was nothing more to it. Nothing clandestine. The Russian officers laughed and they produced a photograph they had taken from a satellite and said, "There he is." They had identified him up there. So from time to time on the mountain, I'd look up and wave to the satellites.

In our search for the exact location of the ark, we turned first to the Russian ALMAZ Radar Remote Sensing Satellite. Launched in 1987, the Russians claim, "No other remote sensing satellite can offer around-the-clock, year-round coverage of the earth's surface—regardless of cloud cover or illumination conditions—with continuous, high-quality, high-resolution imagery."

This sounded exactly like what was needed to pinpoint the ark under the glacial ice of Ararat—

particularly when Bill Wirin, the ALMAZ Radar Applications Director, told us that ALMAZ, orbiting at 300 kilometers above the earth, "will reveal something that's forty-five feet in size. ALMAZ does this by differentiating between ice and snow and the geological features of the mountain. It can reveal sharp edges, which might indicate the location of Noah's ark. An expert analyst viewing these images can detect unusual surfaces or structures beneath the ice and snow which give a hint that an object is there."

Since this was the best satellite spy radar imagery commercially available from any government, we gave the Russians the Mount Ararat summit coordinates and requested that the imagery be shot in September of 1992—generally the month of greatest ice meltback on Ararat. As often happens, however, something was confused in the English-to-Russian translation, and the Russians shot the wrong coordinates, completely missing Mount Ararat. "No problem," they said, and resubmitted the order to direct the satellite to shoot the correct coordinates.

Just when we were expecting to receive our ALMAZ imagery, the following message arrived from Moscow:

I am sorry to inform you that ALMAZ 1 deorbited on October 17, 1992, at 07:28 Moscow time. It is difficult to predict when a successor radar satellite will be launched by the Russians. They did not capture Mount Ararat. I am very sorry this order was never completed.

We, too, became the victims of the "missing photos syndrome" due to an ironic twist of fate—or are the old legends true that God and the angels protect the ark from outsiders?

Spy Photos

Next, the Russians offered us their best declassified spy photographs from their DD-5 Digital Satellite, which takes pictures from 280 kilometers above the earth. This was the first time any government had offered black-and-white photographs with the ability to capture images down to two meters in resolution.

"That's an object six feet in size," said Wirin, the Russians' representative, whose office is located in Palm Springs, California. "The imagery is even better than this resolution. However, they 'dumbed' it up to two meters from what we were told was the ability to read license plates."

As a selling point for these spy photos, they showed us photographs taken of the U.S. Pentagon in which the type of cars could be identified in the parking lot, and employee picnic tables were noted in the inner quad area. We did not pursue this imagery of Ararat due to the expensive cost.

U.S. radar spy satellites can detect objects down to basketball-size from 1,000 kilometers. Photographic satellites operated by the United States are so good that David Hafemeister, a physicist at California Polytechnic University said, "We sometimes read the other guy's mail before he does." During the Iranian hostage crisis in 1980, [satellite] photos were of such high quality that specialists claimed they could identify individual Ayatollahs by the shape of their beards.[1]

Satellite Imagery

We finally turned to French SPOT satellite imagery to definitively locate and measure the size of Noah's ark on Mount Ararat.

"The SPOT satellites orbit at an altitude of over 500 hundred miles and acquire the most detailed imagery that's available commercially in the world," said the SPOT Applications director, Clark Nelson, who probably was not aware of the Russians coming on the market with their DD-5 2-meter resolution imagery.

We acquire both black-and-white and color imagery from every particular point on the earth at about 10:30 in the morning local time. The black-and-white has a 10-meter ground resolution—about half the size of a tennis court. The multi-spectral imagery has 20-meter resolution and includes infrared bands, which are used for vegetation, productivity studies, and other geographic information. The imagery can be used to explore Mount Ararat and could possibly even find Noah's ark.

SPOT imagery has been used for a wide variety of applications. Some of the more exotic applications include overlay databases with the ability, for example, to pick out all of the hamburger fast-food or pizza restaurants in a large city. You could make your dining selections by satellite.

"SPOT satellite data was used quite a bit during the Phoenicia for a variety of things—particularly for flight briefings and target objectives before they flew," SPOT applications technician Sheila Pelczarski explained. "Also, SPOT was used to monitor the Kuwaiti oil fires set by Saddam Hussein. You could actually see the flames from the oil wells from over 500 miles above the earth. Military analysts monitored bombing damage successes against such targets as small bridge spans in the Gulf War."

The SPOT imagery containing the Mount Ararat data was retrieved in September of 1989, the same year Dr. Arslan clicked his photo of the ark after his near-fatal fall and the same year the Shockey FIBER Foundation took still photos of the location from a helicopter. We then took the SPOT imagery to Mike Holman, a physicist, computer scientist, and satellite imagery analyst, to determine if the ark seen by the eyewitnesses could be confirmed by satellite. He reported:

I put the SPOT Ararat imagery on computer, where I could detect objects down to thirty-two feet in size. I examined an "S"-shaped area above Ahora Gorge where photographs taken from a helicopter show a rectangular object extending out of the snow on a rocky ledge. Military satellite information says there is a wooden object at this location.

This "S"-shaped crevasse is about 1,500 feet long and ninety feet wide. In the middle of this crevasse, I saw a defined object approximately eighty feet wide with ninety feet of the length extending out of the snow over a rocky ledge.

It should be noted that the SPOT satellite image and the helicopter photo show the object aligned in the same direction over the ledge; they are the same size in terms of width to length and they show that it is definitely not just a part of the surrounding terrain.

I'm not here to tell you this is Noah's ark or a broken portion of it. But, in my opinion, both the satellite imagery and the helicopter photo enhancement confirm that this object is not part of the natural terrain. According to military satellite information, it is an organic, fibrous object made of wood.

Helicopter Photographs

Exactly what did the 1989 and 1990 Shockey-Baugh expeditions see and photograph from their helicopter? Carl Baugh, author, archaeological excavator, and museum curator, explains their aerial discovery:

In late August of 1990, our team did eleven separate helicopter expeditions around Mount Ararat. We were especially interested in the northeast slope facing Russia. As we flew at approximately 15,000 feet, and approximately 150 feet from the surface of the glacier, I personally saw a huge beam of laminated wood protruding out of the ice and snow.

The beam was variant in color and it had an indenture near the top with extensions at the top and the bottom. It was approximately four feet thick, and about twelve feet of it extended out of the ice and snow.

This was in the Abich Glacier area on the northeast face of Mount Ararat. The geographic location of this wood sighting matches precisely the area of our advance satellite information.

Our advanced satellite information identified this specific Abich Glacier area as the primary artifact location. Then, 800 to 1,200 feet below the primary location were secondary fragments of the same object under the ice and snow. It was in this 800-foot-square area that I saw the beam of laminated wood.

Our advance satellite information identified spectrographic lines of a wooden object under sixty feet of ice and snow, and at the time we flew there, it was under twenty-eight feet of ice and snow.

The satellite information identified a crevice, a cliff that extended, and a wooden object under the ice and snow extending in a north and south direction.

This structure we photographed appears to have a barge-like shape to the end, a deck, a superstructure in the middle, and it continues back into the ice-bank.

It is of special interest to note that there appears to be a platform with an incline leading up to the deck of whatever this vessel might be. Eyewitness accounts in previous decades identified that configuration at the end of this barge-like vessel as a series of steps extending to a platform, all built into the vessel itself. This matches the specific identification in our photograph. It is our opinion that we have located portions of the ark of Noah.

We also took the Shockey-Baugh helicopter photograph to Mike Holman for computer enhancement and analysis to determine if Carl Baugh's conclusions were valid. Was it Noah's ark? Holman says:

As I enhanced the computer image of this object it became apparent that the object was rectangular in shape. And that the object extends over a ledge. I could clearly see the outline of the object with even an icicle hanging over what appears to be a catwalk area. It's not my job or expertise to confirm that it's Noah's ark, but in my opinion, this is clearly a man-made object.

Conclusive Proof

To summarize the findings so far: When enhanced by computer and compared to SPOT satellite data, the Shockey-Baugh helicopter photo gives strong proof that a large wooden ship is located near the Abich Glacier above Ahora Gorge—exactly where eyewitnesses have placed it. In other words, space technology has scientifically confirmed the existence and location of Noah's ark on Mount Ararat.

Furthermore, it's known that the ark is no longer intact but has broken into two to four pieces. The first piece has been identified by ark expeditioner and photo analyst Ray Anderson as being locked in the ice high up in the fishhook area of the eastern plateau of the Ararat summit. Neither SPOT nor military satellite data were able to confirm this Anderson sighting.

The Shockey-Baugh FIBER expeditions placed two pieces of the ark above the Ahora Gorge. The highest portion is at 15,800 feet while the lower portion is at 14,900 feet. In addition, some artifacts appear to be scattered between the two sites. Both SPOT and military satellite data confirm these sites.

Some experts believe an additional portion of the ark is located below the Shockey-Baugh site on the treacherous upper edge of the Ahora Gorge. They say the broken portion of the ark protrudes from the glacier ice and is clearly visible when the weather permits. It was at this location that the late astronaut James Irwin and Dutch National Television crew took an amazing photograph.

Jan van den Bosch, a freelance producer for Dutch National Television, describes what they saw that day in 1986:

We were in a plane with Jim Irwin flying around the Ararat mountain on an afternoon at the end of August. Our excitement was really great when we noticed that the snowcap had melted more than ever before.

Nearly at the end of the trip, we saw an object high up in the Ahora Gorge that looked like the ark of Noah. In fact, it was a boat-shaped object, and so we went for a closer look. We did see an object sticking out of the snowcap.

Our cameraman took all the pictures he could, but our time of flying was running out. We had to go back to our base. Some of us were really convinced this could well be the ark of Noah. It was as big as a soccer field, and part of it was sticking out of the mountain. So, on that very last expedition on that afternoon we think we saw Noah's ark.

When the pictures were developed and Jim Irwin studied them, he said, "I want to be sure that this is really the ark of Noah and for that reason I want to do a ground expedition and do a better survey of the object." That never happened because we weren't able to get permission from the Turkish authorities.

Colonel Irwin didn't want to announce any startling discovery until he could mount a successful ground expedition to film at the site. Unfortunately, Irwin died of a heart attack in 1991 before he could return to Mount Ararat.

His quest to explore space and his incredible accomplishments in that frontier will be remembered for many generations to come. Maybe Irwin's personal, spiritual quest to find Noah's ark has been fulfilled as well. Dutch National Television included the historic photo taken during the flight in a 1987 documentary on Noah's ark. Unfortunately, however, the vital SPOT satellite imagery that could possibly confirm or reject the Irwin photo and sighting was not available for those years.

The photograph has created some controversy among Irwin family members, including Irwin's widow, who says she had never seen the photograph before it appeared on television. We learned that because of Irwin's top-secret security clearance, he often had special knowledge about the ark from secret military files, and had even seen photographs of the ark taken during U.S. reconnaissance operations.

Although some of his expedition associates and family members may not have seen the photograph described, there was an unusual confirmation regarding the photograph in October of 1994.

According to Murray Fisher—a close friend of Col. Irwin's as well as his publicist during a national tour to promote his book—Irwin and his mother visited the Fishers in Orlando, Florida, in 1989 or 1990. During the visit, Col. Irwin showed them a photograph that he believed was of Noah's ark.

"It was the exact same photo or one extremely similar to it," says Fisher. However, Mrs. Fisher recalls that Irwin said the photograph came from government files.

Could it possibly be that the controversial photograph was actually from U.S. government files? Is it possible that the story of Dutch National Television taking it on one of Irwin's expeditions was a cover for Dutch TV releasing it in their news documentary—a show that was never intended for viewing outside of Holland? The real answers surrounding the source of the photograph may never be known.

Advancement of Satellite Technology

Satellite technology has been very useful in the search for Noah's ark since the 1990s when we had lower resolution satellites and higher resolution declassified military photos. But since 2000, the turn of the century, we've been able to obtain high resolution, multi-spectral satellite imagery according to Tom Pickett, a Military Imagery Analyst who provides ongoing remote sensing support to ark researchers. In a 2007 interview he explains the current use and potential of advanced satellite imagery in the search for the ark:

> The multi-spectral imagery allows us to do spectral analysis on the material, which allows for recognition of material using specialized software; and this is very important in the search for Noah's ark and resolving anomalies on the mountain. Satellite imagery has provided us with a number of anomalies on Mt. Ararat. There are probably about half a dozen up there that are more noted than others are, but what needs to be done is to narrow these anomalies down to what they really are.

> Using current satellite technology we can look at the surface of Mt. Ararat, we can convert the imagery into 3D, and visit any location on the mountain instantaneously and analyze it. Future satellites will enable us to look beneath the surface of Mt. Ararat and analyze subsurface features beneath the icecap.

I've been able to take modern tools and apply this imagery to 3D analysis in multi-spectral. Future work would be to put the imagery into layers that would provide 3D surface analysis as well as 3D subsurface analysis.

Of course, what we're dealing with now is surface, and what is needed is to look below the surface. Our choices are—we could wait for a melt-back to occur where more surface feature is exposed, or we could wait for new satellite technology to be launched in the near future that would enable us to look beneath the surface of Mt. Ararat.

It's quite possible that the ark will first be discovered through satellite imagery, which would then serve as a map locater for expeditioners to go up the mountain and find the location. Since the ark may be buried indefinitely deep beneath the ice, out of view and non-accessible to explorers, its existence could be confirmed through subsurface imagery, as the technology advances and becomes available.

In the meantime, advanced satellite imagery is an aid in the planning of expeditions by eliminating anomalies of the mountain that can be explained by natural means, (such as rock formations). This prevents explorers from needless searching in wrong locations based on these false anomalies.

Most Recent Search for Noah's ark

Government red tape, terrorist attacks and political unrest have shut off virtually all access to the mountain for two decades. What's more, no government, it seems, wants to squarely face the issue of what the discovery of Noah's ark could mean to the world.

However, during the 1990s up until the present time, numerous Noah's ark expeditions by American teams and other groups from throughout Europe, Korea, and other countries have been conducted. They have all attempted to go to specific sites on Mt. Ararat to check out anomalies on photographs and satellite images that may be Noah's ark.

There are still many anomaly sites that need to be checked out, but one of the more promising sites is the result of a picture revealing a beam of wood in the Parrot Glacier ice taken in 2002. There is a close up video clip of it that shows it sticking out of an ice mound, out of reach, in the Parrot glacier that has been shared with ark researchers by an Italian expedition team. Efforts to retrieve it in 2003 failed. It had moved and disappeared. It was searched for again in the summer of 2004 but not found.

Claudio Schranz climbed to the Parrot Glacier area with two Kurdish horsemen. He ascended the Parrot glacier alone and between 12–13,000 feet spotted a beam of wood sticking out of an ice mound on the north side of the glacier. He could not climb the ice mound so he videotaped the beam using zoom and different angles to record the find. After descending the mountain, he shared the video with Angelo Palego, ark explorers, and other Swiss researchers who shared it on the Internet.

It is believed that this wood, along with the Navarra wood find in the glacier many years ago, indicate that it is likely that part of the structure of the ark has been broken up on the north-northwest side of the mountain, buried and moved further down the glacier.

Hopefully, continued research in the Parrot Glacier area will result in a future wood find that can later be tested by scientists and scholarly researchers.

Improved melt-back conditions on Mt. Ararat have been occurring during the past ten years—possibly due to global warming or a cyclical warming period. As researchers have explored Mt. Ararat from the 1980s to the present, many have noticed areas that were previously covered by glacial ice are now exposed. There have been no recent, official summer ice and snow coverage studies done, but it is becoming evident that some areas of the mountain are now remaining free of ice that used to be covered during the summer months. If the Ararat ice cap continues to shrink in future years, perhaps some of the remains of the long sought after ark will be openly exposed. Unless subsurface radar imaging of the ice cap is allowed by Turkish officials for some future expedition, this might be the only hope for finding remains of the ark, which has remained hidden under the ice.

The Ultimate Leap of Faith

The man called Noah demonstrated faith in epic proportions. He spent more than a hundred years building the ark—enduring the jeers and laughter of those who refused to believe that God was actually going to judge the world in a catastrophic way.

Noah spent 120 years faithfully constructing and stocking the enormous ark. Some scholars even claim that Noah had another son who refused to believe and was lost.

When the door of the ark was sealed shut, his convictions were further tested. Noah and his family had to spend another seven days with a ship full of

restless animals without any overt sign of the immi-
nent destruction about to take place. He had nothing
to cling to but his faith.

No one inside or outside the ark could conceive of
the enormity of the calamity that was to come. This
is more than just a story about a worldwide Flood
and a mysterious 5,000-year-old shipwreck under
the ice near the top of a mountain in Turkey. This
is the story of an extraordinary man of conviction
and faith who faced and overcame incredible odds
to accomplish the seemingly impossible task God
had given him.

Noah took what could be called the "ultimate
leap of faith," and his courage is a message as
powerful today as it was when his ship "docked" on
a radically changed earth. Noah's life and his 5,000-
year-old ship anchored in ice serve as a powerful
testimony that God always keeps His word.

Judging the Evidence

Is the ark on Mount Ararat? Much of the
evidence is now before you. You've read about
the numerous sightings throughout history, the
eyewitness accounts and their analysis by scientists
and experts in a number of other fields. You've
seen and read about the satellite and photographic
imagery—some of which clearly reveals a great ship
frozen under the ice and snows of Mount Ararat.
Is it Noah's ark?

Inside the great ship, cages and pens have
reportedly been examined by Napoleon's party
and the atheistic English scientists. The interior
and exterior of the ark have also been measured
and photographed by the czar's expedition, the
Turkish earthquake expedition—and possibly by
U.S. scientific organizations unwilling to divulge

their findings. Wood samples have been recovered and tested at labs around the world, and artifacts have been seen and examined by scores of people over the past 5,000 years.

Reports and photographs from pilots of many nations over several decades have been discussed, along with the accounts of people from all walks of life who have seen the photographs. In more recent years advanced satellite imagery and computer analysis have made their contribution.

The evidence is overwhelming, and yet so much of it has mysteriously disappeared that it makes the existence of the ark suspect in some people's eyes.

Press reports, interview excerpts, speeches, and ancient to modern secular and religious books on Noah's ark have been presented in these pages. What conclusions can we draw from all of this? We asked Dr. Tim LaHaye, coauthor of *The Ark on Ararat*, to give us his final thoughts on the matter:

> You can look at all of the stories that come out of that community of nations around Mount Ararat and they all seem to have one central thought that surfaces—the story of Noah. All of the evidence leads us to the fact that the great ship that has been sighted by so many on Mount Ararat has to be the ark of Noah.

Yet, despite all of the evidence and man's efforts, the ark continues to remain elusive. However, recent cyclical warming trends and the effects of Global Warming give promise that major melt backs will unveil the ark's hiding place in the near future. But what significance will that final revelation of the ark hold? We have already mentioned some of the possibilities from the outset of this book.

After many false leads and unsettled accounts of discovery, leading ark researchers and explorers are cautious to accept new finds. The ark's monumental historic significance exempts premature celebration. For thousands of years the ark has remained unearthed. As in the past, time and effort will be invested to investigate and authenticate the most recent claims of success.

Regardless of if or when the ark is ultimately discovered and confirmed, we already have access to a revelation far greater than the ark itself. That revelation has been passed down from the time of Noah up until the present time, and holds the outlook for the future of all mankind. Meanwhile, will we be like Noah, who had no hard evidence other than what God had told him, and take the *ultimate leap of faith*?

Endnotes

1 Stanley N. Wellborn and Robert A. Kittle, "Can Eyes and Ears in Space Monitor an Arms Deal?" *U.S. News and World Report*, November 25, 1985, p. 41.

Thirteen

NOAH'S CONNECTION TO THE END TIMES

I make known the end from the beginning,
from ancient times, what is still to come.
— Isaiah 46:10

AS OUR SCIENTIFIC INVESTIGATION comes to a close, it's important to connect the dots between Noah's ark, the Great Flood, Global Warming, and the End Times. To do this, we need to look at what we can fashionably think of as the "Redemption Code" in the Bible. The Noah Flood story is a link and a part of this code. But before we examine the final messages of the Redemption Code, we need to understand the integrated message system underlying the Bible, and that there is one unifying message that permeates the entire Bible.

An Integrated Message System

Chuck Missler, a former military think-tank analyst turned biblical expositional commentator, explains:

> One of the greatest discoveries you can make is that the Bible is a message system. Sixty-six separate books penned by over forty

authors over a period of several thousand years, and yet we discover it's an integrated message system in which every detail, every number, every place name is there by deliberate, skillful engineering.

A remarkable example is in the earliest book of our Bible, in Genesis Chapter 5, where we read the list of Hebrew names or genealogy of Noah's ancestors. They're listed from "Adam, Seth, Enosh, Kenan, Mahalalel, Jared, Enoch, Methuselah, Lamech and, finally, Noah." The English transliteration of the Hebrew doesn't mean much to us. But if we look at the original Hebrew terms we can, from the Hebrew roots, determine what those names actually mean. In other words, when we look at the English translation of the original word roots, we discover there is a message encoded within it. Adam means "Man," Seth means "Appointed." Enosh means "Mortal," and so forth.

Adam	= Man
Seth	= Appointed
Enosh	= Mortal
Kenan	= Sorrow
Mahalalel	= The Blessed God
Jared	= Shall Come Down
Enoch	= Teaching
Methusaleh	= His Death Shall Bring
Lamech	= Despairing/Lamentation
Noah	= Comfort/Rest

But then, going through each of the names as to what they mean, and putting them together in the list, it spells out a sentence:

"Man is appointed mortal sorrow, but the blessed God shall come down teaching that His death shall bring the despairing comfort or rest." Here we have encrypted into the first genealogy, in the first book of the Bible, a summary of the Christian Gospel. What this message in Genesis demonstrates to us is that God's plan of redemption was not a knee jerk reaction to Adam's failure. God had already laid out from the beginning of the world His plan of redemption for the predicament of mankind. You and I are the beneficiaries of a love story that was written in blood on a wooden cross that was erected in Judea some 2,000 years ago.

So we can begin to understand that the Bible is an integrated message system. Every number, every place name, every detail is there by supernatural engineering, for our learning and discovery. [The meaning and significance of names and words throughout the Bible can be discovered when we go back to the original word translations in their original context. A New Testament example– the English translation for "Jesus," from the transliteration "Yeshua," means "Salvation."] Well, if God has the ability to lay out, thousands of years in advance, His whole plan of redemption–can we not expect that God also has the answers for our problems today?

As we've seen, [from the genealogy example and from the Noah Flood account,] God has a plan, and He communicates that plan in the Bible. And as we begin to understand that plan, the Bible gives us many clues as to what to expect next in our world.

If the Bible is an indisputable integrated message system that clearly spells out the details of the past, present, and future, what does Noah's Flood tell us about our past, our present-day world with its threats of world war and flooding from global warming; and finally, what does Noah's story tell us about the end of the world that could come in our lifetime or the future?

An Integrated Plan

Let's start by looking at the past—the days in which Noah's Flood occurred. There has been a consistent pattern in the biblical history of man which started with Adam and Eve in the Garden of Eden.

According to the opening chapters of Genesis (translated "Beginnings"), in the beginning God created a *good* and perfect world, with man created in God's own image to live in fellowship with Him in the paradise garden of Eden (translated "Delight"). Man asserted his first act of willfully turning away from God by eating of the *Tree of the Knowledge of Good and Evil*, and as a result, evil came into the world, with a consequence of separation from God, and death. Out of mercy, God then dispelled man from the garden, so that he wouldn't eat of the *Tree of Life* and live immortally in this fallen state from which he was originally designed and created.

The consistent pattern of God's relations with man that has repeated cyclically throughout biblical history can be summarized: People rebel and move independently away from God. Then God first sends a warning (i.e., through a direct prophecy or spokesman or written word) and a time period of "grace" or waiting, giving people an opportunity to turn back to Him and from their offensive ways; He then brings an act of judgment (in various ways, such as the Flood and later Israel's exiles and captivities). He then reconciles them back again and they live for a while in harmony, but eventually man is unfaithful and strays again. As a response, God again gives warning and a grace period of waiting before an act of intervention or judgment, followed by redemption and reconciliation once again. What we see in the Bible and world history is this central theme being repeated throughout the past 5,000 to 8,000 years. It is a relationship theme between God and man–God's continual responses to redeem man back. This pattern and "code" of Redemption is woven throughout the entire Bible. Encoded into the story of Noah and the Flood is that pattern of redemption.

Going back to the beginning events of man's history that explain why we are where we are today, the result of man eating of the Tree of Knowledge of Good and Evil was that now the experiential knowledge of *good and evil* coexisted with man. The effects of man's inclination toward evil and waywardness continued to grow with the growing population on earth, so that it increased to the levels of debasement and violence in Noah's day. The people of Noah's generation had become corrupted to the extent that they no longer reflected their original purpose and design. God decided to intervene. His intent was to recreate the earth with a new beginning.

The "wickedness" and "evil" that grieved God included not only the immorality, depravity, violence and injustice, but an attitude and lifestyle of indifference to God, dominated by man's independent self-pursuits. Noah stood apart from the universal condition of the people in his day in that he "walked with God." When he responded to God's warning of a coming Flood by trustingly building the ark, he and his family were saved from the Flood's destruction.

After the worldwide deluge ended, as they exited the ark they entered into a "covenant" relationship with God on the top of the mountain, and were instructed to repopulate the newly created earth that resulted from the Flood activity. [A covenant was a binding contract agreement in ancient times, bringing two parties into league with one another.]

Noah's civilization was the first to experience God's cataclysmic judgment of the world. Significantly, this judgment was followed by a universal covenant, that in the future, regardless of how far man might go in perverting his purposes, God would never again send a Flood as a solution.

Descendents of Noah Form Nations

Let's now relate the Noah Flood account to the present day. All people today are descended from the eight survivors of the Flood that were on the ark. (This explains why every culture of the world had a flood story.) The present races are descended from the three sons of Noah. They were instructed, *"Be fruitful and increase in number and fill the earth"* (Genesis 9:1).

Geologist and Mt. Ararat expeditioner, John Morris, comments on the central location from which the ark inhabitants spread throughout the world:

Using computer programs to calculate the distances between every geographical square area, we've identified the actual geographical center of planet Earth–and the area that is the least distance to every other inhabitable area on planet Earth is right near Mt. Ararat. This would be an ideal place from which to migrate, to spread and fill the Earth. Mt. Ararat is the optimal starting place on planet Earth.

The descendents of the three sons of Noah (Ham, Shem, and Japheth) geographically dispersed to become the seventy nations—Ham, the nations of Africa, (thirty nations); Shem, the Asian nations (twenty-six); and Japheth, the European nations (fourteen). (Over time these three groups spread to larger areas and were divided into language groups after the Tower of Babel incident.)

Each of these basic races have distinguishing traits that can also be seen today. Ham's descendents, who settled in areas south of Palestine—Egypt, Africa, and part of India—are characterized as practical-minded people with great technical ability. They are known to have been great builders and have given the world the standards of measurement, planetary studies and the alphabet.

Shem's descendents are the Israelites and the Arabs, a very religious people. The Hebrew nation, (the Israelites), who gave us the Scriptures, came from Shem's line, and it is the line from which Jesus was descended. The first Christians came from this group as well.

Japheth's descendents, who went north and west of Palestine, inhabit most of the world today and are known to be a prolific and philosophical people, intellectual and academic.

Today's division of races, and the worldwide tensions and political problems, can be traced back to these original diverging groups, as the descendents of Noah's three sons repopulated the earth. (The earliest history of the beginning of the nations is recorded in Genesis 11 and is studied by secular historians as a reliable record.)

The Threat of Global Warming

Currently, one of mankind's biggest concerns is the potential catastrophic effects from Global Warming–the belief that the eight million square miles of polar ice will melt and flood much of the most heavily-populated areas of the world—the continental coastlines extending thousands of miles into the continents—within the next 100 years, drastically affecting life on Earth.

Regardless of the opposing arguments and predictions surrounding the Global Warming issue, the Bible makes it clear that the earth will never again be destroyed by a worldwide flood. Soon after Noah and his family left the ark, a covenant promise was given, not just to Noah, but to all of Earth's inhabitants for all time. Assurance to the present day has been recorded in Genesis 9:12-17:

And God said, "This is the sign of the covenant I am making between me and you and every living creature with you, a covenant for all generations to come: I have set my rainbow in the clouds, and it will be the sign of the covenant between me and the earth. Whenever I bring clouds over the earth and the rainbow appears in the clouds, I will remember my covenant between me and you and all living creatures of every kind never again will the waters become a flood to destroy all life. Whenever the rainbow appears in the clouds, I will see it and remember the everlasting covenant between God and all living creatures of every kind on the earth." So God said to Noah, "This is the sign of the covenant I have established between me and all life on the earth.

The rainbow was the covenant sign of this promise, and the sign of the rainbow also was not given just to Noah, but for all mankind and every living thing. The rainbow can be seen in every part of the world and is a reminder of God's never-ending covenant with man. God was starting his relationship over again with the remnant of mankind who were willing to live in relationship with Him in a newly-created world; and He will never again destroy the world by a flood of waters, regardless of man's attitudes or actions against Him.

As we have already shown, the Bible is an integrated message system from beginning to end. The Old Testament is not just a series of random stories, but a predestined methodical movement toward God's final covenant with mankind. The covenant with Noah was the first relationship covenant that God established as a universal covenant for all future descendents. It prefigured the final universal plan of redemption in Christ. The Old Testament Scriptures purposefully trace the sixty-three generations from Adam to Christ. In Genesis the ancestral line to Christ is traced from Adam to Noah, and then Noah to Abraham. As Noah's descendents strayed from the covenant relationship with God, He again made a covenant, this time with Abraham, in order to bless the entire world through a family. The rest of the Old

Testament is the account of God's relationship with this family, the Hebrew descendents of Abraham. Ultimately, Christ was born into the context of this family, and consummated a universal eternal covenant between God and mankind.

In summary, we can view the repopulation of the earth after the Flood (Genesis 10–11) as a link between Noah and the people God chooses to fulfill His ultimate plan for creation.

Global End Times Destiny

Connecting this biblical history with the present, what does the Noah account reveal to us about our future and the end of this world? Amazingly, there is a significant link between the Noah Flood and the future as it culminates in the End Times.

Jesus explained to his disciples in Matthew 24 that the End Times climax would come in the same manner that God brought judgment to the people of Noah's time:

> No one knows about that day or hour, not even the angels in heaven, nor the Son, but only the Father. As it was in the days of Noah, so it will be at the coming of the Son of Man. For in the days before the Flood, people were eating and drinking, marrying and giving in marriage, up to the day Noah entered the ark; and they knew nothing about what would happen until the Flood came and took them all away. That is how it will be at the coming of the Son of Man. Therefore, keep watch, because you do not know on what day our Lord will come.

So what do we know for sure about the End Times? Jesus listed specific signs in Matthew 24 that would indicate when the final End Time event was near. These "signs" included increase in worldwide strife and wars; storms and changes in the seas and ocean tides; a significant increase in the incidence of major storms, hurricanes, earthquakes and famines, worldwide pestilences and epidemics. We are seeing these "signs" in our time.

Global Warming may even be the contributing cause of some of them. But the final End Time event itself is set apart. It will come like the sudden unexpected 9/11 terrorist attack on New York City—an ordinary weekday morning in September when everyone worldwide was going about their daily routine, unsuspecting and oblivious, and also unprepared. Just like that ordinary day that the Flood of Noah erupted and was set in motion, sweeping away the unsuspecting.

If the Earth isn't going to be destroyed by a flood or devastated worldwide by the effects of Global Warming, how will the sudden end of the earth and this age come about? The Apostle Peter gives the answer:

> First of all, you must understand that in the last days scoffers will come, scoffing and following their own evil desires. They will say, "Where is this 'coming' He promised? Ever since our fathers died, everything goes on as it has since the beginning of creation." But they deliberately forget that long ago by God's word the heavens existed and the earth was formed out of water and by water. *By these waters also the world of that time was deluged and destroyed. By the same word the present heavens and earth are reserved for fire, being kept for the day of judgment and destruction of ungodly men....*

But do not forget this one thing, dear friends: With the Lord a day is like a thousand years, and a thousand years are like a day. The Lord is not slow in keeping his promise, as some understand slowness. He is patient with you, not wanting any to perish, but everyone to come to repentance.

But the day of the Lord will come like a thief. *The heavens will disappear with a roar; the elements will be destroyed by fire, and the earth and everything in it will be laid bare ...*

Since everything will be destroyed in this way, what kind of people ought you to be? You ought to live holy and godly lives as you look forward to the day of God and speed it coming. *That day will bring about the destruction of the heavens by fire, and the elements will melt in the heat. But in keeping with his promise we are looking forward to a new heaven and a new earth, the home of righteousness* (II Peter 3: 2-13).

Both secular and religious philosophers and scientists have predicted the end of the world by methods that are consistent with this biblical description. Albert Barnes, in his commentary on II Peter 3 from *Barnes' Notes on the New Testament*, theorizes the final outcome for our combustible planet:

Modern science has revealed that the interior of the earth is a melted and intensely heated mass of burning materials; that the habitable world is a comparatively thin crust or shell over those internal fires; earthquakes are caused by the vapors caused when that heated mass comes into contact with water;

and volcanoes are openings and vent-holes through which those internal flames make their way to the surface. Whether these fires will everywhere make their way to the surface, and produce a universal conflagration cannot be scientifically predetermined, but God can use whatever cataclysmic trigger to set in motion the outpouring of those burning floods over the earth, as he once caused the waters to spring forth and roll over every mountain. It is probable that such a change produced by fire, and bringing the present order of things to a close, will occur. Such changes are taking place in other worlds.... During the last century more than thirteen fixed stars have disappeared, as observed and documented by astronomers. If such things are occurring in other worlds, it is not improbable or absurd to suppose that they may occur on the earth.

Some say that the trigger event may be an asteroid crashing into the earth; others say it will be a thermal nuclear blast, while others believe it will be a fiery eruption coming from beneath the earth's surface—something like thousands of erupting volcanoes spewing fiery molten lava across the surface of the globe. The picture given is reminiscent of the flood of waters that swept over the entire earth in Noah's Flood—only this time instead of a flood of water, it will be a flood of fire.

A New Earth

But there is hope for mankind—the people who are destined to survive this fiery holocaust of a magnitude beyond multiplication of the 9/11 disaster. The Apostle John prophesies the outcome and conclusion in the closing book of the Bible—the book of Revelations:

> *Then I saw a new heaven and a new earth, for the first heaven and the first earth had passed away, and there was no longer any sea ... And I heard a loud voice from the throne saying, "Now the dwelling of God is with men, and he will live with them. They will be his people, and God himself will be with them and be their God. He will wipe every tear from their eyes. There will be no more death or mourning or crying or pain, for the old order of things has passed away." He who was seated on the throne said, "I am making everything new!" Then he said, "Write this down, for these words are trustworthy and true"* (Revelation 21: 1-5).

"The elements will dissolve ..." Fire will be the mechanism. But not a single particle of matter will ever cease to exist—it will only change its form. The elements of the earth will be transformed, not annihilated. In other words, the form of the earth will change, but its matter will still be in existence. The dramatic "ending" of the Earth and present world age will usher in "a new beginning" in a newly created world. Just as Noah exited the ark into a world that underwent metamorphoses by the Flood, a "new heaven and a new earth" will emerge from the ravishing fires.

The world will be restored to be like the paradise Eden, and God himself will once again live in fellowship with man in the new creation. This will be our permanent home. The cycle of separation and downfall will be ended. Perhaps this sounds like mere idealism in the present tense, but it is the plan that has been set in motion from the very beginning. And this plan of ultimate redemption has been encoded, not only in the account of Noah, but from beginning to end throughout the Bible.

Invited to Enter the Ark

In the days of Noah, eight people—Noah along with his wife, his three sons with their wives along with representatives of all the animal kingdom—escaped judgment aboard Noah's ark. But this time there is no safety boat to board in a world destined to be consumed by fire, so what escape plan exists for people in the Twenty-first Century?

The answer is spelled out in the closing dialogue of the Bible. Just as God commissioned Noah not just to warn the people of his day, but to extend an invitation up until the day that the door of the ark was closed—it is the same universal invitation today:

> The [Holy] Spirit and the Bride [the church, the true Christians] say, Come! And let him who is listening say, Come! And let everyone come who is thirsty [who is painfully conscious of his need of those thing by which the soul is refreshed, supported, and strengthened]; and whoever [earnestly] desires to do it, let him come, take, appropriate, and drink the water of Life without cost (Revelation 22:17, Amplified Bible).

Miraculous Messages:
From Noah's Flood to the End Times

The dots have been connected, from the time of Noah to our time. The door of the ark for our time remains open, inviting any who will enter.

And for those who do, what awaits them on the other side of their journey is a new life in a newly created world.

> *Jesus said "I am the door ... If anyone enters through me, he will be saved"* (John 10:9 NASB).

EPILOGUE

Some have pointed out that the discovery of Noah's ark would be the greatest archaeological discovery of all time and I think that's an accurate statement, because Noah's Flood, if it ever happened, the purpose for it was to wipe out the civilization before the flood. It was so horribly wicked and violent that the Bible reveals that God sent the Flood as a judgment of the sin. And so, if that world was totally annihilated, Noah's ark would be the one remaining link to that pre-Flood world—the greatest archaeological artifact that could ever be found.

John Morris, PhD,
Author/Professor of Geology

If the story of Noah and the ark is true, then that alters our whole perception of the Bible. God has laid out a plan and He has a purpose, and that purpose needs to reprioritize everything in our life, because our eternal destiny will be determined by our relationship to that purpose.

Chuck Missler
Biblical Expositional Commentator

Perhaps one of the greatest potential impacts of the discovery of Noah's ark would be in a more personal realm—the realm of salvation. Because if you recognize what the Bible is talking about, the Bible says that Noah's Flood was a judgment of sin, but God, in His grace, had Noah build the ark as a means by which the believers out of a previous civilization could escape that coming judgment and be placed in a new and better world afterwards.

The exact same situation faces us today. God looks down on this civilization and sees again a rampant, sinful, violent world and He promises judgment. The wages of sin is still death and there is a judgment coming. Not by water this time, but a judgment nonetheless. And yet, in His grace God has given us an Ark of Salvation—Jesus Christ. If we climb aboard that Ark, if we recognize that His death paid the penalty for our sins, we can be forgiven of our sins and have adoption into His family and have eternal life. This is the real message of Noah's ark.

John D. Morris, PhD
Author/Professor of Geology

APPENDIX

The Search for Artifacts and Photos

One of the most puzzling aspects of the Noah's ark mystery is the amount of evidence that has disappeared over the last century.

"How there could be so much evidence and so little proof defies reason," say Dr. Tim LaHaye and Dr. John Morris in their book, *The Ark on Ararat*. "It almost seems that by design, the proof is kept from the hands of those who would make it public."

Everyone loses things from time to time, but the amount of "missing" ark evidence including photographs, artifacts, and wood samples has become phenomenal. For example: When ten people recall seeing the same photo of the ark which then turns up missing no one is too surprised, as this has occurred several times. However, when you multiply that one photo by about fifty people seeing it, you can't help but wonder what's happening in regard to photos of Noah's ark.

Where are the photographs taken by George Greene, Prince Nouri, and the explorers of the czar's expedition? What about the evidence from the Turkish geological mission? Where are the *Stars and Stripes* articles and pictures, or the articles about the deathbed confession of the British scientist? Where are the photos and other evidence seen at the Smithsonian Institution? What about the secret U.S. reconnaissance photos?

Does anyone have copies of these startling photographs or access to them? Will they ever surface again? The new evidence we have recently uncovered is astounding, but the mystery behind the missing evidence continues. If you have or know anyone who has any of these missing photographs or film footage, share that information with the ark explorers and research centers listed below.

Noah's Ark–Ararat Expedition Groups

The following individuals and/or groups conduct research expeditions to Mount Ararat:

Chuck Aaron
President, FX Helicopters, Inc.
1218 Willowgreen Court
Westlake Village, CA 91361
atppilot@aol.com

Dr. Ahmet Ali Arslan
9430 Cloverdale Court
Burke, VA 22015
aaarslan2002@yahoo.com

Dr. Carl Baugh
Creation Evidence Museum
P. O. Box 309
Glen Rose, TX 76043
creation@creationevidence.org

Richard Bright
P. O. Box 505788
Saipan, M.P. 96950
rbright@vzpacifica.net
rcbright@gmail.com

David Larsen
804 E. Mendocino Street
Altadena, CA 91001
Godere8d@juno.com

John McIntosh
President, SEARCH Foundation
P. O. Box 1729
Crestline, CA 92325
jtmomega7777@juno.com

Dr. John Morris
Institute for Creation Research
10946 Woodside Avenue, North
Santee, CA 92071
jmorris@icr.org
www.icr.org

Dr. Don Shockey
P. O. Box 941
Mountainair, NM 87036
drshockey@hisurfer.net

Rex Geissler
2927 Newbury Court
Highlands Ranch, CO 80126-8037
rex@noahsarksearch.com
www.noahsarksearch.com
www.arcimaging.org

B. J. Corbin
31380 Melson Road
Delmar, MD 21875

bjcorbin@gmail.com
www.noahsarksearch.com

Bob Stuplich
Box 85
Crested Butte, CO 81224
bob@crestedbutte.net

Professor Jim Hall
Director, Ark Research Project
107 Buckingham Drive
Lynchburg, VA 24502
profhall@netzero.com
www.arksearch.com

Elfred Lee
4274 Pondhill Court
Riverside, CA 92505
marthaleeart@charter.net

Gerrit Aalten
De Wilderen 10
5581 AD Waalre
The Netherlands
gerrit.ricky@dutchweb.nl
gerrit.aalten@wxs.nl

Giuseppe Rezzonico
VIA Roncaccio 12
6942 Sauosa
Switzerland
gius_arcas@hotmail.com
www.web.ticino.com/arcas

Jeremy Wiles
Quest For Bible Treasures
P. O. Box 93
McDonald, TN 37353
Jeremy@thequestforbibletreasures.com
www.thequestforbibletreasures.com

Alternative Noah's Ark Sites
Robert Cornuke
BASE Institute
P. O. Box 125
Palmer Lake, CO 80133
basebobc@aol.com

Dr. Charles Willis
2490 W. Fir Street
Fresno, CO 93711
cdjapheth@aol.com

Noah's Ark Research Centers
David W. Balsiger
Noah's Ark TV/DVD Productions
Writeway Research International
P. O. Box 1987
Loveland, CO 80539-1987
dwbalsiger@ultrasys.net

Bill Crouse
Christian Information Ministries
2050 N. Collins Boulevard, #100
Richardson, TX 75080
bill@rapidresponsereport.com

Professor Jim Hall
Ark Research Project
Director of ARP

107 Buckingham Drive
Lynchburg, VA 24502
profhall@netzero.com
www.arksearch.com

Rex Geissler
Arcimaging
2927 Newbury Court
Highlands Ranch, CO 80126-8037
rex@noahsarksearch.com
www.noahsarksearch.com
www.arcimaging.org

John McIntosh
SEARCH Foundation
P. O. Box 1729
Crestline, CA 92325
jtmomega7777@juno.com

Ark Theme Parks

Noah's Ark Ministries International
Andrew Yuen
c/o Media Evangelism Ltd.
22/F., Fullerton Centre,
19 Hung To Road,
Kwun Tong, Hong Kong
(852) 2396-1688 Office
(852) 2309-2739
info@media.org.hk
www.media.org.hk

This organization also oversees the Noah's Ark Theme Park, which features Noah's ark built in full biblical dimension. It's a museum, conference center, and hotel.

Floating Noah's Ark—Ark Van Noach
Johan Huibers, Builder
Prins Hendrikkade 24
1721 AK
Broek OP Langedijk
Netherlands
(0031) 06-53-40-68-4
bhubiers@quicknet.nl
www.arkvannoach.com

This replica of Noah's ark actually floats and is moved to different locations around Holland. Visitors can board it and see what conditions would have been like on the ark during Noah's day. The replica is 70 meters long and 13 meters high.

Other Noah's Ark Interests

Caboodle! Toys
1140 Broadway, Suite 907
New York, NY 10001
(866) 222-6635
(866) 224-5712 Fax
steve@caboodletoys.com
www.noahspals.com

Caboodle Toys offers a delightful collection of lovingly sculpted and beautifully painted pairs of collectible animal figures build to a 1:24 scale. Each pair of animals comes with a collectible ID card with educational information about each species. Complete the set with Noah and his ark!

Bibleland Studios
23 High Banks Dr.
Fulton, Ny 13069

(866) 593-3010
(702) 925-7983 Fax
info@BiblelandStudios.com
www.BiblelandStudios.com

Bibleland Studios sells limited edition paper lithographs, canvas lithographs and canvas giclees of Elfred Lee's famous painting "The Invitation." The painting features the building of Noah's ark with Noah giving the invitation to come aboard the ark. It highlights 135 people along with animals and birds. It's a meaningful piece of fine art for your home or office wall. Mention hearing about this painting in this book and you will receive a significant discount.

Related Web Links
http://www.noahsarksearch.com/index.htm
http://www.arksearch.com
http://www.web.ticino.com/arcas
http://arcimaging.org
http://www.arkonararat.com
http://www.genesisfiles.com
http://www.ancientworldfoundation.org
http://answersingenesis.org/home/area/faq/noah.
   asp
http://www.parentcompany.com/search_for_
   noahs_ark/sfna1.htm
http://www.noahsarkfactnotfiction.com
http://www.answersingenesis.org/home/area/faq/
   noah.asp
http://www.mountararat.net/pages/265853/index.
   htm
http://www.rapidresponsereport.com
http://www.wyattmuseum.com
http://www.accuracyingenesis.com/noahark.html

http://www.answersmagazine.com
http://www.arkvannoach.com
http://www.anchorstone.com
http://www.christiananswers.net
http://www.TheNoahark.com
Flood Stories Around the World: http://home.
earthlink.net/~misaak/floods.htm

Index

A

Abas 277, 278, 279, 280, 282
abyss 72
Adam 146
Adams, J.Q. 113
aestivation 49
Africa 76, 161, 162, 228, 229, 327
Aghri Dagh 1, 171, 196
A□rı Da□ı 1, 171
Air War College 63, 298
Alaska 75, 137
Albert Barnes 332
allochthonous process 99
ALMAZ Radar Remote Sensing Satellite 304
American Antiquarian 113
Anatolia 178
Anderson, Newton 114
Ankara, Turkey 178
Apameia Kibotos 97
Apostle John 333
aqueous fluids 79
Aralik 289
Ararat Report xi, 36, 57, 191
Ark Research Project (ARP) 342, 343
Armenia 72, 171, 190, 191, 196, 200, 204, 239
Army Engineer's Special Service Group 276
artifacts 15, 17, 19, 84, 97, 110, 111, 162, 182, 190,
225, 261, 271, 284, 311, 319, 339
Asia Minor 97
Assyrian 81, 94
asteroid 79, 82, 333
astronomy 13
Atalay, Dr. Bulent 304

G

H

N

O

P

ABOUT THE AUTHORS

David W. "Dave" Balsiger, LHD, is a television producer-director and the author of 40 major literary works, including 30 nonfiction books. Additionally, he is the senior producer at Grizzly Adams Productions Inc. (named after the company's Grizzly Adams TV Series), the producers of family friendly and faith-based TV specials, series, and DVDs.

His most recent major TV/DVD specials include *Miraculous Messages: From Noah's Ark to the End Times, The Case for Christ's Resurrection, Heroes Among Us, Miracles Around Us; Fabric of Time: Secrets of the Universe, Miracles in Our Midst, Apocalypse and the End Times, Breaking the Da Vinci Code, Faith in the White House, Miraculous Mission, The Evidence for Heaven, Twelve Ordinary Men, Secrets of the Bible Code Revealed, The Quest for Noah's Ark,* and *The Miracle and Wonder of Prayer.*

His well-known, co-authored multimillion copy best-selling books *In Search of Noah's Ark* (Sunn) and *The Lincoln* Conspiracy (New American Library) have both been made into major movies of the same titles. He has also recently co-authored the books *The Case for Christ's Resurrection* (Bridge-Logos, 2007), *Inspirational Wit and Wisdom from the Internet* (Bridge-Logos 2006), *The Evidence for Heaven* (Bridge-Logos, 2005), *The Incredible Power of Prayer* (Tyndale, 1998), *Ancient Secrets of the Bible* (Dell, 1994), and *The Incredible Discovery of Noah's Ark* (Dell, 1995).

His books and TV/DVD projects have won more than 155 national awards for journalistic, literary, or production excellence. He is listed in 19 achievement directories including eight of the prestigious Marquis Library directories. Mr. Balsiger is also the recipient of an honorary doctoral degree from Lincoln Memorial University (Harrogate, Tennessee) for his historical book *The Lincoln Conspiracy.*

Charles E. "Chuck" Sellier, LHD, is both a writer and television/film producer who has over 30 theatrical feature films to his credit, as well as 450 television shows and pilots that he has written and/or produced. They include such films and series as *Life and Times of Grizzly Adams, Encounters with the Unexplained, Xtreme Mysteries, Knight Rider 2000, Greatest Heroes of the Bible, Desperado, Longarm, Vestige of Honor, Angels Sent on Assignment, Ancient Secrets of the Bible, Friends for Life* and *Miracles and Other Wonders.* His newest network television specials are *The Search for Heaven, Fabric of Time: Secrets of the Universe, Miracles in Our Midst, Apocalypse and the End Times, Twelve Ordinary Men, Friends for Life, Miraculous Messages: From Noah's Ark to the End Times, Breaking the Da Vinci Code, The Untold Story of Flight 93, Secrets of the Bible Code Revealed, The Quest for Noah's Ark, Jesus: The Evidence,* and *The Bible's Greatest Miracles.*

Along with his stunning film record, he has authored or co-authored many best-selling books including *In Search of Noah's Ark,* (4 weeks on the New York Post list), *The Lincoln Conspiracy*

(22 weeks on the New York Times list), *The Life and Times of Grizzly Adams, Hangar 18, Miracles and Other Wonders, Ancient Secrets of the Bible, Incredible Discovery of Noah's Ark,* and *Conspiracy to Kill the President.*

Sellier is the President/CEO of Grizzly Adams Productions, Inc., with operations in Colorado and Oregon. He lives in northern Idaho and is married, with one son.

He is the recipient of an honorary doctoral degree from Lincoln Memorial University for producing the docudrama, *The Lincoln Conspiracy.*

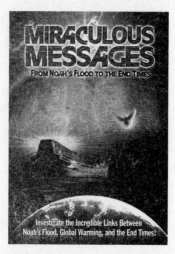

MIRACULOUS MESSAGES:
From Noah's Flood to the End Times

EXECUTIVE PRODUCERS
John Todd, Eric Holmlund, Corey Nathan,
John Gilman, Hickory Knob LLC

SUPERVISING PRODUCER
Charles E. Sellier

PRODUCER
David W. Balsiger

Partially based on the books *In the Beginning: Compelling Evidence for Creation and the Flood* by Walt Brown, Ph.D., and *Miraculous Messages: From Noah's Flood to the End Times* by David W. Balsiger and Charles E. Sellier.

It is a mystery to which all of mankind is seeking the answer. Beginning with the story of Noah and woven throughout the pages of the Bible is a thread that ties together our past, present, and future—a series of supernatural messages that carry the keys to life, death, and eternity.

Can these miraculous messages provide answers to life's most fundamental questions? What is mankind's purpose on Earth? What does the future hold? Will we escape impending End Times catastrophic events?

Our quest for answers to these tough questions leads us to a mountaintop in eastern Turkey, and to the remains of a 5,000-year-old wooden ship. Could this be Noah's Ark?

Join us for a thought-provoking investigation of the links between the Noah Flood story, Global

Warming, and the End Times. You will be amazed at what you discover!

Approximately 120 minutes including Bonus Features plus FaithGrowers™ Curriculum and Pastor's Sermon Outline with Listener's Notes. Spanish Subtitles.

To Order Your DVD
Call (800) 811-0548 toll free
www.grizzlyadams.tv